Hibernate

Hibernate

A J2EE Developer's Guide

Will Iverson

✦ Addison-Wesley

Upper Saddle River, NJ • Boston • Indianapolis • San Francisco
New York • Toronto • Montreal • London • Munich • Paris
Madrid • Capetown • Sydney • Tokyo • Singapore • Mexico City

The publisher offers excellent discounts on this book when ordered in quantity for bulk purchases or special sales, which may include electronic versions and/or custom covers and content particular to your business, training goals, marketing focus, and branding interests. For more information, please contact:

    U. S. Corporate and Government Sales
    (800) 382-3419
    corpsales@pearsontechgroup.com

For sales outside the U. S., please contact:

    International Sales
    international@pearsoned.com

Visit us on the Web: www.awprofessional.com

Library of Congress Cataloging-in-Publication Data:

2004113059

Pearson Education, Inc.
Rights and Contracts Department
One Lake Street
Upper Saddle River, NJ 07458

Text printed on recycled and acid-free paper.

ISBN 0321268199

2 3 4 5 6 7   PH   07 06 05

2nd Printing   January 2005

For Diane

Contents

Acknowledgments

Many, many thanks to Ann Sellers, both for agreeing to do this book and for being such a delight to work with.

Thanks to Ebony Haight for coordinating the technical review (as well as everything else I don't know about).

Thanks to my agent, Laura Lewin of StudioB, without whom this book would not exist.

Thanks to the technical reviewers, including Paul Bain, Kevin Bentley, Evan Campbell, Thomas Duff, Bill Higgins, Bob Kemmerer, Scott Rich, Alex Rosenberg, and Satadip Dutta for taking the time to provide such excellent feedback. I would like to thank Sylvain Gibassier and Kevin Hammond in particular for supplying such excellent feedback. Any remaining mistakes are my own.

On a personal note, thanks to my friends and family for their support. And finally, thanks to Cynthia, Diane, and Mom. You are, quite simply, the best.

Will Iverson

About the Author

Will Iverson has been working in the computer and information technology field professionally since 1990. His diverse background includes developing statistical applications to analyze data from the NASA space shuttle, product management for Apple Computer, and developer relations for Symantec VisualCafé. For nearly five years, Will ran an independent J2EE consulting company with a variety of clients, including Sun, BEA, and Canal+ Technologies. Will currently serves as the application development practice manager for SolutionsIQ. Will lives in Seattle, Washington.

Preface

I got into Hibernate because I'm lazy. Specifically, I got tired of writing my own systems to bridge my Java applications and relational databases. I write both Swing and server-based applications; I can't assume (nor do I enjoy) the complexity of EJB container-managed persistence. I hate writing SQL when all I really want to do is write Java code. I *really* don't like writing endless pages of mindless code, loading my JDBC results into Java objects and back.

Simply put, Hibernate solves all of these problems for me, and it does so in a fast, flexible manner. I can use it with Swing, JSP, or as an EJB BMP solution. I can test my code outside of a container. I can even use it to manage my database schema.

Regardless of your background—whether you are a nothing-but-JDBC developer or a full EJB-level architect—you can save yourself considerable time and effort by adding Hibernate to your skill set, and in the process you can get a *significant* leg up on learning EJB 3.0. You can learn the principal terminology and concepts behind EJB 3.0 today, on the Java 2 (JDK 1.4) JVM you are using now.

Life is short. Spend less time writing code that bridges your database and your Java application and more time adding new features.

Required Skills

Familiarity with Java development, including object-oriented design. If you don't already know Java, this book will be quite unhelpful.

Familiarity with SQL and relational databases. There are many books on both the practical and theoretical sides of relational database design and development. The examples in this book are all done with MySQL, a free, open-source database. If you have never worked with a relational database before, you will almost certainly want to pick up an introductory text on MySQL.

Familiarity with Ant. Many books on Ant are available; if you are a Java developer and haven't already worked with Ant, you should learn.

Other skills, such as familiarity with JSP web application development, are helpful but not required. One example in Chapter 2 assumes the use of a web server such as Tomcat—all other examples can be run from the command-line.

Roadmap

This book can be loosely broken into a few basic sections. Following the introductory chapter, Chapters 2 through 4 illustrate different approaches to Hibernate development: starting from a Hibernate object/relational mapping file, starting from Java code, or starting from an existing database schema. Chapters 5 through 12 cover basic concepts and the use of persistent objects, concluding with chapters on tools, performance, and best practices. Chapter 13 discusses the future of Hibernate.

This book can be read in several ways, depending on your inclination. If you wish to start with real-world examples and then move into general usage and theory, you can more or less read the book in order. If you prefer a higher-level introduction, you may wish to start with Chapters 6 through 9 and then return to the beginning. Regardless of the method you choose, I encourage you to download and work through the examples from *http://www.cascadetg.com/hibernate/*.

Chapter 1 introduces Hibernate. It compares Hibernate to other forms of database access, including JDBC and a variety of other tools. It concludes with a list of required files and where to obtain them.

Chapter 2 illustrates an example of development starting with a Hibernate mapping file. The mapping file is used to generate Java and database schema files.

Chapter 3 shows how to use Hibernate when starting from a Java source file. XDoclet is used to generate the mapping file, and Hibernate is used to generate the database schema.

Chapter 4 shows how to use Middlegen in conjunction with Hibernate when starting from an existing database schema.

Chapter 5 is a reference to the Hibernate mapping file format. While few readers will want to read this chapter from start to finish, this reference will hopefully prove invaluable on a day-to-day basis when using Hibernate.

Chapter 6 contains information on the general use of Hibernate, including basic operations such as creating, finding, refreshing, updating, and deleting objects.

Chapter 7 explains how Hibernate handles both class and database relationship concepts.

Chapter 8 discusses Hibernate's two main query mechanisms, HQL and Criteria, and also shows how native SQL can be integrated.

Chapter 9 covers the various aspects of a Hibernate transaction, illustrating both session and database transaction concepts.

Chapter 10 shows tools for identifying potential Hibernate performance issues.

Chapter 11 discusses how Hibernate can be used to manage an application's schema.

Chapter 12 covers various Hibernate best practices.

Chapter 13 discusses future directions for Hibernate, and also covers potential similarities with EJB 3.0.

Overview

Applications that act on data are a fundamental of computer science. Historically, these applications have been written in wide variety of programming languages, with an equally wide variety of storage mechanisms for the data. Over time, programming languages evolved to use an essentially hierarchical model (part of the suite of advancements encompassed by object-oriented development). In comparison, the most popular form of reasonably scalable data storage is the relational database—a tables, columns, and rows model. Developers wind up developing systems to bridge two worlds—the hierarchical world of a modern programming language and the tabular world of relational databases. The goal of Hibernate is to dramatically reduce the time and energy you spend maintaining this bridge without losing the power and flexibility associated with the two worlds.

Why Object/Relational Mapping?

Let's take a look at what the difference between an object and a relational model means. First, an example of object inheritance, as shown in Figure 1.1.

Consider the data associated with these objects. For example, you may wish to store the fang length for the mammals, and the number of fins on the fish, but you're also keeping track of the height and weight that you would track for all animals. Expressing this hierarchical relationship in an object-oriented programming language is easy, convenient, and efficient.

Relational databases, in comparison, view data in terms of tables. Structured Query Language (SQL) is the standard mechanism for interaction with a relational database. Most critically, data is viewed in terms of tables, columns, and rows. Relational capabilities allow multiple tables to be integrated and perform sophisticated data retrieval, allowing powerful mining and reporting capabilities.

Unfortunately, it is surprisingly difficult to map the tables and queries one might express in SQL to the hierarchical, object-oriented capabilities of a modern

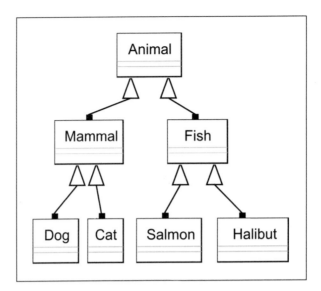

Figure 1.1.   Simple Object Hierarchy

programming language. To store the data associated with an object hierarchy, as shown in Figure 1.1, in a database could require as many as seven tables, with many complex SQL statements required to perform the retrieval of all of the data associated with a single halibut—or a single table with many unused fields, depending on the record entry. Hibernate allows you to easily use any of these potential database structures seamlessly and naturally from Java.

What Is Hibernate?

As stated on the Hibernate Web site, the goal of Hibernate "is to relieve the developer from 95 percent of common data persistence related programming tasks." By combining ordinary Java classes with XML descriptors, Hibernate provides an object-oriented view of a relational database.

As shown in Figure 1.2, most Java applications access a relational database via JDBC (route 1, as indicated in the diagram). By using Hibernate, a developer is freed from writing custom JDBC integration code and can focus on writing the presentation and business logic of the application (route 2). This doesn't have to be an all-or-nothing proposition; you can use an existing JDBC application in conjunction with Hibernate, migrating access as you go along.

Hibernate allows you to choose a development methodology that fits your needs. If you are starting a new project from scratch, you may wish to start with a mapping file, automatically generating both the schema and the Java classes

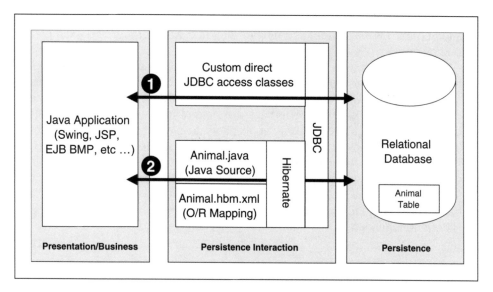

Figure 1.2. Weblog & Post Java Objects

(Chapter 2). Alternatively, you may wish to start from a relational database schema or directly from Java code (Chapters 3 and 4). Each system has pros and cons, as described in the chapter covering it.

There are several conceptual components to Hibernate that will be described in detail in this book. Java classes and XML files are used by Hibernate to bind Java objects to a particular relational database schema (Chapter 5). Straightforward Java-based operations are then used to create, update, query, and delete records (Chapter 6). More complex relationships, including Java collections, class hierarchies, and database one-to-many, many-to-one, and many-to-many relationships can be managed by Hibernate in a very natural manner (Chapter 7). Rich queries can be expressed in terms of both a simple object-oriented query language and a "Criteria" system (Chapter 8). Hibernate has robust support for complex transactions (Chapter 9).

SO MUCH TO LEARN!

When you first start working with Hibernate, it is easy to feel overwhelmed (especially if you haven't already been exposed to an object/relational framework). If you are just starting out, I strongly recommend that you begin by skimming through this text, paying particular attention to sections that outline concepts new to you. Then download the source for this book from my Web site at http://www.cascadetg.com/hibernate/ and work through the examples one by one.

This text assumes a baseline knowledge of Java application development, traditional relational database concepts, and SQL. Many developers (especially those who are largely self-taught) will discover that some of the basic concepts underlying Hibernate are unfamiliar. If you hit such a wall, check with either a recent Java application development text (JDK 1.4 or later) or a solid book on SQL and relational database theory.

I recommend starting with the mapping file–based example described in Chapter 2. Understanding the mapping file is usually the biggest challenge for developers new to Hibernate. By inspecting the Java source and database schema generated by Hibernate, you can quickly understand how Hibernate functions.

Comparing JDBC to Hibernate

If you are reading this book, you almost certainly have either written or maintained applications in which a surprisingly large amount of code is devoted to maintaining the glue between your Java code and your relational database. (From here on, we'll assume that you have chosen to standardize on Java as your preferred programming language, and on SQL as your preferred relational database language. While object/relational technology is available for a variety of other programming environments, Hibernate is a Java-based system.)

Anyone who has built a Java application using JDBC has experienced the difficulties inherent in the mismatch between Java and SQL. Let's look at an example of retrieving data using JDBC, shown in Listing 1.1.

Listing 1.1   Simple JDBC Code

```
package com.cascadetg.ch01;

import java.sql.*;

public class JDBCClient
{

    static void printColumn(String in)
    {
        System.out.print(in);
        System.out.print(" | ");
    }
```

Listing 1.1   Simple JDBC Code (*continued*)

```java
    public static void main(String[] args)
    {
        Driver myDriver = null;
        Connection myConnection = null;
        try
        {
            myDriver = (Driver)Class
                    .forName("com.mysql.jdbc.Driver")
                        .newInstance();

            myConnection = DriverManager.getConnection(
                    "jdbc:mysql://localhost/sample", "root",
                        "");

            Statement myStatement =
                    myConnection.createStatement();

            ResultSet myResults = myStatement.executeQuery(
                    "SELECT ID, weight, name FROM Animal");

            while (myResults.next())
            {
                printColumn(myResults.getLong("ID") + "");
                printColumn(myResults.getInt("weight") + "");
                printColumn(myResults.getString("name"));
                System.out.println();
            }

        } catch (Exception e)
        {
            e.printStackTrace();
        } finally
        {
            try
            {
                if (myConnection != null)
                    myConnection.close();
            } catch (Exception e)
            {
            }
        }
    }
}
```

As you can see, the retrieval of the individual data is both error-prone and time-consuming. It's very easy to make a mistake in any of the hard-coded strings, and more complex SQL can lead to (possibly inadvertent) database-specific code.

Now let's look at a similar retrieval performed using Hibernate, as shown in Listing 1.2. The output of Listing 1.2 (excluding informational messages provided by Hibernate) is identical to that of Listing 1.1.

Listing 1.2   Simple Hibernate Code

```
package com.cascadetg.ch01;

import net.sf.hibernate.*;
import net.sf.hibernate.cfg.*;

public class HibernateClient
{
    static String[] props =
        {
            "hibernate.connection.driver_class",
                "com.mysql.jdbc.Driver",
            "hibernate.connection.url",
                "jdbc:mysql://localhost/sample",
            "hibernate.connection.username", "root",
            "hibernate.connection.password", "",
            "hibernate.dialect",
                "net.sf.hibernate.dialect.MySQLDialect",
            "hibernate.show_sql", "true"
        };

    static void printColumn(String in)
    {
        System.out.print(in);
        System.out.print(" | ");
    }

    public static void main(String[] args)
    {
        try
        {
            // One-time only configuration code, run only
            // during application initialization.
            Configuration myConfiguration = new
                Configuration();
            myConfiguration.addClass(
                com.cascadetg.ch01.Animal.class);
```

Listing 1.2   Simple Hibernate Code (*continued*)

```
for (int i = 0; i < props.length; i = i + 2)
    myConfiguration.setProperty(props[i], props[i
        +1]);

SessionFactory sessionFactory =
    myConfiguration.buildSessionFactory();

Session hibernateSession =
    sessionFactory.openSession();

Criteria query = hibernateSession.createCriteria(
    com.cascadetg.ch01.Animal.class);

// Here we get and loop over the results
java.util.Iterator results =
    query.list().iterator();
while (results.hasNext())
{
    // Notice that the result set is cast to the
    // Animal
    // object directly - no manual binding
    // required.
    Animal myAnimal = (Animal)results.next();

    printColumn(myAnimal.getId() + "");
    printColumn(myAnimal.getWeight() + "");
    printColumn(myAnimal.getName());
}
} catch (Exception e)
{
    e.printStackTrace();
}
    }
}
```

The first thing you should notice when examining the code in Listing 1.2 is that there are no hard-coded SQL strings in the query. In addition, there is no need to retrieve data using JDBC result set queries; you simply work with returned `Animal` objects. In this example, both the Java source for the `Animal` class and the schema for the corresponding `Animal` table are generated automatically by Hibernate.

It's possible to express complex relationships, including one-to-many and even many-to-many, using Hibernate, with Hibernate intelligently loading and caching data, automatically generating potentially very complex joins in order to optimally retrieve the data. This binding of the Java code and database schema is known as object/relational mapping.

Hibernate's Mapping System

Object/relational mapping refers to the notion of binding an object-oriented programming language to a relational database. In lieu of a theoretical discussion of object/relational mapping, let's take a quick look at how this mapping occurs in Hibernate.

The heart of the object/relational mapping system in Hibernate is an XML file, normally named `*.hbm.xml`. This mapping file describes how a database schema is bound to a set of Java classes. Hibernate (and related projects) provide tools for generating `*.hbm.xml` files both from existing database schema and from Java code. Some developers start with the `*.hbm.xml` file because it may be the most straightforward way to describe an application. Once you have a `*.hbm.xml` file, you can generate the supporting Java code, the database schema, or both. Regardless of your approach, it's important to understand the importance of `*.hbm.xml` files when working with Hibernate.

Listing 1.3 shows a simple Hibernate mapping file. A database-oriented developer would interpret this mapping as describing a system with two tables, weblog and post.

Listing 1.3   Example Hibernate Mapping File

```
<?xml version="1.0"?>
<!DOCTYPE hibernate-mapping SYSTEM
"http://hibernate.sourceforge.net/hibernate-mapping-2.0.dtd" >
<hibernate-mapping package="com.cascadetg.ch01">

     <class name="Weblog" table="weblog">
          <id name="id" column="ID" type="long" unsaved-
               value="null">
            <generator class="native"/>
          </id>
          <property name="title" column="title"
               type="string" length="50" not-null="true"/>
          <set name="Posts" lazy="true">
               <key column="weblog_id" />
               <one-to-many class="Post"/>
          </set>
     </class>

     <class name="Post" table="post">
          <id name="id" column="ID" type="long" unsaved-
               value="null">
```

Listing 1.3 Example Hibernate Mapping File (*continued*)

```
                <generator class="native"/>
            </id>
            <property name="title" column="title" type="string"
                    length="50" not-null="true"/>
            <property name="body" column="body" type="string"
                    length="255" not-null="true"/>
            <property name="postTimestamp" column="posttimestamp"
                    type="timestamp" />
            <many-to-one name="Weblog" class="Weblog"
                    column="weblog_id" not-null="true"/>
        </class>
</hibernate-mapping>
```

Listing 1.4 shows the resulting MySQL schema, generated automatically by Hibernate using the `*.hbm.xml` file shown in Listing 1.3. In particular, note the `post.weblog_id` column generated by Hibernate, used to track the relationship between a post and a weblog.

Listing 1.4 MySQL Schema for Weblog and Post

```
mysql> desc post;
+---------------+-------------+------+-----+---------+--------+
| Field         | Type        | Null | Key | Default | Extra  |
+---------------+-------------+------+-----+---------+--------+
| ID            | bigint(20)  |      | PRI | NULL    |        |
                                                auto_increment |
| title         | varchar(50) |      |     |         |        |
| body          | text        |      |     |         |        |
| posttimestamp | datetime    | YES  |     | NULL    |        |
| weblog_id     | bigint(20)  |      | MUL | 0       |        |
+---------------+-------------+------+ -----+---------+--------+

mysql> desc weblog;
+-------+-------------+------+-----+---------+----------------+
| Field | Type        | Null | Key | Default | Extra          |
+-------+-------------+------+-----+---------+----------------+
| ID    | bigint(20)  |      | PRI | NULL    | auto_increment |
| title | varchar(50) |      |     |         |                |
+-------+-------------+------+-----+---------+----------------+
```

Similarly, a set of Java class files generated by Hibernate from the same mapping file is shown in Figure 1.3. The generated Java objects act as data placeholders, but are essentially ordinary Java objects, conforming to standard JavaBean patterns.

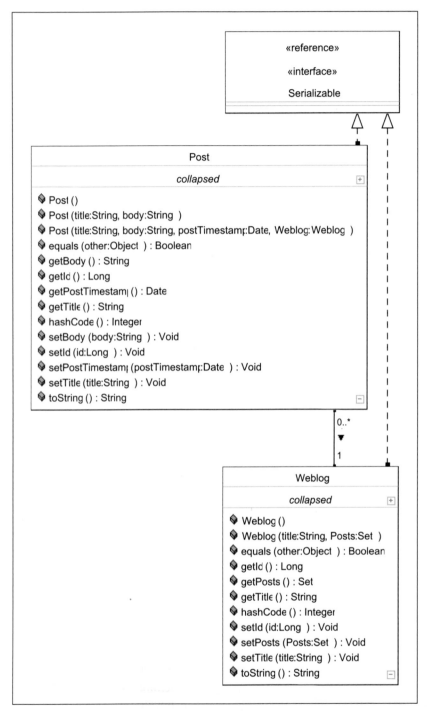

Figure 1.3.   Weblog & Post Java Objects

WHAT ARE JAVABEANS?

JavaBeans refer to the standard, base component model for Java applications. Briefly stated, JavaBeans are Java classes that define properties in the form `String getProperty() /setProperty(String in)`. A broad suite of APIs, tools, and software use JavaBeans as a core pattern. You will need to be familiar with the JavaBeans specification to use Hibernate, JSF, EJB 3.0, Swing, and almost any other significant Java library.

For more information on JavaBeans, consult any introductory Java text or http://java.sun.com/j2se/1.5.0/docs/guide/beans/index.html.

After creating this mapping, a Java developer can use a few simple Hibernate methods to insert, delete, update, and select data using these Java objects. This mapping between Java objects and relational tables is much more than a simplistic one-table-is-one-class system. As shown above, there is a relationship between the two tables: a weblog can have multiple posts. A Java developer can retrieve the posts associated with a given weblog merely by issuing a single `Weblog .getPosts()` call. Hibernate will automatically load the related posts from the database, bundle them into a set, and then return the data as Java objects.

Other Java/Database Integration Solutions

Hibernate represents merely one approach to object/relational mapping. Other programming languages and platforms offer a variety of other options, some similar to Hibernate, others radically different. Focusing on the Java world, here are a few of the popular alternatives.

Enterprise JavaBeans (EJB) 2.X

At the core of the J2EE specification, EJB 2.X attempts to provide a much broader set of features and functionality than Hibernate, at the price of a less robust core persistence model. The portion of J2EE/EJB 2.X most comparable to Hibernate is called container-managed entity persistence (CMP). Typically, CMP describes a system in which the J2EE server manages a single-entity bean class per table with individual-entity bean objects representing individual records. Conceptually, entity beans managed by the J2EE server include sophisticated functionality, such as complex transaction management, distributed caching, and much more. The alternative is bean-managed persistence, in which developer code is used to handle interaction with a database.

While EJB 2.X is suitable for certain large-scale enterprise applications, some developers find it difficult to work with. Most EJB 2.X systems involve a considerable amount of code generation and the need to master a complex suite of terminology. In particular, the implementation of the container-managed persistence layer and other components varies greatly between different application servers, making migration between projects that rely on container-managed persistence difficult. A popular use of Hibernate is as a persistence layer while working within the larger EJB 2.X environment—in effect, Hibernate serves as a replacement for container-managed persistence while leveraging the other portions of the EJB 2.X specification. This allows you to take advantage of many of the powerful features of your J2EE server without worrying about the portability of your object/relational layer.

Enterprise JavaBeans (EJB) 3.0

With an early draft specification first released in mid-2004, EJB 3.0 promises a persistence mechanism very similar to Hibernate. This is not surprising; the key developer of Hibernate was heavily involved in crafting the EJB 3.0 specification. Throughout this text, areas of similarity between EJB 3.0 and Hibernate will be highlighted, and additional comparison is provided in Chapter 13.

Java Data Objects (JDO)

Java Data Objects, or JDO, differ more from Hibernate in terms of implementation than from the interface offered to developers. Specifically, JDO normally requires compile-time pre-processing of the Java byte-code in order to add persistence capability, whereas Hibernate performs similar tasks at runtime when the application is first started. There are also differences in the APIs used to query from the persistence source. In particular, JDO attempts to solve a larger issue of persistence, targeting data stores other than relational databases. The attempt to target a broader range of storage mechanisms leads to a different focus than the relational database-focused Hibernate, with a different set of query capabilities. It's unclear whether the goal of targeting non–relational database persistence engines is worth the tradeoffs.

As of this writing, there has been some discussion of future versions of Hibernate and JDO moving closer together. Hibernate already supports three different interfaces (ODMG, HQL, and Criteria). It's entirely possible that future Hibernate releases may support a JDO style interface as well.

As of this writing, JDO implementations include:

TJDO, or TriActive JDO, is an open-source implementation of the JDO specification. It is explicitly designed to operate as Java persistence layer. In other words, the developer is expected to focus on Java development, with the database schema generated and managed by TJDO. It is not appropriate for situations with an existing schema. For more information, see http://tjdo.sourceforge.net/.

JPOX is another open-source JDO implementation. Unlike TJDO, more emphasis is placed on both schema-centric and Java-centric development. For more information, see http://www.jpox.org/.

JCredo provides a commercial implementation of JDO. A free edition is available for download from the Web site at http://www.jcredo.com/.

Apache OJB, available at http://db.apache.org/ojb/, provides both an ODMB and a JDO interface.

Castor is an open-source data-binding framework. While the implementation doesn't adhere precisely to the Sun JDO specification, it's similar enough that someone familiar with JDO can easily use Castor. For more information on Castor, see http://castor.exolab.org/.

How Does Sun Compare EJB and JDO?

Q. What is container managed persistence, and what are Java data objects?

A. EJB 2.0 CMP is the part of the J2EE component model that provides an object persistence service for EJB Containers. CMP's goal is to provide a standard mechanism for implementing persistent business components. CMP is not a general persistence facility for the Java platform. CMP provides distributed, transactional, secure access to persistent data, with a guaranteed portable interface. CMP is based on a functional set/get data-access model. It does not support transparent Java instance variable persistence.

A. JDO is an architecture that provides a standard way to transparently persist plain Java objects. It is designed to work in multiple tiers of an enterprise architecture, including J2SE, Web tier, and Application Servers. It does not itself provide distributed objects, distributed transactions, or security services, although it might be integrated with an EJB container that provides these services. CMP is for persisting distributed components built specifically to the entity bean component API. JDO is geared toward local, rich object models not tied to any particular API. Developers can choose between these technologies by evaluating their requirements (persistent components or persistent objects).

- From Sun's EJB 2.0 CMP and JDO FAQ, http://java.sun.com/ products/jdo/JDOCMPFAQ.html

---

Other Commercial O/R Tools

There are a variety of commercial object/relational tools, some of which were in existence long before Hibernate, EJB, or JDO. The prices for these tools range from free to tens of thousands of dollars. Options in this arena include Oracle's

TopLink (http://otn.oracle.com/products/ias/toplink/) and Software Tree's JDX (http://www.softwaretree.com/).

How to Obtain and Install

Hibernate can be downloaded for free from http://www.hibernate.org/. The core Hibernate distribution includes both Hibernate itself and several ancillary libraries. In addition to the main distribution, we will also make extensive use of the tools available in the Hibernate Extensions library.

Hibernate Distribution

Hibernate is distributed as a single compressed archive. For the remainder of this book, we will assume that you have decompressed the archive inside a folder called `C:\devenv\`. All screenshots and code in the book will assume that directory as the default installation directory for Hibernate and Hibernate Extensions.

Figure 1.4.   Hibernate.org Website

DIRECTORY CONVENTIONS

On my Windows development system, I install downloaded libraries in a single directory, `C:\devenv\`. This represents my personal repository of downloaded libraries (and associated documentation, samples, etc.). My development source trees are stored in another directory, `C:\devrep\`, which is controlled by a version control system (CVS, soon to be converted to Subversion). As libraries are required by projects, I copy the `.jar` files from the `C:\devenv\` directory into the appropriate location in `C:\devrep\`. Therefore, project-specific dependencies are resolved by relative paths, but on occasion interim development is done with references to the `C:\devenv\` directory. I don't use the `C:\Documents and Settings\<username>` directory because too many packages are confused by spaces in paths.

On UNIX systems, I generally use `~\devrep\` and `~\devenv\`.

There's nothing very magical about this strategy, but it does keep my tools and documentation nicely sorted from my development tree.

Let's explore the Hibernate installation a bit, as shown in Figure 1.5. The `bin` directory contains a couple of batch scripts for generating schema from a `*.hbm.xml` file. The `doc` directory contains a copy of the Hibernate documentation, including both the reference material and the Hibernate javadoc (also available online at http://www.hibernate.org/). The `eg` directory contains a Hibernate-provided example. The `lib` directory contains all of the various libraries that Hibernate either requires or can potentially take advantage of. The `src` directory contains the source for Hibernate itself. The test directory contains a suite of JUnit tests, useful when building or developing Hibernate itself. Similarly, the `build.bat` and `build.xml` files are used to generate your own version of Hibernate from source (a batch file to kick off the build, and an Ant script, respectively). The `changelog.txt` file indicates updates to Hibernate made since the last major revision. The `hibernate2.jar` file, is, of course, the main Hibernate library. The file `hibernate_logo.gif` is simply the logo for Hibernate; you might want to put this on your Web site, with a link back to http://www.hibernate.org/. The `lgpl.txt` file contains the LGPL license for Hibernate, and finally, `readme.txt` contains a variety of useful information tidbits on Hibernate.

LGPL and Hibernate

"Hibernate is Free Software. The LGPL license is sufficiently flexible to allow the use of Hibernate in both open source and commercial projects. Using Hibernate (by importing Hibernate's public interfaces in your Java code), and extending Hibernate (by subclassing) is considered by the authors of Hibernate to be dynamic linking. Hence our interpretation of the LGPL is that the use of the unmodified Hibernate source or binary does not affect the license of your application code.

If you modify Hibernate and redistribute your modifications, the LGPL applies."

- From the Hibernate documentation, http://hibernate.org/196.html

In other words, if you download the Hibernate source, make modifications, and distribute the resulting binaries, you will need to publish the source for the modifications. If you are merely including the original Hibernate libraries with your application, commercial or otherwise, you are under no obligation to release your source.

Depending on your application, you'll need to include the main hibernate2.jar file and supporting libraries to your application's CLASS-PATH.

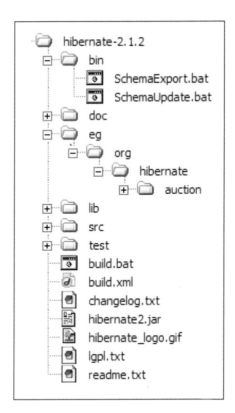

Figure 1.5. Hibernate Distribution

The lib directory of Hibernate contains a large number of libraries. Table 1.1 shows a list of the libraries files included with Hibernate 2.1.2, along with a list of URLs for the original library developers and the use of the library. The latest version of Hibernate, 2.1.5, relies on the same JAR files, but in certain cases a later version is included. Generally speaking, it's easiest to simply rely on the versions included with Hibernate, but you may wish to visit the URL below for additional documentation on that particular component.

Table 1.1. Hibernate Support Libraries

Library	URL	Description
`ant-1.5.3.jar`	http://ant.apache.org/	Build tool (similar to make)
`ant-optional-1.5.3.jar`	http://ant.apache.org/	Supporting features for Ant
`c3p0-0.8.3.jar`	http://sourceforge.net/projects/c3p0	Database connection pool
`cglib-2.0-rc2.jar`	http://cglib.sourceforge.net/	Runtime code-generation library
`commons-collections-2.1.jar`	http://jakarta.apache.org/commons/collections/	Additional collections beyond JDK collections
`commons-dbcp-1.1.jar`	http://jakarta.apache.org/commons/dbcp/	Database connection pool
`commons-lang-1.0.1.jar`	http://jakarta.apache.org/commons/lang/	Wide variety of basic utility functions
`commons-logging-1.0.3.jar`	http://jakarta.apache.org/commons/logging/	Wrapper for a wide variety of logging systems
`commons-pool-1.1.jar`	http://jakarta.apache.org/commons/pool/	Generic object pool
`concurrent-1.3.2.jar`	http://gee.cs.oswego.edu/dl/classes/EDU/ oswego/cs/dl/util/concurrent/intro.html	Doug Lea's concurrent programming utilities
`connector.jar`	http://java.sun.com/j2ee/connector/	Sun specification for integrating enterprise systems.
`dom4j-1.4.jar`	http://dom4j.org/	Library to ease use of XML, XPath, XSLT.
`ehcache-0.6.jar`	http://sourceforge.net/projects/ehcache	In-memory and disk cache, specifically designed for use with Hibernate
`jaas.jar`	http://java.sun.com/products/jaas/	Java authentication and authorization service
`jboss-cache.jar`	http://jboss.org/products/jbosscache	JBoss distributed cache implementation
`jboss-common.jar`	http://jboss.org/	JBoss utilities, including network and logging

(continued)

Table 1.1. Hibernate Support Libraries (*continued*)

Library	URL	Description
jboss-jmx.jar	http://jboss.org/	JBoss JMX implementation
jboss-system.jar	http://jboss.org/	JBoss core, including server and deployment engine
jcs-1.0-dev.jar	http://jakarta.apache.org/turbine/jcs/	Distributed cache system
jdbc2_0-stdext.jar	http://java.sun.com/products/jdbc/	JDBC 2.0 Optional Package, server side data sources
jgroups-2.2.jar	http://www.jgroups.org/	Toolkit for reliable multicast
jta.jar	http://java.sun.com/products/jta/	Java Transaction API, distributed transactions
junit-3.8.1.jar	http://www.junit.org/	Regression testing framework
log4j-1.2.8.jar	http://logging.apache.org/log4j/	Logging framework
odmg-3.0.jar	http://www.odmg.org/ originally, now source can be found at http://db.apache.org/ojb/	ODMG is now considered deprecated in favor of JDO and will probably be removed from a future version of Hibernate
oscache-2.0.jar	http://www.opensymphony.com/oscache/	Cache system
proxool-0.8.3.jar	http://proxool.sourceforge.net/	Database connection pool
swarmcache-1.0rc2.jar	http://swarmcache.sourceforge.net/	Distributed cache system
xalan-2.4.0.jar	http://xml.apache.org/xalan-j/	XSLT processor
xerces-2.4.0.jar	http://xml.apache.org/xerces2-j/	XML parser
xml-apis.jar	http://xml.apache.org/xerces2-j/	JAXP support

The precise collection of libraries you'll need will depend on your use of Hibernate. Aside from space, there's no reason not to copy all of the libraries into your application's path (for example, your \WEB-INF\lib\ directory for a Web application).

Hibernate Extensions Distribution

In addition to the core Hibernate distribution, you should also download and uncompress the Hibernate Extensions library (as of this writing, version 2.0.2). Figure 1.6 shows the distributions.

You may notice that the Hibernate Extensions distribution really consists of two main components: the Hibern8 IDE and a suite of command-line tools. Hibern8 IDE is really more analogous to a SQL monitor tool, allowing you to

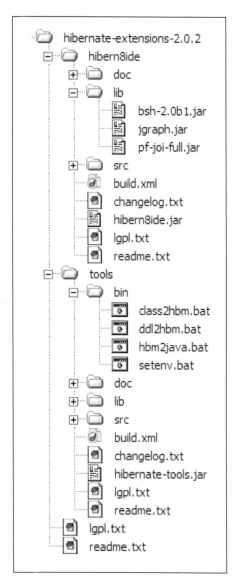

Figure 1.6. Hibernate Extensions Distribution

interactively query and explore object-results, as shown in Figure 1.7. You can use Hibern8 to interactively build your HQL queries, as shown in Chapter 8.

The various items in the tools directory are used to for mechanically generating files. The utility `class2hbm` is used to generate an `hbm.xml` file from compiled `.class` files. This is useful but not a complete solution, because

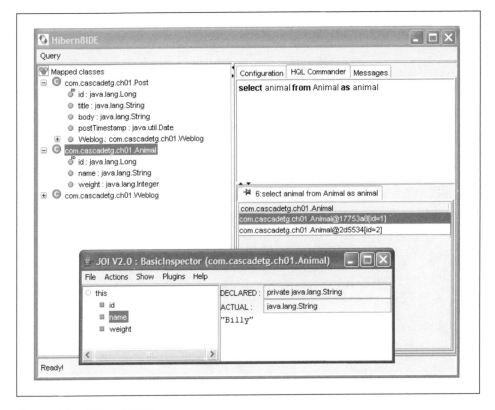

Figure 1.7.   Hibern8 IDE

hand-editing of `hbm.xml` files is still required; instead this book will be focus on the more complete solution provided by XDoclet, as described in Chapter 3. The utility `ddl2hbm` allows for import of an existing schema and automatic generation of an `hbm.xml` file, although this use has been deprecated in favor of a tool called MiddleGen, as will be discussed in Chapter 4. Finally, `hbm2java` generates Java code for you automatically from an existing `hbm.xml` file, as will also be discussed in Chapter 2 and Chapter 4.

Configuration

As we have seen, Hibernate is essentially a clump of libraries—not a full application. In the next chapter, we'll show a fully working Hibernate application, with complete instructions on how to set it up and configure it. If you already have a Hibernate-supported database installed and working, you can skip to Chapter 2 and get started with Hibernate. If you don't have a database set up (or aren't sure if it's supported), continue to the next section for instructions and information on how to get started with a Hibernate-supported database.

Supported Databases

The list of databases supported by Hibernate is maintained at http://hibernate.org/80.html. You would be well advised to visit this site frequently, because it lists a variety of database-specific issues.

As of this writing, the following databases have been tested and are known to work with Hibernate:

- IBM DB2 7.1, 7.2, 8.1
- MySQL 3.23, 4.0
- PostgreSQL 7.1.2, 7.2, 7.3, 7.4
- Oracle 8i, 9i
- Sybase 12.5 (JConnect 5.5)
- Interbase 6.0.1 (Open Source) with Firebird InterClient 2.01
- HypersonicSQL 1.61, 1.7.0
- Microsoft SQL Server 2000
- Mckoi SQL 0.93
- Progress 9
- Pointbase Embedded 4.3
- SAP DB 7.3

The following databases have been used and are thought to be compatible:

- Informix
- Ingres
- FrontBase
- Firebird (1.5 with JayBird 1.01)

The feature of Hibernate most subject to per-database vagaries is the automatic generation of schema. Even if your database is not supported, you can probably generate a DDL that is close, and modify the schema to fit. If you wish to use a database that is not shown, you can create a new dialect (see the `net.sf.hibernate.dialect.*` package).

If you don't already have a database in mind, the popular open-source, cross-platform MySQL is an excellent choice.

NOTE
Throughout the rest of this book, all examples are shown as run against MySQL, installed as described below. With luck, you should be able to run all of the examples against your preferred database merely by adding your database's driver to the CLASSPATH and changing the JDBC connection parameters.

Introduction to MySQL

MySQL can be downloaded for free from the Web site http://www.mysql.com/ (Figure 1.8). You'll want to download two pieces—the server itself, and the driver.

As of this writing, you can download the latest production version at http://www.mysql.com/downloads/mysql-4.0.html. On Windows, just click the download link for the version with installer. The instructions below should work on Windows NT, 2000, and XP. For other versions of Windows (and other operating systems), see the installation instructions on the MySQL Web site. Supported platforms include Linux, Solaris, FreeBSD, Mac OS X, and a variety of other flavors of UNIX (as well as a source release).

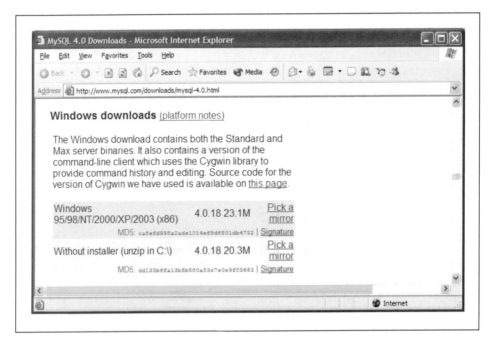

Figure 1.8.   MySQL Download

PLATFORM SUPPORT

I have personally used both Hibernate and MySQL on Windows, Red Hat Linux, and Mac OS X. If you are a Mac OS X developer, you may be interested in my other title, *Mac OS X for Java Geeks* (O'Reilly); it includes information on setting up Apache Jakarta Tomcat, and MySQL on Mac OS X. MySQL is a very common database on Linux; many distributions include it, and RPMs are available directly from the MySQL.com Web site.

While the screenshots and information shown in this text are generally provided for Windows, Mac OS X and Linux users should know that Hibernate works well on all of these platforms. While paths and screenshots shown were done on Windows, all of the software and tools covered in this text can easily be adapted to other platforms.

After downloading the resulting zip file (`mysql-4.0.18-win.zip` as of this writing), uncompress it using an unzip utility (such as WinZIP, http://www.winzip.com/). Inside the uncompressed folder, you should see several files. The only file of interest is the SETUP.EXE file. Double-click this and the installer will launch, as shown in Figure 1.9.

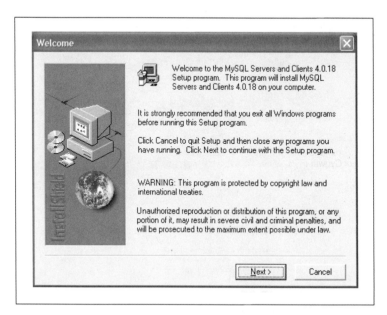

Figure 1.9. Starting the MySQL Installer

Click next several times, accepting the default options.

WARNING
Install MySQL in the default location, `C:\mysql`. Installation in another directory requires additional steps, not described here, even if you are using the MySQL installer.

After installation is complete, click *Start -> Programs -> Accessories -> Command Prompt* to bring up the terminal (on Windows XP; other versions of Windows may differ). At the terminal, use the CD command to change to the `C:\mysql\bin` directory. Then enter the command `mysqld  --install` and press return (this will install MySQL as a Windows service).

```
C:\mysql\bin>mysqld --install
Service successfully installed.
```

Next, click *Start -> Settings -> Control Panel -> Administrative Tools -> Services* (again, on Windows XP; other versions of Windows may differ). This will bring up a window, as shown in Figure 1.10. Right-clicking on the entry for MySQL, you bring up the menu shown to start the server. Note that MySQL is set to Automatic in the Startup Type column; this means that MySQL will start automatically when you restart your computer. You may wish to double-click on the MySQL entry and change this value to Manual if you expect to use MySQL only

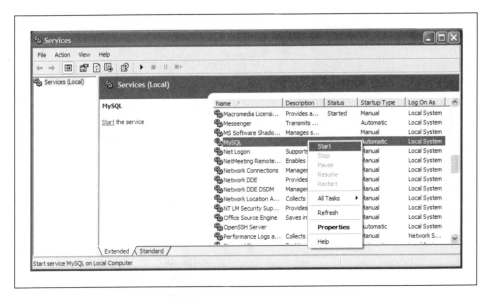

Figure 1.10.   Starting the MySQL Service

rarely—just remember that you'll need to come back to this pane to start the server before starting your development work.

NOTE

Make sure that MySQL is started (the status column in the Services window should read "Started") before continuing.

Now that MySQL has been installed and configured, let's make sure that we can access the monitor. Returning to our command prompt, from inside the `C:\mysql\bin` directory, issue the command `mysql -u root` and press return.

```
C:\mysql\bin>mysql -u root
Welcome to the MySQL monitor.  Commands end with ; or \g.
Your MySQL connection id is 1 to server version: 4.0.18-max-debug

Type 'help;' or '\h' for help. Type '\c' to clear the buffer.

mysql>
```

If you are familiar with SQL, you can now enter SQL commands, creating databases, tables, inserting and selecting records, and so on.

Before continuing, create a test database by entering the command `create database hibernate` and pressing return.

```
mysql> create database hibernate;
Query OK, 1 row affected (0.00 sec)
```

The only thing left to do is download the MySQL driver (called MySQL Connector/J). You can download the latest version of the driver from http://www.mysql.com/products/connector-j/. As of this writing, the production release is version 3.0, with the ZIP file download named `mysql-connector-java-3.0.11-stable.zip`. Inside this ZIP archive, you will find three folders, `clover`, `META-INF`, and `mysql-connector-java-3.0.11-stable`. Inside the `mysql-connector-java-3.0.11-stable` folder, you will find a `mysql-connector-java-3.0.11-stable-bin.jar` file. This is the file you should put on your `CLASSPATH` to connect to MySQL.

NOTE

These instructions create a minimal, insecure installation of MySQL on your system (including a default, local-host-only root account with no password). If you are using MySQL in a production environment, you'll want to do a lot more (beyond the scope of this text) to secure and optimize MySQL.

Table 1.2.   Default MySQL Connection Properties

Hibernate Property	Setting
`hibernate.connection.driver_class`	`com.mysql.jdbc.Driver`
`hibernate.connection.url`	`jdbc:mysql://localhost/` `hibernate`
`hibernate.connection.username`	`root`
`hibernate.connection.password`	*none – set to an empty string*
`hibernate.dialect`	`net.sf.hibernate.dialect` `.MySQLDialect`

If you have configured your system in this fashion, you will use the configuration options shown in Table 1.2 to connect to MySQL. Note the hibernate string at the end of the connection URL; that's a reference to the database we just created.

Now that you've set up and configured MySQL, you're ready to move on to the next chapter and start working with a sample Hibernate application.

Getting Oriented

This chapter provides a non-trivial example of how a developer might use Hibernate in the course of building a simple JSP application. The application in the example is a partial implementation of a simple weblog system. (For an example of a full-blown weblog system, check out http://blogger.com/ or the Hibernate-based http://www.rollerweblogger.org/.)

The example shows how to build an application by starting with Hibernate mapping files (*.hbm.xml). These mapping files are used to generate the database schema and the persistent Java code; as the mapping files are updated, the schema and the persistent Java code are updated as well. This isn't the only way to build an application in Hibernate. In Chapter 3, an application will be built by starting from Java source files, and in Chapter 4, an existing database schema is used to generate both the mapping files and the Java source.

Application Architecture

The application in this chapter is a classic three-tier application—a browser accesses an application server, which in turn accesses a database. Figure 2.1 shows the files used by the application. Note that the application works with persistent objects, not directly with the database. Handcrafted Hibernate mapping files generate the persistent objects and the database definition. The mapping files provide development-time information and also runtime configuration information.

The JSP pages in the application are typical, insofar as each page contains a small amount of persistent logic corresponding to its action. In a larger-scale application, it would be best to move the logic in the JSP pages into Java classes, but for an application of this size the present approach works reasonably well.

The handcrafted portions of the application are the JSP pages, the single Java class, and the two mapping files (*.hbm.xml). The heart of the application is described by two mapping files. As a reminder, you are strongly encouraged to

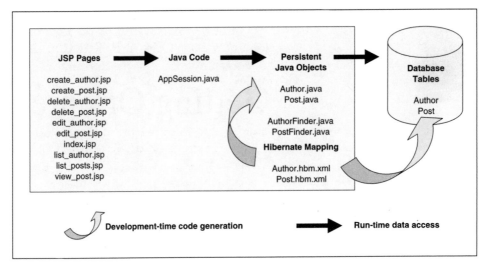

Figure 2.1.   Application Architecture

start by downloading the source for this example from http://www
.cascadetg.com/hibernate/ and then use it to follow along.

Mapping Files

A mapping file is principally concerned with the binding between Java objects and
a database schema. In this application, the mapping files are generating both the
Java objects and the database schema.

WHY START WITH MAPPING FILES?

I feel that it is much easier to learn how Hibernate works by starting with the
mapping files and then looking carefully at the code generated. This may
seem harder (after all, if you're already a Java guru, wouldn't it be easier to
start with Java?), but in practice, it is easier to simply rely on Hibernate's
code generators when you are learning Hibernate.

This approach may seem non-intuitive at first, but almost by definition the
technology you are least likely to be familiar with is the Hibernate mapping
file format. If you have experience with Java and SQL, you will probably
understand the output generated from the mapping file and thereby be able
to form an opinion as to the "correctness" of the result for your purposes.

Starting from Java (as described in Chapter 3) adds the complexity of
XDoclet. Starting from an existing database schema (as described in Chap-

ter 4) adds the complexity of Middlegen. No matter which system you choose, you will need an understanding of the mapping file format to be successful. For all of these reasons, I strongly recommend that your first Hibernate project start with the mapping file.

The mapping files define two classes, a `Post` class and an `Author` class. The idea is simple—an author can write one or more posts. Our application will show how to create, update, insert, and delete records using these two basic classes. Finally, this application will use Hibernate's built-in support for version management to manage situations in which a submitted edit for a post would overwrite changes made by another author.

Mapping Files in Depth

The `Post` and `Author` classes are modeled using two `*.hbm.xml` files, named `Post.hbm.xml` and `Author.hbm.xml`. Each is placed in the proper package folder corresponding to the desired class name. Therefore, the path of the `Post.hbm.xml` file would be `com/cascadetg/ch02/Post.hbm.xml`, next to the corresponding source file. Inspecting Listing 2.1, the `Post` class is mapped to a `post` table. A unique identifier[1] is automatically generated when a `Post` is created. In this example, the unique identifier is a string, but it could be an integer as well. A column is declared in the `post` table, `revision`, which allows Hibernate to keep track of the version number of the `Post`. By using Hibernate's built-in versioning system, our application can easily handle conflicting concurrent modifications.

VERSIONING?

The example uses Hibernate's built-in support for version management to perform optimistic locking (as described in more detail in Chapter 9). If you are just starting to work your way through learning Hibernate, simply be aware that Hibernate has a built-in feature for handling versioning of database records. This functionality is very handy for Web application development in which logical transactions may be spread across a variety of Web browser requests.

---

[1] In database terminology, a primary key

The most confusing part of the `Post` mapping file is the `many-to-one` element. Each `Post` has one (not optional) author. The `many-to-one` element is used to indicate that each `Post` will have a single column pointing to the unique identifier of the author.

For more information on the tags used in a mapping file, see Chapter 5.

ADVANCED COMMENTS

In this example, the `*.hbm.xml` files are stored with the source files and then copied to the class path as part of the deployment process. The mapping files serve both as a compile-time tool (for generating the Java sources) and a runtime descriptor (for binding the resulting Java sources to the database).

If you start with Java source or an existing database, the mapping files are generated for you at compile time and thus serve only as runtime descriptors.

Note that Hibernate supports a variety of strategies for the location of your `*.hbm.xml` files in addition to the `addClass()` method shown (see Chapter 6 for more information).

The `uuid.hex` generator is portable and also works well in a Web application environment. Most of the columns are specified using a `column` attribute, but the `many-to-one` column is specified with a separate element to indicate that the column is `not-null`. The `meta` tags are used by the `hbm2java` code generator to indicate that utility-retrieval methods corresponding to these properties should be generated.

Listing 2.1   Post Mapping

```xml
<?xml version="1.0"?>
<!DOCTYPE hibernate-mapping PUBLIC
    "-//Hibernate/Hibernate Mapping DTD 2.0//EN"
    "http://hibernate.sourceforge.net/hibernate-mapping-
2.0.dtd" >

<hibernate-mapping>

<class name="com.cascadetg.ch02.Post" table="post">

    <id name="id" type="string" column="ID">
        <meta attribute="finder-method">findByID</meta>
        <generator class="uuid.hex" />
    </id>
```

Listing 2.1 Post Mapping (continued*)*

```
    <version column="revision" name="revision" />

    <property name="title" type="string"
         column="title" length="100" />

    <property name="summary" type="string"
         column="summary" length="255" />

    <property name="content" type="text" column="content" />

    <property name="date" type="timestamp" column="date" />

    <many-to-one name="author"
        class="com.cascadetg.ch02.Author">

        <!-- Used by code generator -->
        <meta attribute="finder-method">findByAuthorID</meta>

        <!-- Used as a DDL hint -->
        <column name="authorID" not-null="true" />
    </many-to-one>
  </class>
  </hibernate-mapping>
```

Turning to the `Author.hbm.xml` file shown in Listing 2.2, several elements are seen in common with the `Post.hbm.xml` mapping. The most significant change is the introduction of the `set` tag, which defines the pointer back from an author to zero, one, or more posts. The `set` tag means that an implementation of `java.util.Set` will be used to represent the posts.

Several attributes are used to control how the `java.util.Set` is managed by Hibernate. The `lazy="true"` attribute means that the posts associated with a particular `Author` object won't be automatically fetched with the same SQL query as the `Author` object. The `inverse="true"` attribute is used to indicate that the `Post` is responsible for managing the relationship between authors and posts. The `cascade="delete"` attribute is used to indicate that when a `Author` is deleted, all of the `Author`'s posts should automatically be deleted as well (a powerful and potentially dangerous feature if not used carefully).

LAZY? INVERSE? CASCADE?

These attributes control how Hibernate will integrate the Java object representation with the database. Additional details about these attributes are provided in Chapter 5.

Note the precise declaration of the `set` tag. A `key` column is used to indicate the column in the `Post` table used to refer to the author. The `one-to-many` tag is used to indicate the `Post` object (and therefore, implicitly, the `post` table).

Listing 2.2 Author Mapping

```xml
<?xml version="1.0"?>
<!DOCTYPE hibernate-mapping PUBLIC
    "-//Hibernate/Hibernate Mapping DTD 2.0//EN"
    "http://hibernate.sourceforge.net/hibernate-mapping-
2.0.dtd" >

<hibernate-mapping>

<class name="com.cascadetg.ch02.Author" table="author">

    <id name="id" type="string" column="ID">
        <meta attribute="finder-method">findByID</meta>
        <generator class="uuid.hex" />
    </id>

    <property name="firstName" type="java.lang.String"
        column="first" length="100" />

    <property name="lastName" type="java.lang.String"
        column="last" length="100" />

    <property name="email" type="java.lang.String"
        column="email" length="100">
            <meta attribute="finder-method">findByEmail</meta>
    </property>

    <!-- bi-directional one-to-many association to Post -->
    <set name="posts" lazy="true" inverse="true"
            cascade="delete" >
        <key>
            <column name="authorID" />
        </key>
        <one-to-many class="com.cascadetg.ch02.Post"/>
    </set>

</class>
</hibernate-mapping>
```

As can be seen from the mapping files shown in Listing 2.1 and Listing 2.2, Hibernate possesses a wide (even overwhelming) set of features. The name attributes (used to specify the object-oriented, Java portions of the system) and the table/column attributes (used to specify the database side of affairs) constitute the heart of the mappings. Everything else, more or less, is used to describe additional functionality such as the management of collections, unique identifier generation, and version management.

If you wish to explore the meaning of any of these tags or attributes in more detail before continuing, see Chapter 5.

Generating Java Source

Given the `*.hbm.xml` files shown in Listing 2.1 and Listing 2.2, the next step is to generate the corresponding Java code. This is done with Ant. Listing 2.3 shows the complete Ant `build.xml` file used for this application.

ANT

Ant is a popular open-source build tool. It can be downloaded for free from http://ant.apache.org/. To use Ant, simply unzip or untar the distribution into a directory, place the `/bin` directory on your path, and make sure that your JAVA_HOME variable points to your Java 2 SDK installation.

If you are running on Windows and are not familiar with setting your path, you can invoke Ant directly. For example if Ant has been unzipped into the `C:\devenv\ant\` directory, you could call it by simply typing `C:\devenv\ant\bin\ant`.

Similarly, if you are running on Windows and your JAVA_HOME has not been set, you may find it easiest to simply add a line to the top of the `\bin\ant.bat` file setting JAVA_HOME.

```
set JAVA_HOME=C:\j2sdk1.4.1_03\
```

For Mac OS X and other UNIX systems, check the documentation for your preferred shell for more information on how to set your path and environment variables.

If you don't know how to set your path and environment variables, or don't want to deal with this, you can simply use an integrated development environment (IDE). Both Eclipse (http://www.eclipse.org/) and NetBeans (http://www.netbeans.org/) are free, open-source, multiplatform, and bundle an integrated version of Ant.

Listing 2.3 Ant Build File

```xml
<?xml version="1.0"?>
<project name="ch03" default="all">
```

(continues)

Listing 2.3 Ant Build File (*continued*)

```
    <target name="all" depends="build_hbm,deploy" />

    <description>Hibernate starting with Java</description>

<!-- project name -->
<property name="name" value="chapter2" />

<!-- installation configuration -->
<!-- You'll need to set these depending on your library
    installation directories -->
<property name="hibernate_path"
    value="C:\devenv\hibernate-2.1.2"/>
<property name="hibernate_tool_path"
    value="C:\devenv\hibernate-extensions-2.1\tools"/>

<!-- the generated package info -->
<property name="package" value="com.cascadetg.ch02" />
<property name="package.dir" value="\com\cascadetg\ch02" />

<property name="tomcat.app"
    value="C:\Tomcat5\webapps\weblog\" />
<property name="tomcat.classes.dir"
    value="C:\Tomcat5\webapps\weblog\WEB-INF\classes" />

<path id="project.class.path">
    <pathelement
        location="${hibernate_path}\hibernate2.jar"/>
    <pathelement
        location="${hibernate_tool_path}\hibernate-
        tools.jar"/>
    <pathelement location=
        "${hibernate_path}\lib\commons-collections-2.1.jar"
        />
    <pathelement location=
        "${hibernate_path}\lib\commons-logging-1.0.3.jar"
        />
    <pathelement location=
        "${hibernate_path}\lib\commons-lang-1.0.1.jar" />
    <pathelement location=
        "${hibernate_path}\lib\xerces-2.4.0.jar" />
    <pathelement location=
        "${hibernate_tool_path}\lib\jdom.jar"/>
</path>
```

Listing 2.3   Ant Build File (*continued*)

```
    <!-- Normally, Ant build files are stored at the root of
    the tree.
        The builds for this book are on a per-chapter basis -->
    <property name="base_dir" value="..\..\..\" />

<!-- creates the Java sources from the HBM files. -->
<target name="build_hbm" description="builds the Java
sources">
    <taskdef name="hbm2java"
        classname="net.sf.hibernate.tool.hbm2java
            .Hbm2JavaTask">
        <classpath refid="project.class.path"/>
    </taskdef>

    <mkdir dir="${build.src.dir}"/>
    <hbm2java config="hbm2java_config.xml"
    output="${base_dir}">
        <fileset dir="." includes="*.hbm.xml"/>
    </hbm2java>
</target>

<!-- Builds and copies files into Tomcat WEB-INF classes -->
<target name="deploy" >
    <echo message="compiling..." />
        <javac srcdir="${base_dir}"
        destdir="${tomcat.classes.dir}"
                debug="on" includes="**/ch02/**">
        <classpath refid="project.class.path"/>
    </javac>

    <echo message="copying..." />
    <copy todir="${tomcat.classes.dir}${package.dir}">
        <fileset dir="." casesensitive="yes">
          <include name="**/*.hbm.xml"/>
        </fileset>
    </copy>
    <copy todir="${tomcat.classes.dir}">
        <fileset dir="${base_dir}" casesensitive="yes">
          <include name="*.properties"/>
        </fileset>
    </copy>
</target>

<!-- Used to copy JSP files back into CVS managed folder. -->
<target name="copy_from_jsp">
```

Listing 2.3   Ant Build File *(continued)*

```
        <copy todir="${base_dir}\webapp">
            <fileset dir="${tomcat.app}" casesensitive="yes" />
        </copy>
    </target>
</project>
```

Listing 2.3 contains several tasks. The task of principal interest is the `build_hbm` task, broken out into a separate listing in Listing 2.4. Note that this task relies on the `net.sf.hibernate.tool.hbm2java.Hbm2JavaTask` class, part of the Hibernate `hbm2java` tool suite. The actual function of the tool suite is straightforward; it reads the `*.hbm.xml` files and produces Java files according to rules specified in the `hbm2java_config.xml` file.

Listing 2.4   Building the Java Source

```
<!-- creates the Java sources from the HBM files. -->
<target name="build_hbm" description="builds the Java
sources">
    <taskdef name="hbm2java"
        classname="net.sf.hibernate.tool.hbm2java
            .Hbm2JavaTask">
        <classpath refid="project.class.path"/>
    </taskdef>

    <mkdir dir="${build.src.dir}"/>
    <hbm2java config="hbm2java_config.xml"
    output="${base_dir}">
        <fileset dir="." includes="*.hbm.xml"/>
    </hbm2java>
</target>
```

The `hbm2java_config.xml` file is used to configure additional code-generation features. As shown in Listing 2.5, in addition to the standard Java code generation it will also generate a set of "finder" classes, utility functions that more easily retrieve objects by a specific property value.

Listing 2.5   Configuring hbm2java

```
<?xml version="1.0"?>
<codegen>
```

Listing 2.5 Configuring hbm2java

```
    <generate renderer="net.sf.hibernate.tool.hbm2java
    .BasicRenderer"/>
    <generate
        package="com.cascadetg.ch02.finder"
        suffix="Finder"
        renderer="net.sf.hibernate.tool.hbm2java
        .FinderRenderer"/>
</codegen>
```

Running the Ant task will automatically generate (or regenerate) the Java classes as described in the mapping file.

Generated Persistent Classes

You may be surprised to find that the source generated by Hibernate is simply a set of ordinary JavaBeans (sometimes referred to as plain old Java objects or POJO). Figure 2.2 shows an overview of the generated source (the full argument constructors are omitted for readability).

For the sake of completeness, Listing 2.6 shows the code generated for the `com.cascadetg.ch02.Author` class. Probably the most shocking thing about the generated source is the *lack* of any especially unusual information. The class does implement `java.io.Serializable`, but there is no base class (although implements or extends can optionally be set by the mapping file). This makes Hibernate useful in a wide variety of situations, from an EJB 2.X BMP environment to a Swing client.

Listing 2.6 Author Persistent Object

```
package com.cascadetg.ch02;

import java.io.Serializable;
import java.util.Set;
import org.apache.commons.lang.builder.ToStringBuilder;


/** @author Hibernate CodeGenerator */
public class Author implements Serializable {

    /** identifier field */
    private String id;
```

(continues)

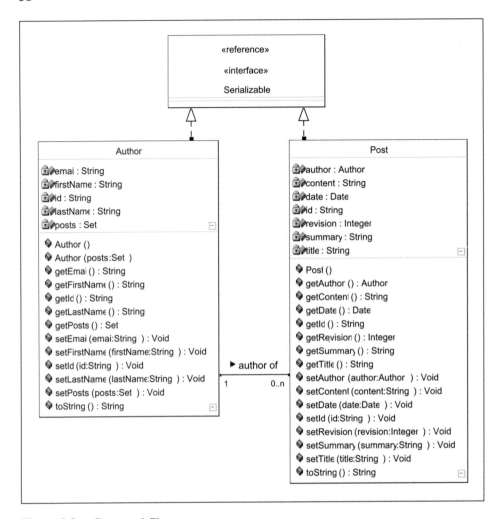

Figure 2.2.   Generated Classes

Listing 2.6   Author Persistent Object (*continued*)

```
/** nullable persistent field */
private String firstName;

/** nullable persistent field */
private String lastName;

/** nullable persistent field */
private String email;
```

Listing 2.6 Author Persistent Object (*continued*)

```java
    /** persistent field */
    private Set posts;

    /** full constructor */
    /*public Author(String firstName, String lastName,
    String email, Set posts) {
        this.firstName = firstName;
        this.lastName = lastName;
        this.email = email;
        this.posts = posts;
    }*/

    /** default constructor */
    public Author() {
    }

    /** minimal constructor */
    public Author(Set posts) { this.posts = posts; }

    public String getId() { return this.id; }

    public void setId(String id) { this.id = id; }

    public String getFirstName() { return this.firstName; }

    public void setFirstName(String firstName) {
        this.firstName = firstName; }

    public String getLastName() { return this.lastName; }

    public void setLastName(String lastName) {
        this.lastName = lastName; }

    public String getEmail() { return this.email; }

    public void setEmail(String email) { this.email = email; }

    public Set getPosts() { return this.posts; }

    public void setPosts(Set posts) { this.posts = posts; }

    public String toString() { return
        new ToStringBuilder(this).append("id",
        getId()).toString(); }

}
```

Now that the application has a set of Java classes corresponding to the database, it needs classes to actually perform work against the database.

Application Configuration

Given the Java source and a set of mapping files, the application needs code in order to actually perform the needed database operations. A set of Hibernate classes (principally those in the `net.sf.hibernate.*` package) is used to handle database operations. The `initialization()` method in Listing 2.7 shows how a Hibernate `net.sf.hibernate.cfg.Configuration` object is used to create an instance of `net.sf.hibernate.SessionFactory`.

The `net.sf.hibernate.cfg.Configuration` object needs a set of mapping files. By using the `Configuration.addClass(Object.class)` method, Hibernate will search the class path for a `directory/*.hbm.xml` file that corresponds to the class name. So, given a `com.cascadetg.ch02.Author` class, Hibernate will look for a `com/cascadetg/ch02/Author.hbm.xml` file somewhere on the current class path. When the application is run and the `Configuration` object is first created, Hibernate will verify that the mapping file and the associated Java class files can actually be bound together.

After a successful configuration, Hibernate returns a `SessionFactory`. A `SessionFactory` is a thread-safe object intended to be shared throughout the application. Later in this chapter, the application will obtain `net.sf.hibernate.Session` objects from this `SessionFactory`.

You may have noticed the reference to `net.sf.hibernate.tool.hbm2ddl.SchemaUpdate`. This single line of code connects to the database and attempts to create tables, column, and key constraints corresponding to the declared mapping files.

ADVANCED COMMENTS

The code given here attempts to update the schema twice and also issues a MySQL specific command to convert the tables to a format that supports modern database features. For more information, consult the MySQL documentation. If you are using a non-MySQL database, you can comment this functionality out.

Even if you do not intend to use MySQL, it is worth noting that Hibernate allows seamless integration of native SQL functionality. Almost every database includes some vendor-specific capability or optimization. As shown, database-specific functionality fits easily into the overall Hibernate development model. It is up to the individual developer to balance the needs of a portable application against vendor-specific extensions.

Listing 2.7   Hibernate Application Configuration

```
package com.cascadetg.ch02;

/** Various Hibernate-related imports */
import net.sf.hibernate.*;
import net.sf.hibernate.cfg.*;

import net.sf.hibernate.tool.hbm2ddl.SchemaUpdate;

public class AppSession
{

    static String fileSep =
        System.getProperty("file.separator");

    /** We use this session factory to create our sessions */
    public static SessionFactory sessionFactory;

    public static Session getSession()
    {
        if (sessionFactory == null) initialization();
        try
        {
            return sessionFactory.openSession();
        } catch (Exception e)
        {
            e.printStackTrace();
            return null;
        }
    }

    /**
     * Loads the Hibernate configuration information, sets up the
     * database and the Hibernate session factory.
     */
    public static void initialization()
    {
        try
        {
            Configuration myConfiguration = new
                Configuration();
            myConfiguration.addClass(Post.class);
            myConfiguration.addClass(Author.class);

            // This is the code that updates the database to the
            // current schema.
```

Listing 2.7   Hibernate Application Configuration (*continued*)

```
            new SchemaUpdate(myConfiguration)
                    .execute(true, true);

            // Sets up the session factory (used in the rest
            // of the application).
            sessionFactory = myConfiguration
                    .buildSessionFactory();

            // MySQL only
            setInnoDB();
            // MySQL only
            new SchemaUpdate(myConfiguration)
                    .execute(true, true);


        } catch (Exception e)
        {
            e.printStackTrace();
        }
    }

    public static void main(String[] args)
    {
        initialization();
    }

    /** MySQL only */
    public static void setInnoDB()
    {
        Session hibernateSession = null;
        Transaction myTransaction = null;

        try
        {
            hibernateSession = sessionFactory.openSession();
            myTransaction =
                hibernateSession.beginTransaction();

            java.sql.Statement myStatement = hibernateSession
                    .connection().createStatement();
            myStatement
                    .execute("ALTER TABLE Author TYPE=InnoDB");
            myStatement.execute("ALTER TABLE Post
                TYPE=InnoDB");
```

Listing 2.7 Hibernate Application Configuration (*continued*)

```
            myTransaction.commit();

            System.out.println();
    } catch (Exception e)
    {
        e.printStackTrace();
        try
        {
            myTransaction.rollback();
        } catch (Exception e2)
        {
            // Silent failure of transaction rollback
        }
    } finally
    {
        try
        {
            if (hibernateSession != null)
                    hibernateSession.close();
        } catch (Exception e)
        {
            // Silent failure of session close
        }
    }

    }

}
```

Using this class to initialize the application makes it easy to port the application to a variety of application servers. The connection underlying the `Session-Factory` can be set to point to many different data sources, from a JNDI connection to a direct JDBC pool (as described in Chapter 6), and can even add a performance monitor (as described in Chapter 10).

Generated Database Schema

The first time a session is obtained (using the code shown in Listing 2.7), the configuration and `SessionFactory` are set up and the database schema is updated. Listing 2.8 shows the schema for the tables as generated by this application's mapping files. In particular, note the `authorID` column, pointing back to the author table.

Listing 2.8   Generated Schema

```
mysql> desc author;
+-------+--------------+------+-----+---------+-------+
| Field | Type         | Null | Key | Default | Extra |
+-------+--------------+------+-----+---------+-------+
| ID    | varchar(255) |      | PRI |         |       |
| first | varchar(100) | YES  |     | NULL    |       |
| last  | varchar(100) | YES  |     | NULL    |       |
| email | varchar(100) | YES  |     | NULL    |       |
+-------+--------------+------+-----+---------+-------+
4 rows in set (0.11 sec)

mysql> desc post;
+----------+--------------+------+-----+---------+-------+
| Field    | Type         | Null | Key | Default | Extra |
+----------+--------------+------+-----+---------+-------+
| ID       | varchar(255) |      | PRI |         |       |
| revision | int(11)      |      |     | 0       |       |
| title    | varchar(100) | YES  |     | NULL    |       |
| summary  | varchar(255) | YES  |     | NULL    |       |
| content  | text         | YES  |     | NULL    |       |
| date     | datetime     | YES  |     | NULL    |       |
| authorID | varchar(255) |      | MUL |         |       |
+----------+--------------+------+-----+---------+-------+
```

Web Application

After the mapping files and Java classes are assembled, the application still needs
a user interface. A Web application defines a specific packaging format. Figure 2.3
shows the various assets in their proper relative directories. All of these files are
included in the download at http://www.cascadetg.com/hibernate/.

Only a subset of the full Hibernate libraries (as described in Chapter 1) is
required for this application. The contents of the WEB-INF/lib directory are:

- c3p0-0.8.3.jar
- cglib-2.0-rc2.jar
- dom4j-1.4.jar
- ehcache-0.6.jar
- hibernate2.jar
- jdbc2_0-stdext.jar

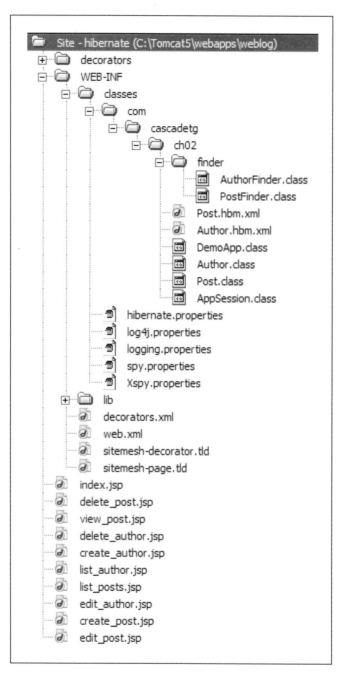

Figure 2.3 Web Application Files

- `jta.jar`
- `log4j-1.2.8.jar`
- `mysql-connector-java-3.0.10-stable-bin.jar`
- `odmg-3.0.jar`
- `sitemesh-2.0.1.jar`

The application includes the JSP pages listed below. The `index.jsp` page simply redirects the user to the `list_posts.jsp` page. The meaning of the pages is self-evident from the name of the file.

- `index.jsp`
- `list_posts.jsp`
- `create_author.jsp`
- `list_author.jsp`
- `create_post.jsp`
- `edit_author.jsp`
- `edit_post.jsp`
- `view_post.jsp`
- `delete_author.jsp`
- `delete_post.jsp`

JSP Interface

A few simple conventions are used in the development of the JSP files used by this application. Identifiers are passed using the values `authorID` and `postID`. All of these files start with a header containing a bit of Java logic, and the rest of the page is concerned with the HTML formatting of the displayed results.

ADVANCED COMMENTS

You may notice that the JSP as displayed in the screenshots looks quite a bit nicer than the raw JSP shown. This is accomplished using a template technology called SiteMesh (http://www.opensymphony.com/sitemesh/). For more information on how SiteMesh works, look for my articles on www .cascadetg.com. SiteMesh has no effect on how these pages work; in this application, it merely serves to provide for nicer formatting and headers.

Figure 2.4. No Posts Listed

List Posts

Our first JSP lists the currently available posts. When the page is first visited, there are no posts. As shown in Figure 2.4, the only real user action at this point is to add a post (which, in turn, requires an author).

After a few authors and posts have been added, the page shows additional functionality for editing and deleting posts, as can be seen in Figure 2.5.

Reviewing the code for this JSP, as shown in Listing 2.9, provides an introduction to Hibernate object retrieval using the Criteria API. A session is retrieved from our `AppSession` factory, a transaction is started, and a query in the form of a `Criteria` object is executed. The post `java.util.Iterator` holds the returned `Post` objects. By setting the sole criteria to the `Post.class`, the application indicates that it wants all of the `Post` objects.

ADVANCED COMMENTS

The Criteria API is one of the two mechanisms for querying objects using Hibernate. The other is Hibernate Query Language, or HQL. Both are described in more detail in Chapter 8. Briefly, the Criteria API allows you to obtain records from the database using Java objects as templates, whereas HQL is a more object-oriented version of SQL. As described in Chapter 8, both query systems have pros and cons.

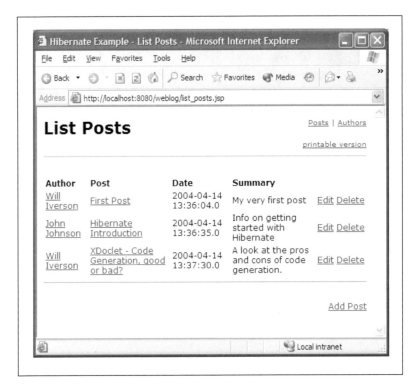

Figure 2.5.   Authors and Posts Added

A more robust application would limit the results returned to a set of perhaps 25 or 50 `Post` objects at a time, and would also add previous/next
functionality. This could easily be done using the `Criteria.setFirst`
`Result()` and `Criteria.setMaxResults()` methods, perhaps in conjunction with an offset parameter.

For more information on the Criteria API, see Chapter 8.

Listing 2.9   Listing Posts Source

```
<%@ page contentType="text/html; charset=utf-8" language="java"
    import="com.cascadetg.ch02.*,net.sf.hibernate.*" %><%

String error = "";
Session hibernateSession = null;
Transaction myTransaction = null;
```

Listing 2.9 Listing Posts Source (*continued*)

```java
java.util.Iterator posts = null;
try
{

    hibernateSession = AppSession.getSession();
    myTransaction = hibernateSession.beginTransaction();

    Criteria query =
        hibernateSession.createCriteria(Post.class);

    posts = query.list().iterator();

    myTransaction.commit();
    hibernateSession.close();

} catch (Exception e) {
    error = e.getMessage(); e.printStackTrace();
    try{ myTransaction.rollback(); }
    catch (Exception e2) {;}
}
finally
{
    try{hibernateSession.close();}
    catch (Exception e) {;}
}
%>
<HTML>
<HEAD>
<TITLE>List Posts</TITLE>
</HEAD>
<BODY>
<%= error %>
<% if(posts == null) { %>
<p>No posts available.</p>
<% } else { %>
<table width="100%"  border="0">
  <tr>
    <td><strong>Author</strong></td>
    <td><strong>Post</strong></td>
  <td><strong>Date</strong></td>
    <td><strong>Summary</strong></td>
  <td> </td>
  <td> </td>
  </tr>
<% while(posts.hasNext()) {
    Post myPost = (Post)posts.next();
```

(*continues*)

Listing 2.9   Listing Posts Source (*continued*)

```
%>
  <tr>
    <td><%

      if(myPost.getAuthor() != null)
      {
            %><a href="edit_author.jsp?authorID=<%=
            myPost.getAuthor().getId()%>"><%=
            myPost.getAuthor().getFirstName()%> <%=
            myPost.getAuthor().getLastName() %></a><%
      }
  %> </td>
    <td><a href="view_post.jsp?postID=<%=
      myPost.getId()%>"><%=myPost.getTitle()%></a> </td>
  <td><%=myPost.getDate().toString()%></td>
    <td><%=myPost.getSummary()%> </td>
  <td>
    <a href="edit_post.jsp?postID=<%=
  myPost.getId()%>">Edit</a></td>
  <td>
    <a href="delete_post.jsp?postID=<%=
            myPost.getId()%>">Delete</a></td>
  </tr>
<% }
}
%>
</table>
<hr />
<p align="right"><a href="create_post.jsp">Add Post </a> </p>
</BODY>
```

Create Author

Before the user can add a post, it is necessary to add an author. Figure 2.6 shows the simple form a user fills out to add an author.

As shown in Listing 2.10, the page simply displays the form unless a user clicks the Submit button. If the page detects the Submit button, the application uses a Hibernate `Session` to save the object. Note that the `Author` object is simply created with a `new` operation, the various properties are set from the request, and the object is passed to the `Session.save()` method. Very straightforward.

Figure 2.6. Adding an Author

Listing 2.10 Creating Author Source

```
<%@ page contentType="text/html; charset=utf-8" language="java"
      import="com.cascadetg.ch02.*,net.sf.hibernate.*" %><%
String error = "";
Session hibernateSession = null;
Transaction myTransaction = null;
java.util.Iterator authors = null;

if(request.getParameter("Submit") != null)
{
      try
      {
            hibernateSession = AppSession.getSession();
            myTransaction = hibernateSession.beginTransaction();

            Author myAuthor = new Author();
            myAuthor.setFirstName(request.getParameter("first"));
            myAuthor.setLastName(request.getParameter("last"));
            myAuthor.setEmail(request.getParameter("email"));

            hibernateSession.save(myAuthor);
```

(continues)

Listing 2.10   Creating Author Source (*continued*)

```
                myTransaction.commit();

                response.sendRedirect("list_author.jsp");
                return;
        } catch (Exception e) {
                error = e.getMessage(); e.printStackTrace();
                try{ myTransaction.rollback(); }
                catch (Exception e2) {;}
        }
        finally
        {
                try{hibernateSession.close();}
                catch (Exception e) {;}
        }
}
%>
<HTML>
<HEAD>
<TITLE>Create Author</TITLE>
<meta name="no_print" content="true" />
</HEAD>
<BODY>
<form name="create_author"
        method="post" action="create_author.jsp">
  <p><%=error%></p>
  <table width="50%"  border="0">
    <tr>
      <td>First Name </td>
      <td><input name="first" type="text" id="first"></td>
    </tr>
    <tr>
      <td>Last Name </td>
      <td><input name="last" type="text" id="last"></td>
    </tr>
    <tr>
      <td>Email</td>
      <td><input name="email" type="text" id="email"></td>
    </tr>
    <tr>
      <td> </td>
      <td><input type="submit" name="Submit" value="Submit"></td>
    </tr>
  </table>
</form>
</BODY>
```

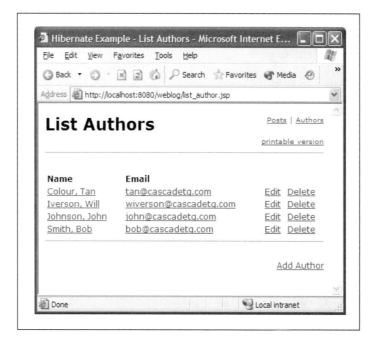

Figure 2.7. Listing Authors

List Authors

After an author is created, the user is returned to a list of authors. Figure 2.7 shows the author list after a few authors have been created.

As can be seen from Listing 2.11, this application uses the Criteria API to retrieve results. The most notable difference is that the results are ordered by last name and first name.

Listing 2.11 Listing Authors Source

```
<%@ page contentType="text/html; charset=utf-8" language="java"
      import="com.cascadetg.ch02.*,net.sf.hibernate.*" %><%
String error = "";
Session hibernateSession = null;
Transaction myTransaction = null;
java.util.Iterator authors = null;
try
{
      hibernateSession = AppSession.getSession();
      myTransaction = hibernateSession.beginTransaction();

      Criteria query =
            hibernateSession.createCriteria(Author.class);
```

(continues)

Listing 2.11 Listing Authors Source (*continued*)

```
        query.addOrder(
                net.sf.hibernate.expression.Order.asc("lastName"));
        query.addOrder(
                net.sf.hibernate.expression.Order.asc("firstName"));

        authors = query.list().iterator();

        myTransaction.commit();
        hibernateSession.close();
}
catch (Exception e) {
        error = e.getMessage(); e.printStackTrace();
        try{ myTransaction.rollback(); }
        catch (Exception e2) {;}
}
finally
{
        try{hibernateSession.close();}
        catch (Exception e2) {;}
}

%><HTML>
<HEAD>
<TITLE>List Authors</TITLE>
</HEAD>
<BODY><%=error%><% if(authors == null) { %>
No authors defined.
<% } else { %>
<table width="100%"  border="0">
  <tr>
    <td><strong>Name</strong></td>
    <td><strong>Email</strong></td>
    <td> </td>
  <td> </td>
  </tr>
  <% while (authors.hasNext()) {
  Author myAuthor = (Author)authors.next(); %>
  <tr>
    <td><a href="edit_author.jsp?authorID=<%=
            myAuthor.getId()%>"><%=
            myAuthor.getLastName()%>, <%=
            myAuthor.getFirstName()%></a></td>
    <td><a href="mailto:<%=
            myAuthor.getEmail()%>"><%=myAuthor.getEmail()%>
    </a></td>
    <td><a href="edit_author.jsp?authorID=<%=
```

Listing 2.11   Listing Authors Source (*continued*)

```
            myAuthor.getId()%>">Edit</a></td>
   <td><a href="delete_author.jsp?authorID=<%=
            myAuthor.getId()%>">Delete</a></td>
   </tr>
   <% } %>
</table>
<% } %>
<hr />
<p align="right"><a href="create_author.jsp">Add Author
</a></p>
</BODY>
```

Edit Author

Everybody makes mistakes, and so it's important to provide a mechanism for fixing mistakes. Figure 2.8 shows the form that enables a user to correct author information.

As can be seen from Listing 2.12, updating an `Author` object is similar to creating one. The biggest changes are the use of the `Session.update()`

Figure 2.8.   Updating an Author

method instead of `Session.save()` and the use of the `authorID` to identify the record to update.

Listing 2.12   Updating an Author Source

```
<%@ page contentType="text/html; charset=utf-8" language="java"
     import="com.cascadetg.ch02.*,net.sf.hibernate.*" %><%
String error = "";
Session hibernateSession = null;
Transaction myTransaction = null;
Author myAuthor = null;

if(request.getParameter("Submit") != null)
{
     boolean done=false;
     try
     {
          hibernateSession = AppSession.getSession();
          myTransaction =
               hibernateSession.beginTransaction();

          myAuthor = new Author();
          myAuthor.setId(request.getParameter("authorID"));
          myAuthor.setFirstName(request.getParameter("first"));
          myAuthor.setLastName(request.getParameter("last"));
          myAuthor.setEmail(request.getParameter("email"));

          hibernateSession.update(myAuthor);

          myTransaction.commit();
          hibernateSession.close();
          done=true;
     } catch (Exception e) {
          error = e.getMessage(); e.printStackTrace();
          try{ myTransaction.rollback(); }
          catch (Exception e2) {;}
     }
     finally
     {
          try{hibernateSession.close();}
          atch (Exception e) {;}
     }


     if(done)
     {
          response.sendRedirect("list_author.jsp");
```

Listing 2.12   Updating an Author Source

```
                return;
    }
}

try
{
        hibernateSession = AppSession.getSession();
        myTransaction = hibernateSession.beginTransaction();

        myAuthor = (Author)hibernateSession.load(
                Author.class, request.getParameter("authorID"));

        myTransaction.commit();
        hibernateSession.close();
} catch (Exception e) { error = e.getMessage(); }
finally
{       try{ myTransaction.rollback(); }
        catch (Exception e) {;}
        finally { hibernateSession.close(); }
}
%>
<HTML>
<HEAD>
<TITLE>Edit Author</TITLE>
<meta name="no_print" content="true" />
</HEAD>
<BODY><%=error%>
<form name="edit_author" method="post"
action="edit_author.jsp">
  <table width="50%"  border="0">
    <tr>
      <td>First Name</td>
      <td><input type="text" name="first" value="<%=
            myAuthor.getFirstName()%>"></td>
    </tr>
    <tr>
      <td>Last Name </td>
      <td><input type="text" name="last" value="<%=
            myAuthor.getLastName()%>"></td>
    </tr>
    <tr>
      <td>Email Address </td>
      <td><input type="text" name="email" value="<%=
            myAuthor.getEmail()%>"></td>
    </tr>
```

(continues)

Listing 2.12   Updating an Author Source (*continued*)

```
    <tr>
      <td> </td>
      <td><input name="authorID" type="hidden"
        value="<%=request.getParameter("authorID")%>"><input
        type="submit" name="Submit" value="Save Changes"></td>
    </tr>
  </table>
</form>
</BODY>
```

Create Post

Once a user has created an author, the author can make posts. Figure 2.9 shows a simple form for the user, with a pop-up to select the author of the post.

Listing 2.13 shows the code for creating a post with this form. Looking over the source, there are two main blocks of Java code at the start of the page. The first is only executed if the form has been submitted. As with the code shown for creating a new author, the most notable change is the use of an Author object to indi-

Figure 2.9.   Creating a Post

cate the post's author. The second block uses the Criteria API to retrieve the list of authors.

Listing 2.13   Source for Creating a Post

```
<%@ page contentType="text/html; charset=utf-8" language="java"
    import="com.cascadetg.ch02.*,net.sf.hibernate.*" %><%
String error = "";
Session hibernateSession = null;
Transaction myTransaction = null;
java.util.Iterator authors = null;

if(request.getParameter("authorID") != null)
if(request.getParameter("authorID").compareTo("null") != 0)
if(request.getParameter("Submit") != null)
{
    boolean done = false;
    String redirect_page = "view_post.jsp?postID=";

    try
    {
        hibernateSession = AppSession.getSession();
        myTransaction = hibernateSession.beginTransaction();

        Post myPost = new Post();
        myPost.setTitle(request.getParameter("title"));
        myPost.setSummary(request.getParameter("summary"));
        myPost.setContent(request.getParameter("content"));
        myPost.setDate(new java.util.Date());

        Author myAuthor = new Author();
        myAuthor.setId(request.getParameter("authorID"));
        myPost.setAuthor(myAuthor);

        hibernateSession.save(myPost);

        myTransaction.commit();

        redirect_page = redirect_page + myPost.getId();
        done=true;
    } catch (Exception e) {
        error = e.getMessage(); e.printStackTrace();
        try{ myTransaction.rollback(); }
        catch (Exception e2) {;}
    }
    finally
```

(continues)

Listing 2.13   Source for Creating a Post (*continued*)

```
    {
        try{hibernateSession.close();}
        catch (Exception e) {;}
    }


    if(done)
    {
        response.sendRedirect(redirect_page);
        return;
    }
}


try
{
    hibernateSession = AppSession.getSession();
    myTransaction = hibernateSession.beginTransaction();

    Criteria query =
        hibernateSession.createCriteria(Author.class);
    query.addOrder(
        net.sf.hibernate.expression.Order.asc("lastName"));
    query.addOrder(
        net.sf.hibernate.expression.Order.asc("firstName"));

    authors = query.list().iterator();

    myTransaction.commit();
    hibernateSession.close();
} catch (Exception e) { error = e.getMessage(); }
finally
{   try{ myTransaction.rollback(); }
    catch (Exception e) {;}
    finally { hibernateSession.close(); }
}

%>
<HTML>
<HEAD>
<TITLE>Create Post</TITLE>
<meta name="no_print" content="true" />
</HEAD>
<BODY><%=error%>
```

Listing 2.13 Source for Creating a Post (*continued*)

```
<form name="create_post" method="post"
action="create_post.jsp">
  <table width="50%"  border="0">
    <tr>
      <td>Author</td>
      <td><select name="authorID">
        <option default value="null">Please select an
        author</option>
                <% if(authors != null) { %>
            <% while(authors.hasNext()) {
            Author myAuthor = (Author)authors.next();%>
        <option default value="<%=
                myAuthor.getId()%>"><%=
                myAuthor.getLastName()%>, <%=
                myAuthor.getFirstName()%></option>
          <% }
            } %>
      </select></td>
    </tr>
    <tr>
      <td>Title</td>
      <td><input name="title" type="text" id="title"></td>
    </tr>
    <tr>
      <td>Summary</td>
      <td><input name="summary" type="text" id="summary"></td>
    </tr>
    <tr>
      <td>Content</td>
      <td><textarea name="content"
      id="content"></textarea></td>
    </tr>
    <tr>
      <td> </td>
      <td><input type="submit" name="Submit"
            value="Create Post"></td>
    </tr>
  </table>
</form>
</BODY>
</HTML>
```

View Post

After the post has been created, the user is given a chance to view it. This allows the user to read the post and optionally click the Edit link to make changes.

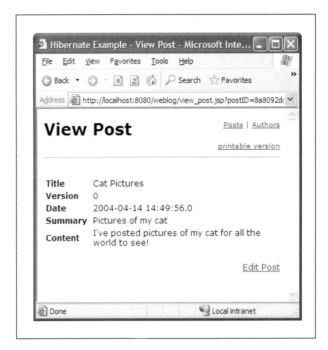

Figure 2.10.   Viewing a Post

Listing 2.14 shows the code for viewing a post. The `Session.get()` method is used to retrieve an object by the supplied identifier.

Listing 2.14   Viewing a Post

```
<%@ page contentType="text/html; charset=utf-8" language="java"
      import="com.cascadetg.ch02.*,net.sf.hibernate.*" %><%

String error = "";
Session hibernateSession = null;
Transaction myTransaction = null;
Post myPost = null;
try
{
      hibernateSession = AppSession.getSession();
      myTransaction = hibernateSession.beginTransaction();

      myPost = (Post)hibernateSession.load(
            Post.class, request.getParameter("postID"));
```

Listing 2.14 Viewing a Post (*continued*)

```
        myTransaction.commit();
        hibernateSession.close();

} catch (Exception e) {
            error = e.getMessage(); e.printStackTrace();
            try{ myTransaction.rollback(); }
            catch (Exception e2) {;}
}
finally
{
        try{hibernateSession.close();}
        catch (Exception e) {;}
}
%><HTML>
<HEAD>
<TITLE>View Post</TITLE>
</HEAD>
<BODY><%=error%>
<table width="100%"  border="0">
  <tr>
    <td width="20%"><strong>Title</strong></td>
    <td><%=myPost.getTitle()%> </td>
  </tr>
  <tr>
    <td width="20%"><strong>Version</strong></td>
    <td><%=myPost.getRevision()%></td>
  </tr>
  <tr>
    <td width="20%"><strong>Date</strong></td>
    <td><%=myPost.getDate()%></td>
  </tr>
  <tr>
    <td width="20%"><strong>Summary</strong></td>
    <td><%=myPost.getSummary()%> </td>
  </tr>
  <tr>
    <td width="20%"><strong>Content</strong></td>
    <td><%=myPost.getContent()%> </td>
  </tr>
</table>

<p align="right"><a href="edit_post.jsp?postID=<%=
      request.getParameter("postID")%>">Edit Post</a> </p>
</BODY>
```

Edit Post

Figure 2.11 shows the standard interface presented when a user chooses to edit a post.

One of the more advanced features of this particular application is the use of Hibernate's built-in support for version management (as specified by the `version` tag in Listing 2.1). This allows Hibernate to verify that no intermediate changes have been made to an object before conducting the update. This powerful feature allows for an optimistic locking strategy (as described in more detail in Chapter 9).

In brief, imagine that two users are isaccessing this application at the same time. The first, Bob, goes to the edit page, and proceeds to spend several hours making lengthy changes. The second, Mary, opens the edit page and makes a minor spelling fix. When Bob attempts to save his revision, the application automatically detects that the version number of Bob's update is out of date (with a single UPDATE statement).

In our application, when this sort of conflict occurs, Bob is presented with both the revision currently in the database and the changes he has submitted. It's up to Bob to take these two revisions and submit a single merged post. Figure 2.12

Figure 2.11.   Editing a Post

Figure 2.12. Conflicting Post Edits

shows the user interface presented to resolve this conflict. The conflict itself is detected with a net.sf.hibernate.StaleObjectStateException.

Listing 2.15 shows the code for editing a post. Pay close attention to the catch of the net.sf.hibernate.StaleObjectStateException. This is the mechanism whereby Hibernate informs the application that the attempt to UPDATE the post has failed because of a problem with the Post version.

Listing 2.15. Editing a Post

```
<%@ page contentType="text/html; charset=utf-8" language="java"
    import="com.cascadetg.ch02.*,net.sf.hibernate.*" %><%

String error = "";
```

(*continues*)

Listing 2.15. Editing a Post (*continued*)

```
boolean conflict = false;
Session hibernateSession = null;
Transaction myTransaction = null;
Post myPost = null;
if(request.getParameter("Submit") != null)
{
      boolean done = false;
      String redirect_page = "view_post.jsp?postID=";
      try
      {
            hibernateSession = AppSession.getSession();
            myTransaction = hibernateSession.beginTransaction();

            myPost = new Post();
            myPost.setId(request.getParameter("postID"));
            myPost.setRevision(
                  new Integer(
                        request.getParameter("revision"))
                              .intValue());
            myPost.setTitle(request.getParameter("title"));
            myPost.setDate(new java.util.Date());
            myPost.setSummary(request.getParameter("summary"));
            myPost.setContent(request.getParameter("content"));

            Author myAuthor = new Author();
            myAuthor.setId(request.getParameter("authorID"));
            myPost.setAuthor(myAuthor);

            hibernateSession.update(myPost);

            myTransaction.commit();
            hibernateSession.close();

            redirect_page =
                  redirect_page + request.getParameter("postID");
            done = true;
      }
      catch (net.sf.hibernate.StaleObjectStateException stale)
      {
            error =
            "This post was updated by another transaction. " +
            "You may either update the existing " +
            "data, or resubmit your changes.";
            conflict=true;
      }
      catch (Exception e) {
            error = e.getMessage(); e.printStackTrace();
```

Listing 2.15. Editing a Post (*continued*)

```
                try{ myTransaction.rollback(); }
                catch (Exception e2) {;}
        }
        finally
        {
                try{hibernateSession.close();}
                catch (Exception e) {;}
        }

        if(done)
        {
                response.sendRedirect(redirect_page);
                return;
        }
}

try
{

        hibernateSession = AppSession.getSession();
        myTransaction = hibernateSession.beginTransaction();

        Criteria query =
                hibernateSession.createCriteria(Post.class);

        myPost = (Post)com.cascadetg.ch02.finder.
                PostFinder.findByID(hibernateSession,
                request.getParameter("postID")).iterator().next();

        myTransaction.commit();
        hibernateSession.close();

} catch (Exception e)
        { error = e.getMessage(); e.printStackTrace(); }
finally
{       try{ myTransaction.rollback(); }
        catch (Exception e) {;}
        finally { hibernateSession.close(); }
}

%>
<HTML>
<HEAD>
<TITLE>Edit Post</TITLE>
<meta name="no_print" content="true" />
</HEAD>
```

Listing 2.15.   Editing a Post (*continued*)

```
<BODY><%=error %>
<% if(conflict) { %>
<p><strong>Current Saved Post</strong></p>
<% } %>
<form name="edit_post" method="post" action="edit_post.jsp">
  <table width="100%"  border="0">
    <tr>
      <td width="25%"><strong>Title</strong></td>
      <td><input name="title" type="text" value="<%=
          myPost.getTitle()%>"></td>
    <td> </td>
    </tr>
    <tr>
      <td width="25%"><strong>Summary</strong></td>
      <td><input name="summary" type="text" id="summary"
          value="<%=myPost.getSummary()%>"></td>
    <td> </td>
    </tr>
    <tr>
      <td width="25%"><strong>Content </strong></td>
      <td><textarea name="content" id="content"><%=
          myPost.getContent()%></textarea></td>
    <td> </td>
    </tr>
    <tr>
      <td width="25%"><strong>Date / Revision</strong></td>
      <td><%=myPost.getDate()%> / <%=myPost.getRevision()%>
          <input name="revision" type="hidden" id="revision"
          value="<%=myPost.getRevision()%>"></td>
    <td> </td>
    </tr>
    <tr>
      <td width="25%"> </td>
      <td><input name="authorID" type="hidden"
          value="<%=myPost.getAuthor().getId()%>"><input
          name="postID" type="hidden"
          value="<%=request.getParameter("postID")%>">
      <input type="submit" name="Submit"
  value="Save Changes"></td>
    <td> </td>
    </tr>
  </table>
</form>
  <% if(conflict) { %>
  <hr>
```

Listing 2.15.   Editing a Post (*continued*)

```
<p>Newly submitted post.</p>
<form name="edit_post" method="post" action="edit_post.jsp">
<table width="100%" border="0">
<tr>
  <td width="25%"><strong>Submitted Title Change
</strong></td>
  <td>
    <input type="text" name="title" value="<%=
          request.getParameter("title") %>"></td>
</tr>
<tr>
  <td width="25%"><strong>Submitted Summary Change
</strong></td>
  <td><input type="text" name="summary" value="<%=
          request.getParameter("summary")%>"></td>
</tr>
<tr>
  <td width="25%"><strong>Submitted Content Change
</strong></td>
  <td><textarea name="content"><%=
                request.getParameter("content")%></textarea>
  <input name="revision" type="hidden"
          id="revision" value="<%=myPost.getRevision()%>">
  <input name="authorID" type="hidden"
          value="<%=myPost.getAuthor().getId()%>">
  <input name="postID" type="hidden"
          value="<%=request.getParameter("postID")%>"></td>

</tr>
<tr>
  <td> </td>
  <td><input type="submit" name="Submit"
          value="Save Submitted Changes"></td>
</tr>
</table>
</form>
  <% } %>

</BODY>
```

Delete Post

Sometimes a post is no longer of interest or covers a topic that the writer wishes had never been brought up. Figure 2.13 shows the simple HTML confirmation form presented when a user wishes to delete a post.

Figure 2.13.   Deleting a Post

Listing 2.16 shows how the post is deleted. As can be seen, deleting a persistent object is a simple one-step method call to the `Session`.

ADVANCED COMMENT

This implementation first executes a load regardless of the delete operation. This is required to delete the post, as the version of the record is required to issue the delete. The application doesn't care about the version; it just wants to delete the post.

Alternatively, the application could retrieve the version number of the post when the form is first displayed and then pass the version along with a hidden field. This would have two advantages—it would allow the delete to occur without the first get, and would ensure that the deleted post is of the proper revision.

Listing 2.16   Deleting a Post

```
<%@ page contentType="text/html; charset=utf-8" language="java"
     import="com.cascadetg.ch02.*,net.sf.hibernate.*" %><%

String error = "";
```

Listing 2.16   Deleting a Post (*continued*)

```
Session hibernateSession = null;
Transaction myTransaction = null;
Post myPost = null;
boolean done = false;
try
{

    hibernateSession = AppSession.getSession();
    myTransaction = hibernateSession.beginTransaction();

    myPost = (Post)hibernateSession.load(Post.class,
        request.getParameter("postID"));
    if(request.getParameter("Submit") != null)
    {
        hibernateSession.delete(myPost);
        done=true;
    } else
    {

    }
    myTransaction.commit();

} catch (Exception e) {
        error = e.getMessage(); e.printStackTrace();
        try{ myTransaction.rollback(); }
        catch (Exception e2) {;}
    }
    finally
    {
        try{hibernateSession.close();}
        catch (Exception e) {;}
    }


if(done)
{
    response.sendRedirect("list_posts.jsp");
    return;
}

%>
<HTML>
<HEAD>
<TITLE>Delete Post</TITLE>
```

(*continues*)

Listing 2.16   Deleting a Post (*continued*)

```
<meta name="no_print" content="true" />
</HEAD>
<BODY><%=error%>
<p>Are you sure you want to delete the post "<b><%=
        myPost.getTitle()%></b>"?</p>
<form name="delete_post" method="post"
action="delete_post.jsp">
<input name="postID" type="hidden" value="<%=
        request.getParameter("postID")%>">
  <input type="submit" name="Submit" value="Delete Post">
</form>
</BODY>
```

Delete Author

Finally, a user may wish to delete an author, as shown in Figure 2.14. Note the warning that all of the author's posts will be deleted as well.

Every post must be assigned to an author. Deleting the author means that any posts pointing to that author are left in an inconsistent state—the foreign key on the authorID column would be violated. Hibernate takes care of this automati-

Figure 2.14.   Deleting an Author

cally. The mapping file in Listing 2.2 declares that the posts are to be deleted when the owning author is deleted (the `cascade="delete"` attribute). Therefore, the code in Listing 2.17 merely issues a single delete and Hibernate automatically deletes both the `Author` and all associated `Post` records.

WARNING

As you can imagine, cascading deletes are both powerful and very dangerous. Make sure that you fully understand (and test) your cascading operations to ensure that the action you get is the action you expect.

Listing 2.17   Deleting an Author

```
<%@ page contentType="text/html; charset=utf-8" language="java"
    import="com.cascadetg.ch02.*,net.sf.hibernate.*" %><%

String error = "";
Session hibernateSession = null;
Transaction myTransaction = null;
Author myAuthor = null;
try
{

    hibernateSession = AppSession.getSession();
    myTransaction = hibernateSession.beginTransaction();

    if(request.getParameter("Submit") != null)
    {
        myAuthor = new Author();
        myAuthor.setId(request.getParameter("authorID"));
        System.out.println(myAuthor.getId());
        hibernateSession.refresh(myAuthor);
        hibernateSession.delete(myAuthor);
        myTransaction.commit();
        response.sendRedirect("list_author.jsp");
        return;
    } else
    {
        myAuthor = (Author)hibernateSession.load(Author.class,
            request.getParameter("authorID"));
        myTransaction.commit();
    }


    } catch (Exception e) {
```

Listing 2.17 Deleting an Author (*continued*)

```
                error = e.getMessage(); e.printStackTrace();
                try{ myTransaction.rollback(); }
                catch (Exception e2) {;}
        }
        finally
        {
                try{hibernateSession.close();}
                catch (Exception e) {;}
        }

%>
<HTML>
<HEAD>
<TITLE>Delete Author</TITLE>
<meta name="no_print" content="true" />
</HEAD>
<BODY><%=error%>
<p>Are you sure you want to delete the author and
all posts written by the author
<b><%=myAuthor.getFirstName()%>
<%=myAuthor.getLastName()%></b>?</p>
<form name="delete_author" method="post"
action="delete_author.jsp">

  <input type="hidden" name="authorID"
      value="<%= request.getParameter("authorID") %>">
  <input type="submit" name="Submit" value="Delete Author">
</form>
</BODY>
</HTML>
```

Next Steps

Now that you've gotten a taste for Hibernate, your next steps depend on your needs and situation. In this chapter the application was built "from the middle out"—a mapping file generated both the persistent Java objects and the database definition. In Chapter 3, an application is built starting from Java, and in Chapter 4, an existing database definition is used. Even if you don't intend to use either of these approaches yourself, the examples shown in Chapters 3 and 4 are used throughout this book as examples. Note that the remaining examples in the book are provided as simple command-line operations and not as full-blown Web applications. This serves to keep the focus on Hibernate as a tool rather than on the idiosyncrasies of Web application development.

CHAPTER **3**

Starting from Java

Combining Hibernate with XDoclet makes it possible to start from Java code when building an application. Using XDoclet markup tags (similar to the tags used by `javadoc`), you can generate the `*.hbm.xml` files required by Hibernate directly from your Java source files.

XDoclet, available from http://xdoclet.sourceforge.net/, is an open-source framework for annotating Java source files with special comments, which are then used to construct configuration files used by a variety of different environments.

Many developers first encounter XDoclet when working with EJB 2.X as a tool to help manage the complexity of EJB 2.X development. XDoclet-style annotations have become so popular that support for similar annotations (as described by JSR 175, http://jcp.org/en/jsr/detail?id=175) is included as a standard extension in the upcoming release of Java (Java 2 Platform, Standard Edition 5.0). The early draft specification for EJB 3.0 uses annotations in lieu of XML descriptors. The upshot is that the use of XDoclet and Hibernate is (as of this writing) a close approximation of the development model being suggested for EJB 3.0.

WARNING
There are three significant downsides to using annotations as your development solution. The first is the addition of (yet another) complex tool to your build process. The second is the relative difficulty of debugging and otherwise tracing the source of problems with the generated mapping file. The third downside of annotations is that configuration information is now stored directly in your Java source files. Given all of these downsides, I have found annotations to be much more error-prone and difficult to work with than simply starting from a mapping file, as described in Chapter 2.

In constructing the application in this chapter, we will start from a set of Java sources and then walk through the rest of the development path.

Java Object Model

This example application models a set of historical artifacts owned by a complex set of owners, including museums, foundations, exhibits, and individual owners. A given artifact may be owned by none, one, or many of these possible owners. Thus the example illustrates how two powerful concepts are used in Hibernate: the use of the Java collection framework to manage the ownership of artifacts by various owners, and the use of a class hierarchy to describe the various kinds of owners.

As shown in Figure 3.1, the application defines an abstract `Owner` class, with four possible concrete implementations. Some of these subclasses in turn may have an owner.

Figure 3.1.   Ownership Object Model

One or more of these possible owners may be connected to a particular Artifact, as shown in Figure 3.2.

Therefore, a given Artifact may be owned by zero or more owners of many different types. For example, a single artifact may be owned by a specific person, be on permanent loan to a museum, be managed by a foundation, and be part of two different exhibitions. This is a complex set of relationships, but not an atypical model, especially for an object-oriented developer.

Java Classes

The Java classes in this application contain several XDoclet tags. Before reviewing the Java classes in this application, a brief introduction to @ tags is required.

The @ symbol is generally used to provide an additional bit of information about a class or method for a source parser such as javadoc or XDoclet. The `@hibernate.` text is used to preface XDoclet Hibernate tags; all the other @ markup tags in this application are used by `javadoc`.

The `@hibernate` tags shown in Figure 3.3 are used in this application. A full list of tags can be found at http://xdoclet.sourceforge.net/tags/hibernate-tags.html. These tags correspond to the relevant HBM tags, as described in more detail in Chapter 5.

Let's start by looking at the abstract `Owner` class, as shown in Listing 3.1. It is superficially an ordinary Java class, but pay close attention to the various @ comment values. Note the convenient `Owner.addArtifact()` methods—not necessary, but helpful.

Listing 3.1   Owner Class

```
package com.cascadetg.ch03;

import java.io.Serializable;

import org.apache.commons.lang.builder.EqualsBuilder;
import org.apache.commons.lang.builder.HashCodeBuilder;

/**
 * @author Will Iverson
 * @hibernate.class
 * @hibernate.discriminator column="discriminator"
 * @since 1.0
 */
public abstract class Owner implements Serializable
{
    long id;
```

(continues on p. 79)

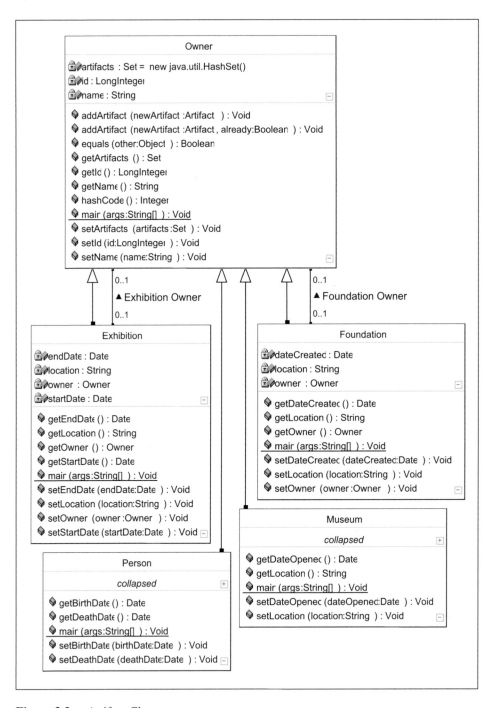

Figure 3.2.   Artifact Class

Table 3.1.   Reference XDoclet Tags

`@hibernate.class`	Indicates that a `*.hbm.xml` file should be generated for this class.
`@hibernate.subclass`	Indicates that the information for this class should be generated using the `subclass` tag. For more information on the `subclass` tag, see Chapter 5.
`@hibernate.discriminator`	Because the application maps multiple classes to a single table, a column is needed in the table for Hibernate to store the class type. For more information, see the `discriminator` tag in Chapter 5.
`@hibernate.property`	Indicates to XDoclet that this `get`/`set` pair should be treated as a persistent property. If you don't use this flag, XDoclet won't generate a persistent property mapping in the `*.hbm.xml` file.
`@hibernate.set`	This application uses a `java.util.Set` to store the association between zero and one or more owners or between zero and one or more artifacts. Hibernate needs to know the table to use as an association table. This tag identifies the table. For descriptions of the `inverse="false"` and `lazy="true"` values, see the `set` tag in Chapter 5, and relationships in Chapter 7.
`@hibernate.collection-key`	This is used to store the id of the referenced artifact.

Listing 3.1   Owner Class (*continued*)

```
    String name;
    java.util.Set artifacts = new java.util.HashSet();

    /**
     * @hibernate.property
     * @return Returns the name.
     */
    public String getName() { return name; }

    /**
     * @param name The name to set.
     */
```

(*continues*)

Listing 3.1   Owner Class (*continued*)

```java
public void setName(String name) { this.name = name; }

/**
  * @hibernate.set table="ownership" inverse="false"
    lazy="true"
  * @hibernate.collection-key column="owner_id"
  * @hibernate.collection-many-to-many column="artifact_id"
    class="com.cascadetg.ch03.Artifact"
  * @return Returns the owners.
  */

public java.util.Set getArtifacts() { return artifacts; }

/**
 * @param owners
 * The owners to set.
 */
public void setArtifacts(java.util.Set artifacts)
{ this.artifacts = artifacts; }

public void addArtifact(Artifact newArtifact, boolean
    already)
{
    artifacts.add(newArtifact);
    if(!already)
        newArtifact.addOwner(this, true);
}

/** Utility function to make adding an artifact easier */
public void addArtifact(Artifact newArtifact)
{ this.addArtifact(newArtifact, true); }

/** Standard Hibernate equality override */
public boolean equals(Object other)
{
    try
    {
        Owner castOther = (Owner)other;
        return new EqualsBuilder()
            .append(this.getId(), castOther.getId())
            .isEquals();
    } catch (Exception e) { return false; }
}

/** Standard Hibernate hash override */
```

Listing 3.1 Owner Class (*continued*)

```
    public int hashCode()
    {
        return new
        HashCodeBuilder().append(getId()).toHashCode();
    }

    /**
     * @hibernate.id generator-class="native"
     * @return Returns the id.
     */
    public long getId() { return id; }

    /**
     * @param id The id to set.
     */
    public void setId(long id) { this.id = id; }

}
```

Given the base `Owner` class, the first subclass, `Exhibition`, is shown in Listing 3.2. This class defines several additional properties over the base `Owner` class.

Listing 3.2 Exhibition Class

```
package com.cascadetg.ch03;

/**
 * @author Will Iverson
 * @hibernate.subclass
 * @since 1.0
 */

public class Exhibition extends Owner
{

    Owner owner;
    String location;
    java.util.Date startDate;
    java.util.Date endDate;

    /**
     * @hibernate.property
```

(*continues*)

Listing 3.2   Exhibition Class (*continued*)

```
    * @return Returns the endDate.
    */
   public java.util.Date getEndDate() { return endDate; }

   /**
    * @param endDate The endDate to set.
    */
   public void setEndDate(java.util.Date endDate)
      { this.endDate = endDate; }

   /**
    * @hibernate.property
    * @return Returns the location.
    */
   public String getLocation() { return location; }

   /**
    * @param location The location to set.
    */
   public void setLocation(String location)
      { this.location = location; }

   /**
    * @hibernate.many-to-one lazy="true"
    * @return Returns the owner.
    */
   public Owner getOwner() { return owner; }

   /**
    * @param owner The owner to set.
    */
   public void setOwner(Owner owner) { this.owner = owner; }

   /**
    * @hibernate.property
    * @return Returns the startDate.
    */
   public java.util.Date getStartDate() { return startDate; }

   /**
    * @param startDate The startDate to set.
    */
   public void setStartDate(java.util.Date startDate)
   { this.startDate = startDate; }
}
```

Listing 3.3 shows the next subclass, `Foundation`. This class defines several additional properties over the base `Owner` class. Some are similar to those described by `Foundation`, others are different.

Listing 3.3   Foundation Class

```
package com.cascadetg.ch03;

/**
 * @author Will Iverson
 * @hibernate.subclass
 * @since 1.0
 */

public class Foundation extends Owner
{
    Owner owner;
    String location;
    java.util.Date dateCreated;

    /**
     * @hibernate.property
     * @return Returns the dateCreated.
     */
    public java.util.Date getDateCreated()
    { return dateCreated; }

    /**
     * @param dateCreated The dateCreated to set.
     */
    public void setDateCreated(java.util.Date dateCreated)
    { this.dateCreated = dateCreated; }

    /**
     * @hibernate.property
     * @return Returns the location.
     */
    public String getLocation()
    { return location; }

    /**
     * @param location The location to set.
     */
    public void setLocation(String location)
    { this.location = location; }

    /**
```

(continues)

Listing 3.3   Foundation Class (*continued*)

```
         * @hibernate.many-to-one
         * @return Returns the owner.
         */
        public Owner getOwner() { return owner; }

        /**
         * @param owner The owner to set.
         */
        public void setOwner(Owner owner) { this.owner = owner; }
    }
```

Listing 3.4 shows the next subclass, Museum. Again, this class defines several additional properties over the base Owner class. Some are similar to those described by other subclasses, others are different.

Listing 3.4   Museum Class

```
package com.cascadetg.ch03;

/**
 * @author Will Iverson
 * @hibernate.subclass
 * @since 1.0
 */

public class Museum extends Owner
{

    String location;
    java.util.Date dateOpened;

    /**
     * @hibernate.property
     * @return Returns the dateOpened.
     */
    public java.util.Date getDateOpened() { return dateOpened;
}

    /**
     * @param dateOpened The dateOpened to set.
     */
    public void setDateOpened(java.util.Date dateOpened)
    { this.dateOpened = dateOpened; }
```

Listing 3.4   Museum Class (*continued*)

```
    /**
     * @hibernate.property
     * @return Returns the location.
     */
    public String getLocation() { return location; }

    /**
     * @param location The location to set.
     */
    public void setLocation(String location)
    { this.location = location; }

}
```

Listing 3.5 shows the final subclass, `Person`. This class also defines several additional properties over the base `Owner` class.

Listing 3.5   Person Class

```
package com.cascadetg.ch03;

import java.util.Date;

/**
 * @author Will Iverson
 * @hibernate.subclass
 * @since 1.0
 */

public class Person extends Owner
{
    Date birthDate;
    Date deathDate;

    /**
     * @hibernate.property
     * @return Returns the birthDate.
     */
    public Date getBirthDate() { return birthDate; }

    /**
     * @param birthDate The birthDate to set.
     */
    public void setBirthDate(Date birthDate)
```

(*continues*)

Listing 3.5   Person Class (*continued*)

```
    { this.birthDate = birthDate; }

    /**
     * @hibernate.property
     * @return Returns the deathDate.
     */
    public Date getDeathDate() { return deathDate; }

    /**
     * @param deathDate The deathDate to set.
     */
    public void setDeathDate(Date deathDate)
        { this.deathDate = deathDate; }

}
```

Working with XDoclet

With Java files properly marked up, XDoclet (in conjunction with Ant, described in Chapter 2) can be used to generate the `*.hbm.xml` mapping files needed by Hibernate.

WHAT ABOUT MAPGENERATOR?

Hibernate includes a tool for generating HBM files from Java class files called `MapGenerator`. `MapGenerator`, unfortunately, does not generate complete `*.hbm.xml` information (but instead makes an incomplete best guess). This means that as you edit and modify your Java class files, you'll need to rerun the MapGenerator and then merge changes back into your existing `*.hbm.xml` file by hand. Using XDoclet lets you generate your `*.hbm.xml` files from your Java source, thereby eliminating the need for hand-merging.

XDoclet can be downloaded from http://xdoclet.sourceforge.net/ (this text was written using xdoclet-bin-1.2). Once XDoclet has been downloaded, simply unzip or untar it into a directory you can easily find. You will then need to modify the `xdoclet_lib_path`, as shown in Listing 3.6, to point to the `lib` directory of the downloaded XDoclet.

The build file shown in Listing 3.6 compiles the Java source and then executes the XDoclet task to generate the `*.hbm.xml` files automatically. Pay close attention to the configuration of the XDoclet task.

Listing 3.6   XDoclet Build File

```xml
<?xml version="1.0"?>
<project name="ch03" default="all">

    <target name="all" depends="compile,build_hbm" />

    <description>Hibernate starting with Java</description>

    <!-- You'll need to set these depending on your library
        installation directories -->
    <property name="hibernate_path"
        value="C:\devenv\hibernate-2.1.2"/>
    <property name="hibernate_tool_path"
        value="C:\devenv\hibernate-extensions-2.1\tools"/>
    <property name="xdoclet_lib_path"
        value="C:\devenv\xdoclet-bin-1.2\lib"/>

    <!-- Normally, build files are stored at the root of the
        tree.
        The builds for this book are on a per-chapter basis -->
    <property name="base_dir" value="..\..\..\" />

    <!-- This defines the Hibernate XDoclet task.  You can
        copy this verbatium, assuming you set the xdoclet
        lib path above -->
    <taskdef name="hibernatedoclet"
        classname="xdoclet.modules.hibernate.Hibernate
        DocletTask">
            <classpath>
                <fileset dir="${xdoclet_lib_path}">
                    <include name="*.jar"/>
                </fileset>
            </classpath>
    </taskdef>

    <path id="project.class.path">
        <pathelement
            location="${hibernate_path}\hibernate2.jar"/>
        <pathelement
            location="${hibernate_tool_path}\hibernate-
            tools.jar"/>
        <pathelement location=
            "${hibernate_path}\lib\commons-collections-2.1.jar"
            />
```

(continues)

Listing 3.6   XDoclet Build File (*continued*)

```
            <pathelement location=
                "${hibernate_path}\lib\commons-logging-1.0.3.jar"
                />
            <pathelement location=
                "${hibernate_path}\lib\commons-lang-1.0.1.jar" />
            <pathelement location=
                "${hibernate_path}\lib\xerces-2.4.0.jar" />
            <pathelement location=
                "${hibernate_tool_path}\lib\jdom.jar"/>
        </path>

  <!-- Compiles the code using javac.  If the files won't
        compile, you won't be able to generate HBM files. -->
  <target name="compile">
        <javac srcdir="${base_dir}" destdir="${base_dir}">
            <include name="**\ch03\*.java" />
                         <classpath refid="project.class.path"/>
        </javac>
  </target>


  <!--   The force attribute causes the system to regenerate the
         files every time the task is run.

         Merge dir can be used to specify text that should be
         automatically included with the generated HBM files.

         If you don't specify the version as 2.0, you will get
         out-of-date v1.x HBM files -->
         <target name="build_hbm"
            description="builds_hbm_file" depends="compile">
            <hibernatedoclet
                destdir="${base_dir}"
                excludedtags="@version,@author,@todo"
                force="true"
                mergedir="${base_dir}"
                verbose="true">
                    <fileset dir="${base_dir}">
                            <include name="**\ch03\*.java" />
                    </fileset>
                    <hibernate version="2.0"/>
            </hibernatedoclet>
        </target>
</project>
```

Generated Mapping Files

The XDoclet tags generate mapping files for you automatically. Despite our five classes, XDoclet only generates two mapping documents and stores the subclasses in the same document as the base class. Therefore, the application only has an `Owner.hbm.xml` file and an `Artifact.hbm.xml`.

Listing 3.7 shows the `Artifact` mapping file, with some of the extraneous white space removed. For additional details on the various attributes and elements, see Chapter 5.

Listing 3.7   Artifact Mapping File

```xml
<?xml version="1.0"?>

<!DOCTYPE hibernate-mapping PUBLIC
    "-//Hibernate/Hibernate Mapping DTD 2.0//EN"
    "http://hibernate.sourceforge.net/hibernate-mapping-
2.0.dtd">

<hibernate-mapping>
    <class name="com.cascadetg.ch03.Artifact"
        dynamic-update="false"
        dynamic-insert="false">

        <id name="id" column="id" type="long">
            <generator class="native" />
        </id>

        <property name="comments" type="java.lang.String"
            update="true" insert="true" column="comments"/>

        <property name="dateCreated" type="java.util.Date"
            update="true" insert="true" column="dateCreated" />

        <property name="dateDiscovered" type="java.util.Date"
            update="true" insert="true" column="dateDiscovered"
            />

        <property name="description" type="java.lang.String"
            update="true" insert="true" column="description" />

        <property name="location" type="java.lang.String"
            update="true" insert="true" column="location" />

        <set name="owners" table="ownership" lazy="false"
```

(continues)

Listing 3.7   Artifact Mapping File (*continued*)

```
            ·  inverse="true" cascade="none" sort="unsorted">
                <key column="artifact_id" />
                <many-to-many class="com.cascadetg.ch03.Owner"
                    column="owner_id" outer-join="auto" />
            </set>

            <property name="title" type="java.lang.String"
                update="true" insert="true" column="title" />

            <!--
            To add non XDoclet property mappings, create a
            file named hibernate-properties-Artifact.xml
            containing the additional properties and place
            it in your merge dir.
            -->
        </class>
</hibernate-mapping>
```

The mapping file for `Owner` and the subclasses, as shown in Listing 3.8, is significantly more complex than the one for `Artifact`. In addition to the properties of the `Owner` class, each subclass is listed with the properties unique to that class. You are more or less allowed to build hierarchies of arbitrary complexity—subclasses of subclasses are allowed, for example. As may be imagined, you can build very complex hierarchies.

Listing 3.8   Owner (and Subclasses) Mapping File

```
<?xml version="1.0"?>

<!DOCTYPE hibernate-mapping PUBLIC
    "-//Hibernate/Hibernate Mapping DTD 2.0//EN"
    "http://hibernate.sourceforge.net/hibernate-mapping-
    2.0.dtd">

<hibernate-mapping>
    <class name="com.cascadetg.ch03.Owner"
        dynamic-update="false" dynamic-insert="false" >

        <id name="id" column="id" type="long">
            <generator class="native" />
        </id>
```

Listing 3.8 Owner (and subclasses) Mapping File (*continued*)

```
<discriminator column="discriminator" type="string" />

<property name="name" type="java.lang.String"
    update="true" insert="true" column="name" />

<set name="artifacts" table="ownership" lazy="true"
    inverse="false" cascade="none" sort="unsorted">
      <key column="owner_id" />

      <many-to-many class="com.cascadetg.ch03.Artifact"
          column="artifact_id" outer-join="auto" />
</set>

<!--
    To add non XDoclet property mappings, create a file
    named
    hibernate-properties-Owner.xml
    containing the additional properties
    and place it in your merge dir.
-->
<subclass name="com.cascadetg.ch03.Foundation"
    dynamic-update="false" dynamic-insert="false" >

<property name="dateCreated" type="java.util.Date"
    update="true" insert="true" column="dateCreated" />

<property name="location" type="java.lang.String"
    update="true" insert="true" column="location" />

<many-to-one name="owner"
class="com.cascadetg.ch03.Owner"
    cascade="none" outer-join="auto" update="true"
    insert="true" column="owner" />
  <!--
          To add non XDoclet property mappings,
          create a file named
          hibernate-properties-Foundation.xml
          containing the additional properties and
          place it in your merge dir.
  -->
</subclass>
<subclass name="com.cascadetg.ch03.Exhibition"
    dynamic-update="false" dynamic-insert="false" >

<property name="endDate" type="java.util.Date"
```

(*continues*)

Listing 3.8   Owner (and subclasses) Mapping File (*continued*)

```
            update="true" insert="true" column="endDate" />

<property name="location" type="java.lang.String"
    update="true" insert="true" column="location" />

<many-to-one name="owner"
class="com.cascadetg.ch03.Owner"
    cascade="none" outer-join="auto" update="true"
    insert="true" column="owner" />

<property name="startDate" type="java.util.Date"
    update="true" insert="true" column="startDate" />
<!--
    To add non XDoclet property mappings, create a file
    named hibernate-properties-Exhibition.xml
    containing the additional properties and
    place it in your merge dir.
-->
</subclass>
<subclass name="com.cascadetg.ch03.Museum"
    dynamic-update="false" dynamic-insert="false" >

<property name="dateOpened" type="java.util.Date"
    update="true" insert="true" column="dateOpened" />

<property name="location" type="java.lang.String"
    update="true" insert="true" column="location" />
<!--
    To add non XDoclet property mappings, create a file
    named hibernate-properties-Museum.xml
    containing the additional properties and
    place it in your merge dir.
-->
</subclass>
<subclass name="com.cascadetg.ch03.Person"
    dynamic-update="false" dynamic-insert="false" >

<property name="birthDate" type="java.util.Date"
    update="true" insert="true" column="birthDate" />

<property name="deathDate" type="java.util.Date"
    update="true" insert="true" column="deathDate" />
    <!--
```

Listing 3.8   Owner (and Subclasses) Mapping File (*continued*)

```
                To add non XDoclet property mappings, create a file
                named hibernate-properties-Person.xml
                containing the additional properties and
                place it in your merge dir.
            -->
            </subclass>
        </class>
</hibernate-mapping>
```

Generated Schema

The application in this chapter is intended to generate the database schema from the mapping files, generated in turn from the Java source. The representation of the `Artifact` object in a database is fairly straightforward, as shown in Listing 3.9.

Listing 3.9   Artifact Table Definition

```
mysql> desc artifact;
+---------------+--------------+------+-----+---------+------+
| Field         | Type         | Null | Key | Default | Extra
|
+---------------+--------------+------+-----+---------+------+
| id            | bigint(20)   |      | PRI | NULL    |
                                               auto_increment |
| comments      | varchar(255) | YES  |     | NULL    |      |
| dateCreated   | datetime     | YES  |     | NULL    |      |
| dateDiscovered| datetime     | YES  |     | NULL    |      |
| description   | varchar(255) | YES  |     | NULL    |      |
| location      | varchar(255) | YES  |     | NULL    |      |
| title         | varchar(255) | YES  |     | NULL    |      |
+---------------+--------------+------+-----+---------+------+
7 rows in set (0.00 sec)
```

The representation of the Owner class and the related subclasses, however, is a bit more complex, as shown in Listing 3.10.

Listing 3.10   Owner Table Definition

```
mysql> desc owner;
+---------------+--------------+------+-----+---------+-------+
| Field         | Type         | Null | Key | Default | Extra |
+---------------+--------------+------+-----+---------+-------+
| id            | bigint(20)   |      | PRI | NULL    | auto_ |
|               |              |      |     |         | increment |
| discriminator | varchar(255) |      |     |         |       |
| name          | varchar(255) | YES  |     | NULL    |       |
| dateCreated   | datetime     | YES  |     | NULL    |       |
| location      | varchar(255) | YES  |     | NULL    |       |
| owner         | bigint(20)   | YES  | MUL | NULL    |       |
| endDate       | datetime     | YES  |     | NULL    |       |
| startDate     | datetime     | YES  |     | NULL    |       |
| dateOpened    | datetime     | YES  |     | NULL    |       |
| birthDate     | datetime     | YES  |     | NULL    |       |
| deathDate     | datetime     | YES  |     | NULL    |       |
+---------------+--------------+------+-----+---------+-------+
```

Looking at the `owner` table in Listing 3.10 more closely, several interesting details emerge. The `discriminator` column is used to store the class type information regarding the record. Listing 3.11 shows an example of several records stored in the owner table; note the class information.

Listing 3.11   Sample Owner Records

```
mysql> select id, discriminator, name from owner;
+----+----------------------------+---------------------+
| id | discriminator              | name                |
+----+----------------------------+---------------------+
|  1 | com.cascadetg.ch03.Person  | Smith, Bob          |
|  2 | com.cascadetg.ch03.Foundation | Smith Foundation |
|  3 | com.cascadetg.ch03.Museum  | Waldendorf          |
|  4 | com.cascadetg.ch03.Exhibition | New Acquisitions 2005 |
+----+----------------------------+---------------------+
4 rows in set (0.00 sec)
```

Any column not relevant to a particular subclass is set to `null`. For example, a `Person` has no date-opened property, and therefore the `dateOpened` column for `Person` records is set to `null`.

Hibernate automatically manages the discriminator for you as you work with persistent objects. For example, when Hibernate retrieves the four records shown in Listing 3.11, it will automatically instantiate the proper object and set the values for you, returning a set of `Owner` objects with the proper underlying class.

In addition to the expected two tables, Hibernate also uses a third table to manage the relationships between artifacts and their owners, as shown in Listing 3.12. This table isn't mapped to a particular Java class; it is instead implied by the bidirectional `set` references on both `Owner` and `Artifact`. In database terminology, this is a many-to-many relationship. For more information on the link between a set collection and a many-to-many database relationship, see Chapter 7.

Listing 3.12   Ownership Table

```
mysql> desc ownership;
+------------+------------+------+-----+---------+-----------+
| Field      | Type       | Null | Key | Default | Extra     |
+------------+------------+------+-----+---------+-----------+
| owner_id   | bigint(20) |      | PRI | 0       |           |
| artifact_id| bigint(20) |      | PRI | 0       |           |
+------------+------------+------+-----+---------+-----------+
2 rows in set (0.00 sec)
```

Working with Artifacts and Owners

This final section of the chapter provides a sample set of operations. The entire class is shown in Listing 3.13, broken up to allow for commentary.

The code shown in Listing 3.13 shows the primary flow for the test application. A `SessionFactory` is shared throughout the execution of the application. An array of strings is used to describe a set of basic objects. The `main()` method tests the creation, update, and deletion of a set of objects.

Listing 3.13   Setting Up the Code

```
package com.cascadetg.ch03;

/** Note that we leverage a JDBC connection for
 * our mass delete code.
 */
import java.sql.Connection;
import java.sql.Statement;

/** Various Hibernate-related imports */
import net.sf.hibernate.*;
import net.sf.hibernate.cfg.*;
import net.sf.hibernate.tool.hbm2ddl.SchemaUpdate;
```

(continues)

Listing 3.13   Setting Up the Code (*continued*)

```java
import net.sf.hibernate.expression.Order;

public class TestSuite
{
    /** We use this session factory to create our sessions */
    public static SessionFactory sessionFactory;

    /** Our artifact data */
    public static String[] artifactNames =
        {
            "Bast Figurine, Faience",
            "Obsidian Spearpoint, Maglenian Period",
            "Lion Bowl, Unidentified",
            "Golden Torq, Six Inch Diameter",
            "Silver Ring, Roman" };

    static long update_id;

    public static void main(String[] args)
    {
        initialization();
        if (currentCount() == 0)
            System.out.println("initialization OK");

        createObjects();
        if (currentCount() == 5)
            System.out.println("createObjects OK");

        loadAllArtifacts();
        if (currentCount() == 5)
            System.out.println("loadAllArtifacts OK");

        updateOneObject();
        if (currentCount() == 5)
            System.out.println("updateOneObject OK");

        deleteObjects();
        if (currentCount() == 4)
            System.out.println("deleteObjects OK");

        massDelete();
        if (currentCount() == 0)
            System.out.println("massDelete OK");
    }
```

Listing 3.14 shows the use of HQL to determine the number of artifacts currently in the system. For more information on HQL, see Chapter 8.

Listing 3.14   Obtaining the Current Count

```
public static int currentCount()
{
    System.out.println();
    Session hibernateSession = null;
    Transaction myTransaction = null;
    Integer result = null;
    try
    {
        hibernateSession = sessionFactory.openSession();
        myTransaction =
            hibernateSession.beginTransaction();

        String hql =
        "select count(artifact) from Artifact as artifact";

        Query myQuery = hibernateSession.createQuery(hql);

        result = (Integer)myQuery.uniqueResult();
        System.out.println(
            "Current count: " + result.toString());

        myTransaction.commit();

    } catch (Exception e)
    {
        e.printStackTrace();
        try
        {
            myTransaction.rollback();
        } catch (Exception e2)
        {
            // Silent failure of transaction rollback
        }
    } finally
    {
        try
        {
            if (hibernateSession != null)
                hibernateSession.close();
        } catch (Exception e)
        {
```

(continues)

Listing 3.14   Obtaining the Current Count (*continued*)

```
                // Silent failure of session close
        }
    }
    return result.intValue();
}
```

   Listing 3.15 shows the standard initialization of a Hibernate application. Note the use of the `SchemaUpdate` class to ensure that the database schema is brought in line with the current mapping files (see Chapter 11 for more information on schema management).

Listing 3.15   Setting Up the Code

```
/** Loads the Hibernate configuration information,
 * sets up the database and the Hibernate session factory.
 */
public static void initialization()
{
    //System.setErr(System.out);
    System.out.println("initialization");
    try
    {
        Configuration myConfiguration = new
            Configuration();

        myConfiguration.addClass(Owner.class);
        myConfiguration.addClass(Artifact.class);

        // This is the code that updates the database to
        // the current schema.
        new SchemaUpdate(myConfiguration).execute(true,
            true);

        // Sets up the session factory (used in the rest
        // of the application).
        sessionFactory =
            myConfiguration.buildSessionFactory();

    } catch (Exception e)
    {
        e.printStackTrace();
    }
}
```

Listing 3.16 shows the creation of a set of objects, along with the establishment of the relationships between various objects. Note that nowhere is the `ownership` table referenced by name; the relationships are instead managed by Hibernate. For more information on the management of relationships by Hibernate, see Chapter 7.

Listing 3.16　Creating Objects

```
public static void createObjects()
{
    System.out.println();
    System.out.println("createObjects");

    Session hibernateSession = null;
    Transaction myTransaction = null;
    try
    {
        hibernateSession = sessionFactory.openSession();
        myTransaction =
            hibernateSession.beginTransaction();

        Owner myExhibition = new Exhibition();
        myExhibition.setName("New Acquisitions 2005");

        Person myPerson = new Person();
        myPerson.setName("Smith, Bob");

        Foundation myFoundation = new Foundation();
        myFoundation.setName("Smith Foundation");
        myFoundation.setOwner(myPerson);

        Museum myMuseum = new Museum();
        myMuseum.setName("Waldendorf");
        myMuseum.setDateOpened(new java.util.Date());

        hibernateSession.save(myPerson);
        hibernateSession.save(myFoundation);
        hibernateSession.save(myMuseum);
        hibernateSession.flush();
        myTransaction.commit();

        myTransaction = hibernateSession.beginTransaction
            ();

        for (int i = 0; i < artifactNames.length; i++)
        {
```

(continues)

Listing 3.16   Creating Objects (*continued*)

```java
                    Artifact myArtifact = new Artifact();
                    myArtifact.setTitle(artifactNames[i]);
                    hibernateSession.save(myArtifact);

                    // Important to issue the save first,
                    // so the ID of the artifact is set.
                    myArtifact.addOwner(myExhibition);
                    myArtifact.addOwner(myFoundation);
                    myArtifact.addOwner(myMuseum);

                    hibernateSession.save(myExhibition);
                    hibernateSession.save(myFoundation);
                    hibernateSession.save(myMuseum);

                    hibernateSession.flush();
                }

                myTransaction.commit();
            } catch (Exception e)
            {
                e.printStackTrace();
                try
                {
                    myTransaction.rollback();
                } catch (Exception e2)
                {
                    // Silent failure of transaction rollback
                }
            } finally
            {
                try
                {
                    hibernateSession.close();
                } catch (Exception e2)
                {
                    // Silent failure of session close
                }
            }
        }
```

Listing 3.17 shows the use of the Criteria API to fetch both the Artifact and all of the associated Owners with a single SQL statement. For more information on the Criteria API, see Chapter 8.

Listing 3.17   Loading the Artifacts and Owners

```
public static void loadAllArtifacts()
{
    System.out.println();
    System.out.println("loadAllArtifacts");

    Session hibernateSession = null;
    Transaction myTransaction = null;

    try
    {
        hibernateSession = sessionFactory.openSession();
        myTransaction =
            hibernateSession.beginTransaction();

        // In this example, we use the Criteria API.
        // We could also have used the HQL, but the
        // Criteria API allows us to express this
        // query more easily. First indicate that
        // we want to grab all of the artifacts.
        Criteria query =
            hibernateSession.createCriteria(Artifact
                .class);

        // Now, specify sorting by the artifact title
        query.addOrder(Order.asc("title"));

        // Indicate that we want to grab all of the
        // associated owners of artifacts as well.
        // This lets us pull of the data in a single
        // SQL statement!
        query.setFetchMode("owners", FetchMode.EAGER);

        // This actually performs the database request,
        // based on the query we've built.
        java.util.Iterator results =
            query.list().iterator();
                Artifact myArtifact;

        // Because we are grabbing all of the artifacts and
```

(continues)

Listing 3.17   Loading the Artifacts and Owners (*continued*)

```java
                    // artifact owners, we need to store the returned
                    // artifacts

                    java.util.LinkedList retrievedArtifacts =
                        new java.util.LinkedList();
                    while (results.hasNext())
                    {
                        // Note that the result set is cast to the
                        // Animal object directly—no manual
                        // binding required.
                        myArtifact = (Artifact)results.next();
                        if (!retrievedArtifacts.contains(myArtifact))
                            retrievedArtifacts.add(myArtifact);

                        update_id = myArtifact.getId();
                    }

                    java.util.Iterator results2 =
                        retrievedArtifacts.iterator();
                    while (results2.hasNext())
                    {
                        myArtifact = (Artifact)results2.next();
                        if (false)
                        {
                            System.out.println(myArtifact.getId() + "");
                            System.out.println(myArtifact.getTitle() +
                                "");
                        }
                        java.util.Set myOwners =
                            myArtifact.getOwners();
                        java.util.Iterator myOwnersIterator =
                            myOwners.iterator();
                        if (false)
                            while (myOwnersIterator.hasNext())
                                System.out.println(
                                    ((Owner)myOwnersIterator.next())
                                        .getName());
                    }

                myTransaction.commit();
            } catch (Exception e)
            {
                e.printStackTrace();
                try
                {
```

Listing 3.17   Loading the Artifacts and Owners (*continued*)

```
                myTransaction.rollback();
        } catch (Exception e2)
        {
            // Silent failure of transaction rollback
        }
    } finally
    {
        try
        {
            if (hibernateSession != null)
                hibernateSession.close();
        } catch (Exception e)
        {
            // Silent failure of session close
        }
    }
}
```

Listing 3.18 shows a single object, loaded and then updated after a minor change.

Listing 3.18   Updating a Single Object

```
public static void updateOneObject()
{
    System.out.println();
    System.out.println("updateOneObject");

    Session hibernateSession = null;
    Transaction myTransaction = null;

    try
    {
        hibernateSession = sessionFactory.openSession();
        myTransaction = hibernateSession
            .beginTransaction();

        Artifact myArtifact =
            (Artifact)hibernateSession.get(
                Artifact.class,
                new Long(update_id));

        myArtifact.setTitle("Test");
```

(*continues*)

Listing 3.18   Updating a Single Object (*continued*)

```
            hibernateSession.update(myArtifact);

            myTransaction.commit();

    } catch (Exception e)
    {
        e.printStackTrace();
        try
        {
            myTransaction.rollback();
        } catch (Exception e2)
        {
            // Silent failure of transaction rollback
        }
    } finally
    {
        try
        {
            if (hibernateSession != null)
                hibernateSession.close();
        } catch (Exception e)
        {
            // Silent failure of session close
        }
    }
}
```

Listing 3.19 shows the deletion of a set of objects that meet a particular HQL query (in this case, items that happen to have a title starting with "Golden").

Note the commented-out call to `Session.find()` prior to the `Session.delete()`. Whenever you are deleting objects, it's a good idea to test this out in advance, making sure that the objects being deleted are the objects you actually *want* to delete.

Listing 3.19   Deleting Particular Objects

```
    public static void deleteObjects()
    {
        System.out.println();
        System.out.println("deleteObjects");

        Session hibernateSession = null;
        Transaction myTransaction = null;
```

Listing 3.19 Deleting Particular Objects (*continued*)

```
try
{
    hibernateSession = sessionFactory.openSession();
    myTransaction =
        hibernateSession.beginTransaction();

    String hql =
        "from Artifact as artifact where "
            + "artifact.title like 'Golden%'";

    java.util.List myArtifacts =
        hibernateSession.find(hql);

    hibernateSession.delete(hql);

    hibernateSession.flush();

    String sql =
"DELETE ownership FROM ownership LEFT JOIN artifact "
+ "ON ownership.artifact_id=artifact.id "
+ "WHERE artifact.id IS NULL";

    Connection myConnection =
        hibernateSession.connection();
    Statement myStatement =
        myConnection.createStatement();
    System.out.println(myStatement.execute(sql));
    System.out.println(myStatement.getUpdateCount());
    myTransaction.commit();

} catch (Exception e)
{
    e.printStackTrace();
    try
    {
        myTransaction.rollback();
    } catch (Exception e2)
    {
        // Silent failure of transaction rollback
    }
} finally
{
    try
    {
```

(*continues*)

Listing 3.19   Deleting Particular Objects (*continued*)

```
                    if (hibernateSession != null)
                        hibernateSession.close();
            } catch (Exception e)
            {
                // Silent failure of session close
            }
        }
    }
```

You may sometimes wish to perform SQL operations on the database directly, instead of relying on HQL or the Criteria API. This is especially true when performing a mass insert, but Listing 3.20 shows the use of SQL to perform a bulk deletion.

Listing 3.20   Deleting Many Objects at Once Using SQL

```
    public static void massDelete()
    {
        System.out.println();
        System.out.println("massDelete");
        Session hibernateSession = null;
        Transaction myTransaction = null;

        try
        {
            hibernateSession = sessionFactory.openSession();
            myTransaction =
                hibernateSession.beginTransaction();
            Connection myConnection =
                hibernateSession.connection();
            Statement myStatement =
                myConnection.createStatement();

            String sql = "delete from artifact";
            System.out.println(sql);
            myStatement.execute(sql);

            sql = "delete from owner";
            System.out.println(sql);
            myStatement.execute(sql);

            sql = "delete from ownership";
            System.out.println(sql);
            myStatement.execute(sql);
```

Listing 3.20   Deleting Many Objects at Once Using SQL (*continued*)

```
                myTransaction.commit();

        } catch (Exception e)
        {
            e.printStackTrace();
            try
            {
                myTransaction.rollback();
            } catch (Exception e2)
            {
                // Silent failure of transaction rollback
            }
        } finally
        {
            try
            {
                if (hibernateSession != null)
                    hibernateSession.close();
            } catch (Exception e)
            {
                // Silent failure of session close
            }
        }

    }

}
```

Assuming that everything is working properly, the output of this test application should be as shown in Listing 3.21.

NOTE

The final step of this program is the deletion of all the data in the tables—you may wish to comment out the references to the deleteObjects() and/or mass Delete() methods in the main() method to explore the data generated in the database.

Listing 3.21   Successful Output

```
Current count: 0
initialization OK
```

(*continues*)

Listing 3.21   Successful Output (*continued*)

```
createObjects

Current count: 5
createObjects OK

loadAllArtifacts

Current count: 5
loadAllArtifacts OK

updateOneObject

Current count: 5
updateOneObject OK

deleteObjects
false
3

Current count: 4
deleteObjects OK

massDelete
delete from artifact
delete from owner
delete from ownership

Current count: 0
massDelete OK
```

CHAPTER 4

Starting from
an Existing Schema

In many enterprise environments, applications will be based on an existing database schema, not the other way around. Hibernate, in conjunction with a tool called Middlegen, supports this development model. In this chapter, persistent objects will be derived from an existing MySQL schema, using Middlegen to generate the Hibernate mapping files; these will in turn be used to generate Java source files.

The example in this chapter should be familiar to anyone who has ever attended school. The database schema models a set of courses and students, tracking exams and exam results for each student. Many books on relational database design include this example—especially some of the more academic texts.

Initial Schema

In this scenario, development is based on an existing schema. Application designers are often not allowed to significantly update or change a schema, perhaps because it is in use by other applications, or because the database is a legacy system, or for any number of other possible reasons. The point is that the database design in this scenario drives the application development. A schema is given, and may occasionally be embroidered (for example, adding a column), but the overall structure is fixed prior to application development.

Listing 4.1 shows the script used to generate the schema for the database in this chapter. Note that this script is written to automatically drop and recreate the tables used in the chapter each time it is run, destroying any data present in the tables (obviously this would not be used in a "real" system).

The schema in this example includes several MySQL specific commands. For example, the `TYPE=InnoDB` command tells MySQL to convert the tables to the InnoDB format, a more modern format for storing database data than the default MySQL format. Similarly, the foreign-key checks are disabled to avoid errors when dropping the tables. The schema described in this chapter is based on MySQL 4.0.18. Depending on the database you are using, you may need to modify this schema script to be able to execute it. Alternatively, you may wish to use the graphical administrative tool included with your database (if any) to create this schema.

PORTABLE SCHEMA SCRIPTS

If you are used to another database, the MySQL schema commands below may look unfamiliar. Worse, unless you are running MySQL, you'll almost certainly have to edit the script for your own database.

This is yet another reason why I strongly prefer working from a mapping file if possible. Hibernate includes schema management functionality (as described in Chapter 11). This allows you to define a common schema structure in your mapping file and rely on Hibernate to generate dialect-specific scripts for a suite of databases.

Pay close attention to the commands to create indexes and foreign key constraints at the end of the script. Middlegen (the tool used later in this chapter) reads these constraints and uses them to generate relationship mappings. In other words, Middlegen reads these key relationships and uses them to establish relationships in the generated Hibernate mapping files (and from there in the generated Java source).

If you wish to see a graphical representation of the tables generated by this script, you may wish to skip ahead to glance at the tables in Figure 4.2.

Listing 4.1   Schema Generation Script

```
USE hibernate;

SET FOREIGN_KEY_CHECKS=0;
DROP TABLE IF EXISTS Course;
DROP TABLE IF EXISTS Student;
DROP TABLE IF EXISTS Exam;
DROP TABLE IF EXISTS ExamResult;
SET FOREIGN_KEY_CHECKS=1;
```

Listing 4.1   Schema Generation Script (*continued*)

```
CREATE TABLE Course
(
     ID BIGINT UNSIGNED AUTO_INCREMENT NOT NULL PRIMARY KEY
);
ALTER TABLE Course ADD title CHAR(100);
ALTER TABLE Course ADD quarter CHAR(4);

CREATE TABLE Student
(
     ID BIGINT UNSIGNED AUTO_INCREMENT NOT NULL PRIMARY KEY
);
ALTER TABLE Student ADD firstName CHAR(100);
ALTER TABLE Student ADD lastName CHAR(100);
ALTER TABLE Student ADD idString CHAR(20);

CREATE TABLE Exam
(
     ID BIGINT UNSIGNED AUTO_INCREMENT NOT NULL PRIMARY KEY
);
ALTER TABLE Exam ADD courseID BIGINT UNSIGNED;
ALTER TABLE Exam ADD date TIMESTAMP;
ALTER TABLE Exam ADD comment CHAR(255);

CREATE TABLE ExamResult
(
     ID BIGINT UNSIGNED AUTO_INCREMENT NOT NULL PRIMARY KEY
);
ALTER TABLE ExamResult ADD score INT;
ALTER TABLE ExamResult ADD studentID BIGINT UNSIGNED;
ALTER TABLE ExamResult ADD examID BIGINT UNSIGNED;


ALTER TABLE Course TYPE=InnoDB;
ALTER TABLE Student TYPE=InnoDB;
ALTER TABLE Exam TYPE=InnoDB;
ALTER TABLE ExamResult TYPE=InnoDB;

ALTER TABLE Exam ADD INDEX (courseID);
ALTER TABLE ExamResult ADD INDEX (studentID);
ALTER TABLE ExamResult ADD INDEX (examID);

ALTER TABLE Exam ADD CONSTRAINT FK_exam_courseID FOREIGN KEY
(courseID) REFERENCES Course (ID);
ALTER TABLE ExamResult ADD CONSTRAINT FK_examresult_studentID
FOREIGN KEY (studentID) REFERENCES Student (ID);
```

(*continues*)

Listing 4.1   Schema Generation Script (*continued*)

```
ALTER TABLE ExamResult ADD CONSTRAINT FK_examresult_examID
FOREIGN KEY (examID) REFERENCES Exam (ID);

SHOW TABLES;
```

Using Middlegen

Assuming that the script has been used to generate the schema in the database, the next step is to set up and configure Middlegen. Middlegen is a tool for generating mapping files and other artifacts from an existing database schema. It can be used to generate bindings for a variety of other technologies (including EJB 2.X) in addition to Hibernate. That's what Middlegen does—generate developer artifacts (for the "middle tier") from a relational database.

Middlegen uses JDBC to connect to a database and then generate application resources and code from that database. Although this may seem counter-intuitive, Ant is used as the engine for launching and configuring Middlegen. The advantage of using Ant is that the graphical user interface and the command-line build process can share a single configuration.

Obtaining Middlegen

You can download the complete Middlegen release from SourceForge.net at http://sourceforge.net/projects/middlegen. Unfortunately, the default download includes a large suite of files unnecessary for use with Hibernate (for example, extensive support for EJB CMP 2.0 and JDO). A great many complex build files are included, as well as a large suite of libraries. To make it easier to understand, this chapter will use a somewhat stripped down version of the Middlegen 2.0 VO files, available for download at http://www.cascadetg.com/hibernate/.

Figure 4.1 shows the files contained in the archive. The `lib` directory contains the `*.jar` files needed by the project. The Commons, log4j, Middlegen, and Velocity JAR files are included with the Middlegen 2.0 VO project, and the MySQL driver is available for download from http://www.mysql.com/.

As you will have noticed, there are several other folders in the distribution. The `prefs` directory contains the `preferences` generated by the Middlegen GUI. The `hbm` directory contains the `*.hbm.xml` files generated by Middlegen. Similarly, the `src` directory contains Java source files generated from the `*.hbm.xml` files by an Ant task.

The `build.xml` file is an Ant script used to launch the Middlegen GUI (see Chapter 2 for more information on Ant). The `schema.sql` file contains the

Figure 4.1. Middlegen Directories and Files

MySQL SQL statements, as shown in Listing 4.1. The various log files are generated during the run of the Ant script, and may be useful if you encounter problems.

Configuring Middlegen

The most important file in the distribution is the `build.xml` file. If you are accustomed to working with Ant, you may expect `build.xml` to serve primarily as a tool for performing automated builds. Middlegen, however, uses Ant and `build.xml` as a configuration tool for the graphical user interface and the automated build process. When you are first building your application, you will use the Middlegen user interface, but later you may wish to merely use Middlegen as an automated build tool.

ANT FOR LAUNCHING MIDDLEGEN?

If you are accustomed to simply double-clicking an application to launch it, the use of Ant to configure and launch Middlegen may feel strange. Those

(continues)

who favor this approach argue that it allows you to reuse a common configuration setting for both the graphic user interface and the command-line version. In practice, it probably would be better for Middlegen to operate as an ordinary application, saving and loading configuration as a standalone XML file, which could then be referenced by the build task. This would allow for a shorter build file and a more accessible first impression when using Middlegen.

Middlegen is open-source, so feel free to download it and start working.

Listing 4.2 show the header for the `build.xml` file, containing the various configuration options for the build script. Of particular interest are the package settings (allowing you to control the package for the generated source) and the JDBC connectivity settings.

Listing 4.2   Ant Build and Run Script

```
<project default="all">

    <!-- project name -->
    <property name="name" value="chapter4" />

    <!-- installation configuration -->
    <property name="hibernate_path"
        value="C:\devenv\hibernate-2.1.2"/>
    <property name="hibernate_tool_path"
        value="C:\devenv\hibernate-extensions-2.0.2\tools"/>
    <property name="project.dir"
        value=
"C:\devenv\eclipsev3_M4\workspace\hibernate\com\cascadetg\ch04"
/>

    <!-- the generated package info -->
    <property name="package" value="com.cascadetg.ch04" />
    <property name="package.dir" value="\com\cascadetg\ch04" />

    <!-- various sub directories -->
    <property name="lib.dir" value=".\lib" />
    <property name="prefs.dir" value=".\prefs" />
    <property name="build.hbm.dir" value=".\hbm" />
    <property name="build.src.dir" value=".\src" />

    <!-- name of the database script -->
    <property name="database.script.file" value="schema.sql" />
```

Listing 4.2   Ant Build and Run Script (*continued*)

```
        <!-- JDBC connectivity information -->
        <property name="database.driver.file"
 value="${lib.dir}\mysql-connector-java-3.0.10-stable-bin.jar"/>
        <property name="database.driver.classpath"
              value="${database.driver.file}"/>
        <property name="database.driver"
              value="com.mysql.jdbc.Driver"/>
        <property name="database.url"
              value="jdbc:mysql://localhost/hibernate"/>
        <property name="database.userid"    value="root"/>
        <property name="database.password" value=""/>
        <property name="database.schema"    value=""/>
        <property name="database.catalog"   value=""/>
```

As shown in Listing 4.3, the default `all` target will build the tables in the database by executing a script containing the commands, as shown in Listing 4.1, then invoke Middlegen (generating the `*.hbm.xml` files), create the Java sources from the `*.hbm.xml` files, and finally copy the files into the project development tree.

Listing 4.3   Building Tables

```
<!-- default target -->
<target name="all"
      depends="build_tables,middlegen,build_hbm,copy_files" />

<!-- calls and executes the schema script -->
<target name="build_tables">
      <sql
      classpath="${database.driver.classpath}"
      driver="${database.driver}"
      url="${database.url}"
      userid="${database.userid}"
      password="${database.password}"
      print="true"
      output="build_tables_result.log">
            <transaction src="${database.script.file}" />
      </sql>
</target>
```

Listing 4.4 shows the target to launch and configure Middlegen. First, a Middlegen Ant task definition is specified, and then the Middlegen task is configured.

A single output `plugin` is used to indicate that the application uses Hibernate (Middlegen can also create EJB or JDO mappings, using other plugins).

Note that the four tables described by the schema are explicitly named in the file. Middlegen will load these tables and attempt to deduce the relationships between them from the JDBC driver metadata. If the relationship is sufficiently complex, it can specify additional configuration data.

COMPLEX RELATIONSHIPS WITH MIDDLEGEN

You can use additional tags to describe many-to-many relationships (as described in Chapter 7) or relationships that are not described by foreign-key constraints (useful if your database doesn't support foreign keys).

For more information on these options, see http://boss.bekk.no/ boss/middlegen/ant/index.html. For example, to use a many-to-many association table without an independent generated class, you can use the `many2many` configuration tag. Alternatively, you might use `crossref` sub-elements of the table tag to declare foreign-key relationships. There are multiple ways to model most relationships, many of which may be equally useful.

Listing 4.4   Middlegen Task

```
<!-- Target to run Middlegen -->
<target name="middlegen"
      description="Run Middlegen"
      unless="middlegen.skip">

      <mkdir dir="${prefs.dir}"/>
      <echo message="Class path = ${basedir}"/>

      <taskdef name="middlegen"
          classname="middlegen.MiddlegenTask">
            <classpath>
                <fileset dir="${lib.dir}">
                    <include name="*.jar"/>
                    <include name="*.properties"/>
                </fileset>
            </classpath>
      </taskdef>

      <!-- Note the gui=true value. Set this to false to use in
      a command-line fashion -->
      <middlegen
          appname="${name}"
```

Listing 4.4 Middlegen Task (*continued*)

```
                prefsdir="${prefs.dir}"
                gui="true"
                databaseurl="${database.url}"
                driver="${database.driver}"
                username="${database.userid}"
                password="${database.password}"
                chema="${database.schema}"
                catalog="${database.catalog}"
        >

                <!-- The hibernate plugin-->
                <hibernate
                    destination="${build.hbm.dir}"
                    package="${package}"
                    javaTypeMapper=
            "middlegen.plugins.hibernate.HibernateJavaTypeMapper"
                />

                <table name="student" />
                <table name="course" />
                <table name="exam" />
                <table name="examresult" />

                <!-- You can declare additional tables and
                relationships here. You can use this to
                override or add to the JDBC derived information
                -->
                <!-- For example...
                <many2many>
                <tablea name="student"/>
                <jointable name="examresult" generate="false"/>
                <tableb name="class"/>
                </many2many>
                -->
        </middlegen>
    </target>
```

Listing 4.5 shows the target that generates the Java sources from the * .hbm.xml
files (similar to the files shown in Chapter 2) after Middlegen exits from the GUI.

Listing 4.5 Building Java Source Files

```
<!-- creates the Java sources from the HBM files.
<target name="build_hbm" description="builds the Java sources">
```

(continues)

Listing 4.5   Building Java Source Files (*continued*)

```
        <mkdir dir="${build.src.dir}"/>
        <echo message="src dir = ${build.src.dir}"/>
        <echo message="target hbm
            files = ${build.hbm.dir}${package.dir}\" />

        <taskdef name="hbm2java"
            classname="net.sf.hibernate.tool.hbm2java.Hbm2JavaTask">
            <classpath>
              <pathelement
    location="${hibernate_path}\hibernate2.jar"/>
              <pathelement
    location="${hibernate_tool_path}\hibernate-tools.jar"/>
              <pathelement
    location=
    "${hibernate_path}\lib\commons-collections-2.1.jar" />
              <pathelement
    location="${hibernate_path}\lib\commons-logging-1.0.3.jar" />
              <pathelement
    location="${hibernate_path}\lib\commons-lang-1.0.1.jar" />
              <pathelement
    location="${hibernate_path}\lib\xerces-2.4.0.jar" />
              <pathelement
    location="${hibernate_tool_path}\lib\jdom.jar"/>
            </classpath>
        </taskdef>

        <hbm2java config="hbm2java_config.xml"
            output="${build.src.dir}">
      <fileset
      dir="${build.hbm.dir}${package.dir}" includes="*.hbm.xml"/>
        </hbm2java>
  </target>
```

Finally, as shown in Listing 4.6 the project provides a task to copy the resulting source and mapping files from the generated projects into the development tree.

Listing 4.6   Building Java Source Files

```
<!-- copies the results to your project source tree.
Note that you need both the Java source and the
HBM files. -->
<target name="copy_files" description="copies results to
project">
        <copy todir="${project.dir}">
```

Listing 4.6   Building Java Source Files (*continued*)

```
                <fileset dir="hbm\${package.dir}" />
                <fileset dir="${build.src.dir}\${package.dir}" />
                <fileset file="${database.script.file}" />
        </copy>
    </target>

</project>
```

Finally, as shown in Listing 4.6, the project provides a task to copy the resulting source and mapping files from the generated projects into the development tree.

Running Middlegen

Before running Middlegen as shown, you must have first successfully installed MySQL, created a database named `hibernate`, and installed Ant. Once you have done all this, simple open a terminal, change to the directory containing the build file, type `ant`, and press return.

The terminal will begin by generating output, as shown in Listing 4.7, and then will launch the Middlegen graphical interface.

Listing 4.7   Initial Middlegen Output

```
C:\devenv\cascadetg-middlegen-2.0-vo>ant
Buildfile: build.xml

build_tables:
      [sql] Executing file: C:\devenv\cascadetg-middlegen-2.0-
vo\schema.sql
      [sql] 33 of 33 SQL statements executed successfully

middlegen:
      [echo] Class path = C:\devenv\cascadetg-middlegen-2.0-vo
[middlegen] log4j:WARN No appenders could be found for logger
(middlegen.Middlegen).
[middlegen] log4j:WARN Please initialize the log4j system
properly.
[middlegen] Database URL:jdbc:mysql://localhost/hibernate
[middlegen]
```

(continues)

Listing 4.7   Initial Middlegen Output (*continued*)

```
* * * * * * * * * * * * * * * * * * * * * * * * * * * * * * * * * * * * * * * * * * * * * * * * * * * * * * * *
[middlegen] * CTRL-Click relations to modify their cardinality
*
[middlegen] * SHIFT-Click relations to modify their
directionality *
[middlegen]
* * * * * * * * * * * * * * * * * * * * * * * * * * * * * * * * * * * * * * * * * * * * * * * * * * * * * * * *
<GUI launches>
```

Figure 4.2 shows the Middlegen user interface in action. The boxes can be organized to fit aesthetic requirements. Clicking on a table will let you set table-specific configuration options; clicking on a column name will allow you to set column-specific configuration options.

By interacting with the Middlegen interface, you configure the `*.hbm.xml` files that will be generated by Middlegen. While the interface allows you to modify the cardinality and direction of the bindings, you can't create or delete associations—this must be done in the database via foreign keys or via the Middlegen `build.xml` file.

The following modifications were made in the Middlegen interface for this application.

- The key generator for all four tables is changed from assigned to native. For more information on these options, see the generator tag in Chapter 5.

- Change the `score` Java type from `java.lang.Long` to `int`.

After these changes are made, the Generate button should be clicked to actually generate the `*.hbm.xml` files. The close box is used to exit. After Middlegen exits, the Ant build script will continue, as shown in Listing 4.8.

Listing 4.8   Concluding Middlegen Output

```
<GUI terminates>
[middlegen] Updated preferences in C:\devenv\cascadetg-
middlegen-2.0-vo\prefs\chapter4-prefs.pr

build_hbm:

copy_files:
    [copy] Copying 4 files to
C:\devenv\eclipsev3_M4\workspace\hibernate\com\cascadetg\ch04
```

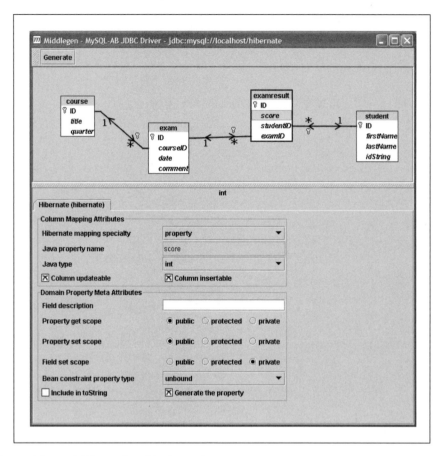

Figure 4.2. Middlegen Graphical Interface

Listing 4.8 Concluding Middlegen Output (*continued*)

```
all:

BUILD SUCCESSFUL
Total time: 11 minutes 38 seconds
C:\devenv\cascadetg-middlegen-2.0-vo>
```

Generated Mapping Files

As seen in Figure 4.2, the `examresult` table is a many-to-many join with an additional data attribute. Because of the additional data (the score value), we can't model this using Hibernate's built-in many-to-many functionality. Instead it must be modeled as a separate class.

Listing 4.9 shows the generated * . hbm . xml file for the Examresult class (the white space has been reformatted slightly to make it more readable). Note the two many-to-one associations; these are used in lieu of a Hibernate many-to-many relationship.

Listing 4.9   Generated Many-to-Many Examresult Class

```xml
<?xml version="1.0"?>
<!DOCTYPE hibernate-mapping PUBLIC
    "-//Hibernate/Hibernate Mapping DTD 2.0//EN"
    "http://hibernate.sourceforge.net/hibernate-mapping-
2.0.dtd" >

<hibernate-mapping>
<!--
    Created by the Middlegen Hibernate plugin

    http://boss.bekk.no/boss/middlegen/
    http://hibernate.sourceforge.net/
-->

<class name="com.cascadetg.ch04.Examresult" table="examresult">

    <id name="id" type="java.lang.Long" column="ID">
        <generator class="native" />
    </id>

    <property name="score" type="int" column="score"
        length="11" />

    <!-- associations -->
    <!-- bi-directional many-to-one association to Student -->
    <many-to-one name="student"
        class="com.cascadetg.ch04.Student"
        not-null="true">
        <column name="studentID" />
    </many-to-one>

    <!-- bi-directional many-to-one association to Exam -->
    <many-to-one name="exam" class="com.cascadetg.ch04.Exam"
        not-null="true" >
        <column name="examID" />
    </many-to-one>

</class>
</hibernate-mapping>
```

The flip side of the association with `Examresult` is shown in Listing 4.10 (again, the white space has been reformatted to make it more readable). The `Exam` mapping uses a `set` to manage the relationship. For more information on the `set` tag and the other nested portions of the mapping, see Chapter 5.

Listing 4.10   Generated Exam Mapping

```xml
<?xml version="1.0"?>
<!DOCTYPE hibernate-mapping PUBLIC
    "-//Hibernate/Hibernate Mapping DTD 2.0//EN"
    "http://hibernate.sourceforge.net/hibernate-mapping-
2.0.dtd" >

<hibernate-mapping>
<!--
    Created by the Middlegen Hibernate plugin

    http://boss.bekk.no/boss/middlegen/
    http://hibernate.sourceforge.net/
-->

<class name="com.cascadetg.ch04.Exam" table="exam">

    <id name="id" type="java.lang.Long" column="ID" >
        <generator class="native" />
    </id>

    <property name="date" type="java.sql.Timestamp"
        column="date" length="14" />
    <property name="comment" type="java.lang.String"
        column="comment" length="255" />

    <!-- associations -->
    <!-- bi-directional many-to-one association to Course -->
    <many-to-one name="course"
        class="com.cascadetg.ch04.Course"
        not-null="true" >
        <column name="courseID" />
    </many-to-one>

    <!-- bi-directional one-to-many association to Examresult -->
    <set name="examresults" lazy="true" inverse="true" >
        <key>
            <column name="examID" />
        </key>
        <one-to-many class="com.cascadetg.ch04.Examresult" />
```

(continues)

Listing 4.10   Generated Exam Mapping (*continued*)

```
    </set>

</class>
</hibernate-mapping>
```

The mapping generated for the student table is shown in Listing 4.11 (extraneous white space removed).

Listing 4.11   Generated Student Mapping

```xml
<?xml version="1.0"?>
<!DOCTYPE hibernate-mapping PUBLIC
    "-//Hibernate/Hibernate Mapping DTD 2.0//EN"
    "http://hibernate.sourceforge.net/hibernate-mapping-
2.0.dtd" >

<hibernate-mapping>
<!--
    Created by the Middlegen Hibernate plugin

    http://boss.bekk.no/boss/middlegen/
    http://hibernate.sourceforge.net/
-->

<class name="com.cascadetg.ch04.Student" table="student">

    <id name="id" type="java.lang.Long" column="ID" >
        <generator class="native" />
    </id>

    <property name="firstName" type="java.lang.String"
        column="firstName" length="100" />
    <property name="lastName" type="java.lang.String"
        column="lastName" length="100" />
    <property name="idString" type="java.lang.String"
        column="idString" length="20" />

    <!-- associations -->
    <!-- bi-directional one-to-many association to Examresult -->
    <set name="examresults" lazy="true" inverse="true">
        <key>
            <column name="studentID" />
        </key>
```

Listing 4.11 Generated Student Mapping

```
        <one-to-many class="com.cascadetg.ch04.Examresult" />
    </set>

</class>
</hibernate-mapping>
```

The mapping generated for the final table, `course`, is shown in Listing 4.12 (white space edited).

Listing 4.12 Generated Course Mapping

```
<?xml version="1.0"?>
<!DOCTYPE hibernate-mapping PUBLIC
    "--//Hibernate/Hibernate Mapping DTD 2.0//EN"
    "http://hibernate.sourceforge.net/hibernate-mapping-
2.0.dtd" >

<hibernate-mapping>
<!--
    Created by the Middlegen Hibernate plugin

    http://boss.bekk.no/boss/middlegen/
    http://hibernate.sourceforge.net/
-->

<class name="com.cascadetg.ch04.Course" table="course" >

    <id name="id" type="java.lang.Long" column="ID" >
        <generator class="native" />
    </id>

    <property name="title" type="java.lang.String"
        column="title" length="100" />
    <property name="quarter" type="java.lang.String"
        column="quarter" length="4" />

    <!-- associations -->
    <!-- bi-directional one-to-many association to Exam -->
    <set name="exams" lazy="true" inverse="true" >
        <key>
            <column name="courseID" />
        </key>
        <one-to-many class="com.cascadetg.ch04.Exam"/>
```

(continues)

Listing 4.12   Generated Course Mapping

```
    </set>

</class>
</hibernate-mapping>
```

Generated Java

Given the mapping files, Ant and Hibernate automatically generate the corresponding Java source from the `*.hbm.xml` files. Figure 4.3 shows an overview of the generated source.

REVIEWING THE GENERATED FILES

You would be well advised to open the generated HBM files in a text editor and go through them in conjunction with the tag reference given in Chapter 5—you should be comfortable with the various configuration options as you work with Hibernate. Keep in mind that the `*.hbm.xml` files (and hence the corresponding Java sources) are generated by Middlegen. If you wish to change an option in a `*.hbm.xml` file, you should update the `build.xml` file or the proper option in the Middlegen graphical interface, not the generated `*.hbm.xml` file (unless you no longer wish to use Middlegen).

Working with the Database

The application now has both `*.hbm.xml` files and corresponding Java source files. Given these files, it's a simple matter to use Hibernate to perform database operations. The sample code shown in the remainder of this chapter will use the generated files to populate the database with some data and then produce a report based on that data.

From the perspective of the classes manipulating the database via Hibernate, these are just additional examples of manipulating data with Hibernate, independent of the build system that generated the Java and mapping files.

Two classes, as shown in Figure 4.4, are used to manipulate the data. The first, `GenerateData`, populates the database with some test data. The second, `GenerateReports`, generates a tab-delimited text file, suitable for use with a spreadsheet.

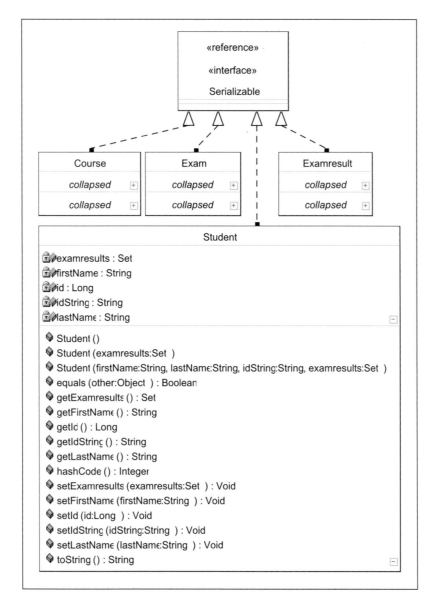

Figure 4.3.   Generated Java Source

Listing 4.13 demonstrates the insertion of data. Note the use of `java.util.HashSet` as a concrete implementation of `java.util.Set`. The latter is only an interface, whereas the former is a concrete implementation. For more information on sets and relationships, see Chapter 7.

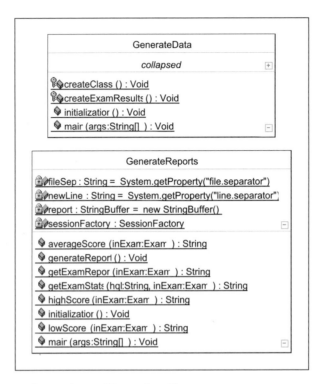

Figure 4.4. Data Generation and Reporting Classes

Listing 4.13 Generating Data

```
package com.cascadetg.ch04;

import java.util.HashSet;

/** Various Hibernate-related imports */
import net.sf.hibernate.*;
import net.sf.hibernate.cfg.*;

public class GenerateData
{
    /** We use this session factory to create our sessions */
    public static SessionFactory sessionFactory;

    static String[] students =
        {
            "Smith",
            "Bob",
```

Listing 4.13 Generating Data (*continued*)

```
            "123-45-6789",
            "Stevens",
            "John",
            "456-78-9012",
            "Almara",
            "Betty",
            "098-76-5432" };

    static Student[] createdStudents = new Student[3];
    static Exam midterm;
    static Exam coursefinal;

    /** Loads the Hibernate configuration information,
     * sets up the database and the Hibernate session factory.
     */
    public static void initialization()
    {
        //System.setErr(System.out);
        System.out.println("initialization");
        try
        {
            Configuration myConfiguration = new
                Configuration();

            myConfiguration.addClass(Course.class);
            myConfiguration.addClass(Exam.class);
            myConfiguration.addClass(Examresult.class);
            myConfiguration.addClass(Student.class);

            // Sets up the session factory (used in the rest
            // of the application).
            sessionFactory =
                myConfiguration.buildSessionFactory();

        } catch (Exception e)
        {
            e.printStackTrace();
        }
    }

    public static void main(String[] args)
    {
        initialization();
        createClass();
        createExamResults();
```

(*continues*)

Listing 4.13   Generating Data (*continued*)

```
    }

    static void createClass()
    {
        System.out.println();
        System.out.println("createClass");

        Session hibernateSession = null;
        Transaction myTransaction = null;
        try
        {
            hibernateSession = sessionFactory.openSession();
            myTransaction =
                hibernateSession.beginTransaction();

            Course myCourse = new Course();
            myCourse.setQuarter("Q12005");
            myCourse.setTitle("Introduction To Hibernate");
            hibernateSession.save(myCourse);

            midterm = new Exam();
            midterm.setComment("First midterm");
            midterm.setCourse(myCourse);
            hibernateSession.save(midterm);

            coursefinal = new Exam();
            coursefinal.setComment("Course final");
            coursefinal.setCourse(myCourse);
            hibernateSession.save(coursefinal);

            HashSet myExams = new HashSet();
            myExams.add(midterm);
            myExams.add(coursefinal);
            myCourse.setExams(myExams);
            hibernateSession.save(myCourse);

            for (int i = 0; i < students.length; i = i + 3)
            {
                Student newStudent = new Student();
                newStudent.setLastName(students[i]);
                newStudent.setFirstName(students[i + 1]);
                newStudent.setIdString(students[i + 2]);
                hibernateSession.save(newStudent);

                createdStudents[i / 3] = newStudent;
```

Listing 4.13   Generating Data (*continued*)

```
            }

            hibernateSession.flush();
            myTransaction.commit();

        } catch (Exception e)
        {
            e.printStackTrace();
            try
            {
                myTransaction.rollback();
            } catch (Exception e2)
            {
                // Silent failure of transaction rollback
            }
        } finally
        {
            try
            {
                hibernateSession.close();
            } catch (Exception e2)
            {
                // Silent failure of session close
            }
        }

    }

    static void createExamResults()
    {
        System.out.println();
        System.out.println("createExamResults");

        Session hibernateSession = null;
        Transaction myTransaction = null;
        try
        {
            hibernateSession = sessionFactory.openSession();
            myTransaction =
                    hibernateSession.beginTransaction();

            for (int i = 0; i < createdStudents.length; i++)
            {
                Student myStudent = createdStudents[i];
```

(*continues*)

Listing 4.13   Generating Data (*continued*)

```
                    Examresult myExamResult = new Examresult();
                    myExamResult.setScore(85 + i * 4);
                    myExamResult.setStudent(myStudent);
                    myExamResult.setExam(midterm);
                    hibernateSession.save(myExamResult);
            }

            for (int i = 0; i < createdStudents.length; i++)
            {
                    Student myStudent = createdStudents[i];

                    Examresult myExamResult = new Examresult();
                    myExamResult.setScore(75 + i * 8);
                    myExamResult.setStudent(myStudent);
                    myExamResult.setExam(coursefinal);
                    hibernateSession.save(myExamResult);
            }

            hibernateSession.flush();
            myTransaction.commit();

    } catch (Exception e)
    {
        e.printStackTrace();
        try
        {
            myTransaction.rollback();
        } catch (Exception e2)
        {
            // Silent failure of transaction rollback
        }
    } finally
    {
        try
        {
            hibernateSession.close();
        } catch (Exception e2)
        {
            // Silent failure of session close
        }
    }
  }
}
```

Once data is loaded into the database, generating a report is only a matter of retrieving data from the database. Listing 4.14 shows how the report is generated, including the use of HQL to obtain statistical information. For more information on HQL, see Chapter 8.

COMMITTING AND BOOKKEEPING

You may have noticed that the uses of Hibernate in the examples in this book all explicitly commit the transactions (for example, `myTransaction .commit()`). This explicit call to commit a transaction isn't strictly necessary, but it's best to get into the habit of using it. On the other hand, you may eventually get tired of doing the bookkeeping associated with opening a session, committing a transaction, handling exceptions, and closing sessions. For a discussion of one strategy to deal with this, check out inversion-of-control as described in Chapter 12.

Listing 4.14   Generating the Report

```
package com.cascadetg.ch04;

/** Various Hibernate-related imports */
import java.io.FileOutputStream;
import java.util.Iterator;

import net.sf.hibernate.*;
import net.sf.hibernate.cfg.*;
import net.sf.hibernate.expression.*;

public class GenerateReports
{
    /** This is used to store the resulting report */
    static StringBuffer report = new StringBuffer();

    // System constants for the new line and directory tokens
    static String newLine =
        System.getProperty("line.separator");
    static String fileSep =
        System.getProperty("file.separator");

    /** We use this session factory to create our sessions */
    static SessionFactory sessionFactory;

    static public String highScore(Exam inExam)
```

(continues)

Listing 4.14   Generating the Report (*continued*)

```
{
    String hql =
        "select max(result.score) from Examresult "
            + "as result where result.exam=?";
    return getExamStats(hql, inExam);
}

static public String lowScore(Exam inExam)
{
    String hql =
        "select min(result.score) from Examresult "
            + "as result where result.exam=?";
    return getExamStats(hql, inExam);
}

static public String averageScore(Exam inExam)
{
    String hql =
        "select avg(result.score) from Examresult "
            + "as result where result.exam=?";
    return getExamStats(hql, inExam);
}

static public String getExamStats(String hql, Exam inExam)
{

    Session hibernateSession = null;
    Transaction myTransaction = null;

    String returnVal = "0";
    try
    {
        hibernateSession = sessionFactory.openSession();
        myTransaction =
            hibernateSession.beginTransaction();

        Query myQuery = hibernateSession.createQuery(hql);
        myQuery.setLong(0, inExam.getId().longValue());

        returnVal = myQuery.iterate().next().toString();

        myTransaction.commit();

    } catch (Exception e)
    {
```

Listing 4.14   Generating the Report (*continued*)

```
            e.printStackTrace();
            try
            {
                myTransaction.rollback();
            } catch (Exception e2)
            {
                // Silent failure of transaction rollback
            }
        } finally
        {
            try
            {
                if (hibernateSession != null)
                    hibernateSession.close();
            } catch (Exception e)
            {
                // Silent failure of session close
            }
        }
        return returnVal;
    }

    static public String getExamReport(Exam inExam)
    {

        Session hibernateSession = null;
        Transaction myTransaction = null;

        java.util.Iterator result = null;
        String returnVal = "0";
        try
        {
            hibernateSession = sessionFactory.openSession();
            myTransaction =
                hibernateSession.beginTransaction();

            // In this example, we use the Criteria API.  We
            // could also have used the HQL, but the
            // Criteria API allows us to express this query
            // more easily.

            Criteria query =
            hibernateSession.createCriteria(Examresult.class);
```

(*continues*)

Listing 4.14   Generating the Report (*continued*)

```java
        query.add(Expression.like("exam", inExam));
        // Now, specify sorting by the score
        query.addOrder(Order.desc("score"));

        // Indicate that we want to grab all of the
        // associated student IDs as well.  This
        // lets us pull all of the data in a single
        // SQL statement!
        query.setFetchMode("student.idString",
            FetchMode.EAGER);

        // This actually performs the database request,
        // based on the query we've built.
        result = query.list().iterator();

        while (result.hasNext())
        {
            Examresult myExamResult =
                (Examresult)result.next();
            report.append(myExamResult.
                getStudent().getIdString());
            report.append("\t");
            report.append(myExamResult.getScore());
            report.append(newLine);
        }

        myTransaction.commit();

    } catch (Exception e)
    {
        e.printStackTrace();
        try
        {
            myTransaction.rollback();
        } catch (Exception e2)
        {
            // Silent failure of transaction rollback
        }
    } finally
    {
        try
        {
            if (hibernateSession != null)
                hibernateSession.close();
```

Listing 4.14   Generating the Report (*continued*)

```
        } catch (Exception e)
        {
            // Silent failure of session close
        }
    }
    return returnVal;
}

static public void generateReport()
{
    Session hibernateSession = null;
    Transaction myTransaction = null;

    java.util.Iterator result = null;
    try
    {
        hibernateSession = sessionFactory.openSession();
        myTransaction =
            hibernateSession.beginTransaction();

        // In this example, we use the Criteria API.  We
        // could also have used the HQL, but the
        // Criteria API allows us to express this query
        // more easily.

        Criteria myQuery =
            hibernateSession.createCriteria(Course.class);

        result = myQuery.list().iterator();

        while (result.hasNext())
        {
            Course myCourse = (Course)result.next();
            Iterator exams =
                myCourse.getExams().iterator();

            report.append(myCourse.getTitle());
            report.append(newLine);
            report.append(myCourse.getQuarter());
            report.append(newLine);
            report.append(newLine);

            while (exams.hasNext())
            {
```

(*continues*)

Listing 4.14   Generating the Report (*continued*)

```
                    Exam myExam = (Exam)exams.next();
                    report.append(myExam.getComment());
                    report.append(newLine);

                    report.append("High Score: \t");
                    report.append(highScore(myExam));
                    report.append(newLine);

                    report.append("Low Score: \t");
                    report.append(lowScore(myExam));
                    report.append(newLine);

                    report.append("Average Score: \t");
                    report.append(averageScore(myExam));
                    report.append(newLine);
                    report.append(newLine);

                    getExamReport(myExam);
                    report.append(newLine);
                }

            }

        myTransaction.commit();

    } catch (Exception e)
    {
        e.printStackTrace();
        try
        {
            myTransaction.rollback();
        } catch (Exception e2)
        {
            // Silent failure of transaction rollback
        }
    } finally
    {
        try
        {
            if (hibernateSession != null)
                hibernateSession.close();
        } catch (Exception e)
        {
            // Silent failure of session close
        }
```

Listing 4.14   Generating the Report (*continued*)

```
        }
    }

    static public void initialization()
    {
        try
        {
            Configuration myConfiguration = new
                Configuration();

            myConfiguration.addClass(Course.class);
            myConfiguration.addClass(Exam.class);
            myConfiguration.addClass(Examresult.class);
            myConfiguration.addClass(Student.class);

            // Sets up the session factory (used in the rest
            // of the application).
            sessionFactory =
                myConfiguration.buildSessionFactory();

        } catch (Exception e)
        {
            e.printStackTrace();
        }
    }

    public static void main(String[] args)
    {
        // Places the generated report in the same directory
        // as this Java source file.
        java.io.File reportFile =
            new java.io.File(
                "com"
                    + fileSep
                    + "cascadetg"
                    + fileSep
                    + "ch04"
                    + fileSep
                    + "report.txt");

        // If the report file doesn't exist, generate the
        // default data set.
        if (!reportFile.exists())
        {
            GenerateData.main(null);
```

(*continues*)

Listing 4.14   Generating the Report (*continued*)

```
        }

        // Set up our session factory
        initialization();

        // Do all of the report generation
        generateReport();

        // Echo the results to the console
        System.out.println(report.toString());

        // Try to write the results to the report file
        try
        {
            FileOutputStream myOutputStream =
                new FileOutputStream(reportFile);
            myOutputStream.write(report.toString().getBytes());
        } catch (Exception e)
        {
            e.printStackTrace();
        }
    }
}
```

When this application runs, it will generate the report file. Before looking at the report, Listing 4.15 shows the SQL generated by Hibernate during the course of the run. While the SQL shown may seem complex, it's a lot easier to look at this generated SQL than to write the SQL by hand. Several statements are much more complex than what one might easily write—in particular, the single lengthy statement which fetches both the Examresults and the associated Student records with a single query. Compare that SQL statement with the generating code, as shown in the GenerateReports.getExamReport().

Listing 4.15   SQL Generated by Hibernate

```
Hibernate: select this.ID as ID0_, this.title as title0_,
this.quarter as quarter0_ from course this where 1=1
Hibernate: select exams0_.ID as ID__, exams0_.courseID as
courseID__, exams0_.ID as ID0_, exams0_.date as date0_,
exams0_.comment as comment0_, exams0_.courseID as courseID0_
from exam exams0_ where exams0_.courseID=?
Hibernate: select max(examresult0_.score) as x0_0_ from
examresult examresult0_ where (examresult0_.examID=? )
```

Listing 4.15 SQL Generated by Hibernate (*continued*)

```
Hibernate: select min(examresult0_.score) as x0_0_ from
examresult examresult0_ where (examresult0_.examID=? )
Hibernate: select avg(examresult0_.score) as x0_0_ from
examresult examresult0_ where (examresult0_.examID=? )
Hibernate: select this.ID as ID3_, this.score as score3_,
this.studentID as studentID3_, this.examID as examID3_,
student1_.ID as ID0_, student1_.firstName as firstName0_,
student1_.lastName as lastName0_, student1_.idString as
idString0_, exam2_.ID as ID1_, exam2_.date as date1_,
exam2_.comment as comment1_, exam2_.courseID as courseID1_,
course3_.ID as ID2_, course3_.title as title2_,
course3_.quarter as quarter2_ from examresult this left outer
```

(*continues*)

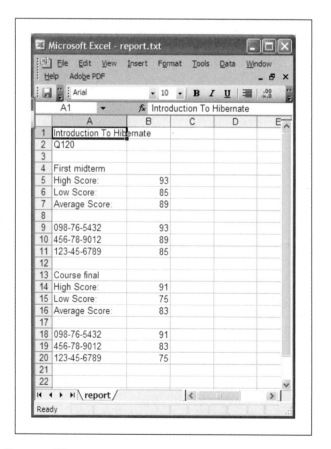

Figure 4.5. Generated Report

Listing 4.15   SQL Generated by Hibernate (*continued*)

```
outer join exam exam2_ on this.examID=exam2_.ID left outer join
join student student1_ on this.studentID=student1_.ID left
course course3_ on exam2_.courseID=course3_.ID where
this.examID like ? order by this.score desc
Hibernate: select max(examresult0_.score) as x0_0_ from
examresult examresult0_ where (examresult0_.examID=? )
Hibernate: select min(examresult0_.score) as x0_0_ from
examresult examresult0_ where (examresult0_.examID=? )
Hibernate: select avg(examresult0_.score) as x0_0_ from
examresult examresult0_ where (examresult0_.examID=? )
Hibernate: select this.ID as ID3_, this.score as score3_,
this.studentID as studentID3_, this.examID as examID3_,
student1_.ID as ID0_, student1_.firstName as firstName0_,
student1_.lastName as lastName0_, student1_.idString as
idString0_, exam2_.ID as ID1_, exam2_.date as date1_,
exam2_.comment as comment1_, exam2_.courseID as courseID1_,
course3_.ID as ID2_, course3_.title as title2_,
course3_.quarter as quarter2_ from examresult this left outer
join student student1_ on this.studentID=student1_.ID left
outer join exam exam2_ on this.examID=exam2_.ID left outer join
course course3_ on exam2_.courseID=course3_.ID where
this.examID like ? order by this.score desc
```

Finally, the generated report, a tab-delimited text file, can easily be opened in any popular spreadsheet software and formatted and edited as needed, as shown in Figure 4.5.

CHAPTER 5

Mapping Files

As can be seen from the examples in Chapters 1 through 4, the `*.hbm.xml` files are at the heart of an application's use of Hibernate. Depending on your needs, you may or may not work with `*.hbm.xml` files directly (for example, you may prefer to work with Java code and use XDoclet, as shown in Chapter 3, or to start from an existing database, as shown in Chapter 4), but it's vital to understand the structure and options available in a `*.hbm.xml` mapping files. The options presented in XDoclet and Middlegen are based on the options available in these mapping files.

This chapter is intended as a reference, organized alphabetically, by tag. A description of each tag is included, as well as some notes and comments on usage where appropriate. If you are just orienting yourself to Hibernate, you may wish to skip or skim this chapter and instead go on to the conceptual elements and tools covered in the remainder of this book. Regardless, at some point you will almost certainly need to consult this reference to make full use of Hibernate or to understand the meaning of one or another attribute.

The vast majority of the tags discussed in this chapter deal with relationship management. For an overall view of the Java and database relationship strategies supported by Hibernate, consult Chapter 7.

Basic Structure

The basic format of a `*.hbm.xml` mapping file is shown in Listing 5.1. The first line is a standard XML declaration. The `DOCTYPE` specifies a `DTD` (defining the structure of the mapping document). This `DTD` is included in the main `hibernate2.jar` file and is also available online. If you are using the standard XML parsing libraries included with the Hibernate distribution, Hibernate will use the `DTD` included in the `hibernate2.jar` file, not the online file. Opening the file in a strict XML editor or viewer, however, may result in an error if no Internet connection is available.

Listing 5.1   Basic Mapping File Declaration

```
<?xml version='1.0' encoding='utf-8'?>
<!DOCTYPE hibernate-mapping PUBLIC
        "-//Hibernate/Hibernate Mapping DTD 2.0//EN"
        "http://hibernate.sourceforge.net/hibernate-mapping-
2.0.dtd">
<hibernate-mapping>
...
</hibernate-mapping>
```

Depending on your needs, you may wish to replace the PUBLIC DOCTYPE declaration with a SYSTEM declaration pointing to a file on the local file system, as shown in Listing 5.2. This should only be done during development, and should be avoided if possible.

Obviously, the location of the DTD on your local file system may vary.

Listing 5.2   Mapping File with Local DTD Declaration

```
<?xml version="1.0"?>
<!DOCTYPE hibernate-mapping SYSTEM "C:\devenv\hibernate-
2.1.2\src\net\sf\hibernate\hibernate-mapping-2.0.dtd">
<hibernate-mapping>
...
</hibernate-mapping>
```

The root element is hibernate-mapping. Most often, you will find one or more class declaration elements in a hibernate-mapping, as well as import declarations to bring in other classes, queries, and other information. For the full range of options, see the hibernate-mapping tag below.

Mapping File Reference

The remainder of this chapter serves as a reference for *.hbm.xml files, organized alphabetically by tag. Each tag notes where the tag may appear, the contents of the tag (i.e., what nested tags are permitted and/or required), required attributes, and optional attributes.

any

The any association allows you to map a single foreign key to any other class.

For example, let's say that you wish to use a single table to keep track of who is creating new records in a database relating to users, groups, and roles. When a new permission is created, you want to log the primary key and the type of new permission (even though a single table is used). By using two columns, you create a foreign-key binding to this new record (the first column is the discriminator, the second is the foreign key).

The concept of an any association is difficult to understand outside the context of Hibernate's handling of class hierarchy relationships. You are strongly encouraged to review the subclass tag and also Chapter 7 for a detailed description of how Hibernate handles class relationships.

Used By

class, subclass, joined-subclass, component, dynamic-component, composite-element, nested-composite-element

Contents

meta	Optionally, one or more meta tags.
meta-value	Optionally, one or more tags. Only needed if you specify a meta-type attribute other than class.
column	A minimum of two column tags are required (and possibly more for a composite identifier). The first column effectively serves as the discriminator (see the subclass tag for a detailed description of the use and purpose of a discriminator). The second (and other) columns store the identifier.

Required Attributes

id-type   The type of the identifier (in other words, the type of the second and later columns).

name   The name of the property. Use an initial lowercase character. For more information, see the property tag, name attribute.

Optional Attributes

access (optional, defaults to property)   Possible values are field, property, or a fully qualified class name. See the tag hibernate-mapping, attribute default-access for more information.

cascade (optional, defaults to none)   Possible values are none, all, save-update, or delete. For more information, see the many-to-one tag, cascade attribute.

meta-type (optional, defaults to class)   The type of the discriminator (the first column). For a discussion of possible types, see the property tag, type attribute. If you set this to a basic type, such as string or integer, you will need to specify the mapping of the value to a type using the meta-value tag.

array

An array is a basic element in the Java programming language—you will see it in use when you write your first *static public void main(String[] args)* statement. An `array` tag is used to map this basic data type to the database, where the contents of the array are of an arbitrary object type (if you are only working with Java language primitives in the array, see the `primitive-array` tag). In practice an array is similar to a list, with the important distinction that an array cannot be lazily loaded—it must be loaded as part of the containing object.

Used By

class, subclass, joined-subclass, component, dynamic-component

Contents

meta	Optionally, one or more meta-tags.
cache	Optional, one tag only.
key	A single key tag must be specified.
index	Required. For lists, this column contains sequential integers numbered from zero.
element | one-to-many | many-to-many | composite-element | many-to-any	A single relationship tag must be specified. For more information, see the appropriate tag and Chapter 7.

Required Attributes

name   The name of the property. Use an initial lowercase character. For more information, see the property tag, name attribute.

Optional Attributes

access (defaults to property)   Possible values are `field`, `property`, and a fully qualified class name. See the tag `hibernate-mapping`, attribute `default-access` for more information.

table (defaults to name value)   Use this attribute to specify the table for the collection data.

schema (defaults to none)   Used to specify the schema name. Overrides the `hibernate-mapping` setting (see the `schema` attribute in `hibernate-mapping` for more information).

cascade (defaults to none)   The possible values for this attribute are `none`, `all`, `save-update`, `delete`, `all-delete-orphan`, and `delete-orphan`. For more information, see the `map` tag, `cascade` attribute.

inverse (defaults to false) If set to `true`, this association is marked as the many end of a one-to-many bi-directional relationship or as one end of a bi-directional many-to-many relationship. For more information, see the `inverse` attribute, map tag, and Chapter 7.

order-by (defaults to none) Typically, this will be one or more `column_name` `asc` or `column_name desc` strings, expressed as SQL (not HQL).

where (defaults to none) Use this attribute to specify an arbitrary SQL `WHERE` condition to be used when retrieving or deleting data for the collection.

batch-size (defaults to 1) This allows you to specify the number of elements to be retrieved when data is retrieved via lazy instantiation.

outer-join (defaults to auto) Possible values are `true`, `false`, or `auto`. For more information, see the tag `many-to-one`, attribute `outer-join`.

check (defaults to none) Used only during schema generation/update. For more information, see the `check` attribute of the `column` tag.

element-class Used to specify the fully qualified class name for the type of the objects in the array.

bag

A bag is one of the many ways to represent what in database terminology would be referred to as a foreign-key relationship. A Java programmer would think of this as a way to persist the pure notion of a `java.util.Collection`. Simply put, a bag is an unordered collection that may contain duplicate elements.
Note that according to the official Hibernate documentation, large Hibernate bags mapped with `inverse="false"` are inefficient and should be avoided. Because there is no key that may be used to identify an individual row, rows cannot be created, deleted or updated individually.

For more information on collections, see Chapter 7.

Used By
`class`, `subclass`, `joined-subclass`, `component`, `dynamic-component`

Contents

`meta`	Optionally, one or more meta-tags.
`cache`	Optional, one only.
`key`	A single key tag must be specified.
`element` | `one-to-many` | `many-to-many` | `composite-element` | `many-to-any`	A single relationship tag must be specified.

Required Attributes

name   The name of the property. Use an initial lowercase character. For more information, see the property tag, name attribute.

Optional Attributes

access (defaults to property)   Possible values are `field`, `property`, and a fully qualified class name. See the tag `hibernate-mapping`, attribute `default-access` for more information.

batch-size (defaults to 1)   This allows you to specify the number of elements to be retrieved when data is retrieved via lazy instantiation.

cascade (defaults to none)   The possible values for this attribute are `none`, `all`, `save-update`, `delete`, `all-delete-orphan`, and `delete-orphan`. For more information, see the map tag, `cascade` attribute.

check (defaults to none)   Used only during schema generation/update. For more information, see the `check` attribute of the `column` tag.

inverse (defaults to false)   If set to true, this association is marked as the many end of a one-to-many bi-directional relationship or one end of a bi-directional many-to-many relationship. For more information, see the `inverse` attribute, map tag.

lazy (defaults to false)   If set to `true`, the class won't actually load data from the database until specifically requested. For more information, see the `lazy` attribute of the `class` tag.

order-by (defaults to none)   Typically, this will be one or more `column_name` `asc` or `column_name` `desc` strings, expressed as SQL (not HQL).

outer-join (defaults to auto)   Possible values are `true`, `false`, or `auto`. For more information, see the tag `many-to-one`, attribute `outer-join`.

table (defaults to name value)   Use this attribute to specify the table for the collection data.

schema (defaults to none)   Used to specify the schema name. Overrides the `hibernate-mapping` setting (see the `schema` attribute in `hibernate-mapping` for more information).

where (defaults to none)   Use this attribute to specify an arbitrary SQL WHERE condition to be used when retrieving or deleting data for the collection.

cache

Specifying a cache allows Hibernate to know more about a particular entity, enabling it to retain more memory in data (and therefore minimizing database access).

If you are using a `hibernate.cfg.xml` file instead of `hibernate.properties`, you may wish to specify cache information using `<class-cache>` and `<collection-cache>` elements in that file.

Contents
A cache tag has no content or nested tags.

Used By
`class`, `map`, `set`, `bag`, `idbag`, `list`, `array`, `primitive-array`

Required Attributes

usage   Possible values are `read-only`, `read-write`, `nonstrict-read-write`, and `transactional`. For more on choosing a strategy (and other performance-related information), see Chapter 10.

class

This is the basic declaration of a mapping file. Conceptually, each class tag describes a table, with a wide variety of options.

Used By
`hibernate-mapping`

Contents
A class only contains nested tags. The tags should appear in the following order:

`meta`	Optional. One or more tags.
`cache`	Optional. One tag only.
`id` | `composite-id`	One or the other is required (but not both).
`discriminator`	Optional. Only one possible. Only needed if you intend to map multiple classes to a single table. See Chapter 2 for an example of use.
`version` | `timestamp`	Optional. Only one possible. Only needed if you intend to track object versioning. See Chapter 2 for an example of use, Chapter 9 for more information.

property | many-to-one | one-to-one | component | dynamic-component | any | map | set | list |bag | idbag | array | primitive-array	All of these are optional, and they can appear in any order, as needed.
subclass | joined-subclass	Optional. You can declare one or more subclasses OR one or more joined-subclasses, but you can't mix the use of subclass and joined-subclass in a single class declaration. Requires a discriminator attribute.

Required Attributes

name   The fully qualified class name. For example, com.example.Order.

Optional Attributes

batch-size (defaults to 1)   The number of objects to be retrieved in a single fetch from the database.

check (defaults to none)   This attribute is only used during schema generation. For more information, see the column tag, check attribute.

discriminator-value (defaults to fully qualified class name)   This attribute specifies a strategy for distinguishing this class from other classes in a persisted class hierarchy.

For example, let's say you wish to persist the following classes: com.example.Animal, com.example.Cat, and com.example.Dog. Cat and Dog both extend Animal, and Animal is considered a concrete class. You wish to persist all three objects to the same table. Hibernate uses a column in the table, as specified by the discriminator tag, to keep track of the type information for the record. By default, the value stored in the database for this column would be com.example.Animal, com.example.Cat, or com.example.Dog.

You may find that this is inefficient, or inelegant, or you may have existing data that uses a different model. For example, you may wish to merely store the values A, C, and D instead of the full class name. This attribute lets you specify the binding between this class and the discriminator value. Continuing the example, the com.example.Cat class would then specify discriminator-value="C".

dynamic-insert (defaults to false)   A true/false attribute. Similar to dynamic-update below, if set to true, Hibernate will generate SQL at runtime, persisting only the non-null fields. Note that dynamic-insert is less prone to versioning complexity (an example of which is shown in Chapter 2) and can be used in a wider variety of situations.

dynamic-update (defaults to false) A `true`/`false` attribute. If set to `true`, causes the class to generate specific SQL for the changes in an object at runtime, as opposed to simply automatically persisting the whole object. In certain situations (but not all), this may improve performance. If you wish to use `dynamic-update`, you will need to be aware of the issues around optimistic locking (see the `optimistic-lock` attribute, below).

lazy (defaults to false) If set to `true`, the class won't actually load data from the database until specifically requested. This is a very important, useful attribute (especially for collections and properties). For example, you may wish to load a `Customer` object without actually loading all of the related `Orders`. By specifying that a class or property is `lazy`, Hibernate will generate a proxy object that, when requested, will actually retrieve the data.

Specifying `lazy=true` is the same as setting the proxy to the same class. Thus, for example, `<class name="com.example.MyObject" proxy="com.example.MyObject">` and `<class name="com.example.MyObject" lazy="true">` are equivalent.

mutable (defaults to true) If set to `false`, the values of this class cannot be changed. Hibernate is able to perform some optimizations if this is set to `false`.

optimistic-lock (defaults to version) Possible values for this attribute are `none`, `version`, `dirty`, and `all`. You will want to set this (and be aware of the implications of the various strategies) both for use by the `dynamic-update` attribute and as a general tool. For an example of versioning, see Chapter 2. For more information on optimistic locking, see Chapter 9.

persister (defaults to Hibernate internal) This attribute allows the class to use a custom implementation of the `net.sf.hibernate.persister.Class Persister` interface. This allows you to specify a wholly new mechanism for saving a persistent object. In theory, you could create a new `ClassPersister` implementation that uses XML, LDAP, stored procedures, or even Web services. In practice, it's often easier to just use native APIs for these data stores.

polymorphism (defaults to implicit) Possible values are `implicit` and `explicit`. By default, Hibernate will return all objects that match a request for a given superclass. For example, in a hierarchy containing `com.example.Animal`, `com.example.Cat`, and `com.example.Dog`, a request for all `com.example.Animal` objects will return all `com.example.Animal`, `com.example.Cat`, and `com.example.Dog` objects. Normally, this is appropriate and correct.

Setting this attribute to `explicit` means that you will have to specifically name the subclasses to retrieve them. For example, `com.example.Animal` requests will only return `com.example.Animal` objects. You would have to explicitly name `com.example.Dog` and `com.example.Cat` to retrieve those objects as well.

Generally speaking, it's better to leave this set to implicit, and if you wish to retrieve a subset, simply specify that in the query.

proxy (defaults to none)   Normally, you won't need this attribute—just use the `lazy="true"` attribute instead.

BEHIND THE SCENES WITH PROXY

Hibernate allows you to perform lazy data retrieval using proxy objects. For example, let's say that you are defining a class for a weblog (`com.example.Weblog`). You may not always want to retrieve all of the associated weblog posts (`com.example.Post`) every time you retrieve the weblog. By declaring a proxy, a proxy object (`com.example.UnloadedPost`) is returned instead when you retrieve a `Weblog`. Using the CGLIB library, Hibernate automatically enhances the `com.example.Weblog` to seamlessly replace the `com.example.UnloadedPost` when the posts are requested by a client using the `com.example.Weblog` object.

In practice you will rarely use this attribute and will instead simply use the `lazy` attribute. You'll only need to consider the proxy attribute (and worry about writing your own implementation) if for some reason you feel you require greater control over lazy-loaded objects. Before considering this approach, make sure that you understand how to use mapping files and queries to control loading of objects (see Chapter 8).

---

schema (defaults to none)   Used to specify the schema name. Overrides the `hibernate-mapping` setting (see the `schema` attribute in `hibernate-mapping` for more information).

select-before-update (defaults to false)   If set to true, Hibernate won't actually send an update unless it is certain that the object has been modified (potentially a useful performance enhancement). If the object was used outside the session and then associated using net.sf.hibernate.Session.update(), Hibernate will first issue a SQL SELECT before updating the object.

table (defaults to unqualified name)   Use this to specify the table mapped to this class. By default, this will be the unqualified class name. For example, if the name is specified as `com.example.Order`, the default table name would be `Order`.

where (defaults to none)   Allows you to specify an arbitrary SQL `WHERE` clause when retrieving an object.

collection-id

A `collection-id` tag is used to specify a primary key column and `generator` for an `idbag`. For more information, see the tag `idbag` and the tag `id`.

Used By
`idbag`

Contents

`meta`	Optionally, one or more meta-tags.
`column`	Optionally, one or more column tags may be specified.
`generator`	A single `generator` tag is required.

Required Attributes

column   The name of the database column.

type   Specify the type for the unique identifier (using a Hibernate type, as described in the property tag sidebar). Any basic type except `binary`, `blob`, and `clob` is allowed. Make sure that the choice of type matches the type of the `generator`. Popular choices include `long` and `string`. For more information on possible types, see the tag `property`, attribute `type`.

Optional Attributes

length (defaults to 255)   Used when Hibernate is asked to generate or update the schema. For more information, see the `property` tag, `length` attribute.

column

The `column` element may be used to specify additional details about a column over the `column` attributes afforded by a variety of other tags. In particular, the `column` tag allows for much greater control over the schema generation.

For certain tags, such as `any`, `many-to-any`, and `index-many-to-any`, you will need to specify multiple `column` tags to properly configure the relationship.

Used By
id, discriminator, property, many-to-one, key-property, key-many-to-one, any, element, many-to-many, key, index, index-many-to-many, many-to-any, index-many-to-any, collection-id

Contents
A column tag has no content or nested tags.

Required Attributes

name   The name of the column.

Optional Attributes

check (defaults to none)   This attribute is only used during schema generation. It allows you to specify an arbitrary constraint that should be put on the table. Note that the implications of this are database-specific, so it should be used with care.

index (defaults to none)   Used during schema update and generation, this attribute can specify the name of a multi-column index.

length (defaults to 255)   Used when Hibernate is asked to generate or update the schema. For more information, see the property tag, length attribute.

not-null (defaults to false unless in an id)   A true/false attribute. If this value is set to true, values of null may not be stored in the database for this property. Only used when Hibernate is asked to generate or update the schema.

sql-type (defaults to value specified by the parent tag)   Use this attribute to specify a specific SQL type to be used when generating or updating this column.

unique (defaults to false unless in an id)   A true/false attribute. Allows you to specify a constraint in the database. Only used when Hibernate is asked to generate or update the schema.

unique-key (defaults to none)   Only used during schema update and generation. Used to specify the name of a multi-column unique constraint.

component

A component is primarily a mechanism for managing the complexity of a table with many columns. For example, imagine a table with 20 columns used to store information about a person. Five columns are used to track information about the person's medical information. You could use the component tag to clump these five columns into a single medical information object.

The component has a strict one-to-one, parent/child relationship with the wrapping class. You can use a `parent` tag to add a reference property pointing to the wrapping class (using the example above, this would let a medical record get back to the owning person object). If all of the properties of a component are set to `null`, the component can be considered `null`.

For more information, including an example of the use of components, see Chapter 7.

Used By

`class`, `subclass`, `joined-subclass`, `component`, `dynamic-component`

Contents

`meta`	Optionally, one or more meta-tags.
`parent`	Optionally, a single parent tag may be present. If this tag is present, a property will be generated that allows a component to retrieve the parent object.
`property` | `many-to-one` | `one-to-one` | `component` | `dynamic-component` | `any` | `map` |`set` | `list` | `bag` | `idbag` | `array` | `primitive-array`	May be included in any order.

Required Attributes

name   The name of the component. Unlike a property, you should use an initial uppercase character, because the component will be mapped to a class.

Optional Attributes

access (defaults to property)   Possible values are `field`, `property`, and a fully qualified class name. See the tag `hibernate-mapping`, attribute `default-access` for more information.

class   Specify the fully qualified class name for the class of this component.

insert (defaults to true)   If set to `false`, this component will be ignored when a SQL `INSERT` is issued for this class. This can only be specified for the component as a whole, not the properties of the component.

update (defaults to true)   If set to false, this component will be ignored when a SQL `UPDATE` is issued for this class. This can only be specified for the component as a whole, not the properties of the component.

composite-element

A `composite-element` allows you to specify a class, instead of simple properties, for the values of a collection. In many ways, a `composite-element` is to a collection as a `component` is to a `class`. Indeed, much of the behavior of a `composite-element` is like that of a `component` (see the `component` tag for more information). For more information on this (and the related `nested-composite-element` tag), see Chapter 7.

Let's say that you want to use a new class to hold the returned elements of a `set`. Much like a `component`, you define the class, properties, and so on, using `composite-element`, but the `composite-element` isn't explicitly bound to a specific table (like a `class`); instead, it's bound to the table specified to the collection tag.

Composite elements may not hold nested collections. If you wish to use a `component` in a `composite-element`, use the `nested-composite-element` tag instead (and you might want to rethink the complexity of your model in this situation).

Used By

map, set, bag, idbag, list, array

Contents

parent	Optionally, a `parent` tag may be specified to provide a property to retrieve the owning collection. For more information, see the `component` and `parent` tags.
property | many-to-one | any | nested-composite-element	One or more of these may be specified.

Required Attributes

class   The name of the class to be used to wrap the properties.

composite-id

A composite key allows you to specify a primary key by "gluing" together other properties. For example, let's say that you know that your users are going to be tracked by social security number (a nine-digit number in the United States) and by driver's license (an eight-digit string in California). Instead of using an `id` tag, you would use the `composite-id` tag to for object identity.

THINKING ABOUT COMPOSITE-ID

I must confess that I have never needed to use a composite-id. A synthetic long or GUID identifier (see the `generator` tag for more information) has always worked quite well for me; it generally outperforms a `composite-id` and is easier to work with. The obvious exception is for collection tables (as described in more detail in Chapter 7), but in Hibernate these are typically modeled implicitly using collection tags, not explicitly as composites.

You may specify a composite key by using the `name`, `class`, and `unsaved-value` attributes. If you do this, in effect you are using the `composite-id` as a `component` (see the `component` tag for more information).

If you wish to specify a composite key using the `name`, `class`, and `unsaved-value` attributes, the class containing the `composite-id` should contain a property for each key column, implement the `java.io.Serializable` interface, and provide correct implementations of the `equals()` and `hashCode()` methods (as described in Chapter 6). If you use this strategy, to load an object you would first need to instantiate it, set the proper values, and then call `Session.load()`.

Used By
class

Contents

meta	Optional, one or more.
key-property | key-many-to-one	At least one of these required.

Optional Attributes

access (defaults to property) See the tag `class`, attribute `default-access` for more information.

class (optional unless a name and unsaved-value also specified) Specifies the class (used as a component) to represent the identifier.

name (optional unless a name and unsaved-value also specified) Specifies the property name for the class.

unsaved-value (defaults to none) If set to `any`, then new transient instances (not associated with a given persistent record) are considered newly instantiated. For more information, see the `id` tag, `unsaved-value` attribute.

composite-index

A `composite-index` allows you to map a key to a `component` (instead of, say, the primary key). Imagine, for instance, that you have defined a person class with a component containing the social security number. You could use the `composite-index` tag to refer to the component containing the social security number while also including the other relevant properties (using the `key-property` and `key-many-to-one` tags).

> **WARNING**
> This tag is not commonly used. Generally speaking, it means that you are using a table with many columns (as described by the `component` tag and in Chapter 7) **and** that you are also using composite keys (two or more columns to uniquely identify a record in another table, as described under the `composite-id` tag). If this is your situation, I would strongly recommend that you consider a redesign of your database schema.

Used By

`` `map ``

Contents

A `composite-index` must contain at least one (and optionally more) `key-property` and/or `key-many-to-one` tags.

Required Attributes

class The fully qualified name of the target component class.

discriminator

A `discriminator` tag is used to specify the column to be used to determine the class of the loaded object when a single table is used to store a class hierarchy. For an example of the use of the `discriminator` tag, see Chapter 3. For more information, see the tag `subclass`.

Used By

`class`

Contents

Normally, no contents, although a `column` tag may be used instead of the `column` attributes.

Optional Attributes

column (defaults to class) Name of the column to be used to store the `discriminator`.

force (defaults to false)   This `true`/`false` attribute is only useful if you have records in the table that don't map to a persistent class. For example, you may have a table that contains `Animal`, `Cat`, `Dog`, and `Fish` records, but no `Fish` persistent class is available. Therefore, you do not want to load any `Fish` records when you request `Animal` objects. In this situation, specify `force=true`, and Hibernate will ignore the `Fish` records.

length (defaults to 255)   Length of the column. For more information, see the tag `property`, attribute `length`.

not-null (defaults to true)   A `true`/`false` attribute. Normally, this should be left to `true`, unless you are using a specific legacy data that uses a `null` type for a column (for example, you might have legacy data where a `null` column value is used to map to the base class).

type (defaults to string)   Type of the column to be used. For more information, see the tag `property`, attribute `class`.

dynamic-component

At times, you may want to decouple the properties of an object from your application code. For example, imagine that you don't know all the properties you want to associate with a person object (or, in database terminology, you don't know the columns on the person table). You can make changes as needed to the database and the `*.hbm.xml` file (editing the various properties nested in the `dynamic-component` tag), but your Java code will work with the component as if it were simply a `java.util.Map` containing the specified properties (for more information on `java.util.Map`, see Chapter 7). The property names refer to the map keys, and the values to the returned results.

Used By
`class, subclass, joined-subclass, component, dynamic-component`

Contents

`property` | `many-to-one` | `one-to-one` | `component` | `dynamic-component` | `any` | `map` | `set` | `list` | `bag` | `array` | `primitive-array`	Any of these tags may be may be included in any order.

Required Attributes

name (required)   The name of the property. Use an initial lowercase character. For more information, see the `property` tag, `name` attribute.

Optional Attributes

access (defaults to property) Possible values are `field`, `property`, and a fully qualified class name. See the tag `hibernate-mapping`, attribute `default-access` for more information.

update (defaults to true) If set to `false`, this property/column will be ignored when a SQL `UPDATE` is issued for this component. This is only usable for properties of a `class` (not a `component` tag).

insert (defaults to true) If set to `false`, this property/column will be ignored when a SQL `INSERT` is issued for this component. This is only usable for properties of a `class` (not a `component` tag).

element

This tag is used to declare the data types and columns for the elements of collections. In many ways, an element's relationship to a collection is similar to the relationship between a `property` and a `class`—it's a way to bind the contained objects to a specific set of columns. You don't specify the name for an element; you'll get the results back as part of the collection only.

The element tag is used when you don't want or need to wrap the contents of a collection in another object type. For example, if you want to represent a collection of primitive `int` values, you would use the element tag to indicate the column and type of the collection.

Used By
`map`, `set`, `bag`, `idbag`, `list`, `array`, `primitive-array`

Contents
An element (much like a property) can optionally contain one or more `column` tags.

Required Attributes

Type The `type` attribute can be set according to the following rules, as described in the `property` tag sidebar, Hibernate Supported Data Types.

Optional Attributes

column The name of the database column.

length Used when Hibernate is asked to generate or update the schema. For more information, see the `property` tag, `length` attribute.

not-null (defaults to false)   A `true`/`false` attribute. For more information, see the `property` tag, `not-null` attribute.

unique (defaults to false)   A `true`/`false` attribute. Only used when Hibernate is asked to generate or update the schema. For more information, see the `property` tag, `unique` attribute.

generator

A `generator` is used to specify a unique identifier (typically for use as a primary key). You use this tag to specify the implementation of `net.sf`
`.hibernate.id.IdentifierGenerator` to be used to generate the primary key when the object is added or saved. For more information on built-in Hibernate generators, see Chapter 6.

Used By
`id`, `collection-id`

Contents

`param`	Depending on the class you specify as a `generator`, you may need to pass one or more `param` tags to properly configure the class.

Required Attributes

class   Either a Hibernate shortcut name or the fully qualified class name of an implementation of `net.sf.hibernate.id.IdentifierGenerator`. For more information on possible generators, see Chapter 6, Built-In Hibernate Generators.

hibernate-mapping

This tag serves as the root element for a `*.hbm.xml` mapping file. Most commonly, this tag will include one or more `class` declarations. If you have more than a few classes, it's considered good form to break up your `*.hbm.xml` file on a per-class basis, but if you are just starting out with a few classes, you can declare them in a single `*.hbm.xml` file.

Contents
You are only allowed to include the following tags in the order shown. You may include as many of each tag as you need.

`meta`	Zero, one, or more tags.
`import`	Zero, one, or more tags.

`class, subclass, joined-subclass`	Zero, one or more of these tags. If using a subclass or joined-subclass directly inside a hibernate-mapping, use the import tag to declare the base class.
`query`	Used to externalize a HQL query in the mapping file (as opposed to in your Java code). See Chapter 8 for more information.
`sql-query`	Used to externalize a SQL query in the mapping file (as opposed to in your Java code). See Chapter 8 for more information.

Optional Attributes

auto-import (defaults to true)   The possible values are `true` and `false`. Allows you to use unqualified class names in the query language. Normally, the only reason you'd set this to `false` is if you have two classes with the same name and only distinguished by the class package—obviously, you are strongly discouraged against doing this, because it is likely to run into confusion and unpredictable results in other areas.

The `auto-import` tag does not affect Java code generation. You'll need to declare the full class name for classes, subclasses, and other entities in your mapping.

default-access (defaults to property)   By default, Hibernate will use standard JavaBean style get/set pairs to access properties, not direct access to the private variables. By setting this attribute to the value `field`, Hibernate will use simple primitive attribute values to directly modify class data. Put another way, `property` access means using `myObject.setName()`, whereas `field` access means using `myObject.name` field directly. This affects both Java code generation and also the manner in which Hibernate will access the object.

default-cascade (defaults to none)   The possible values for this attribute are `none`, `save-update`, and `all`. This attribute is used to determine the settings for collections and properties. For more information, see the various collection declarations (for example, `set`, `list`, `map`, `bag`, `array`, `primitive-array`) and Chapter 7.

package (default to none)   Allows you to specify the package prefix for unqualified names in class declarations. Note that this attribute does not affect code generation. Even if you set it, you'll still need to declare the full package and class name in your classes.

schema (defaults to none)   This attribute is used to specify a specific schema name. This functionality should be considered database-specific.

id

As a matter of course, every object and record has a notion of an identifier, or id. Typically, this is a single integer or string allowing for a quick and easy way to access an object. Normally, this identifier should have no real meaning other than bookkeeping in the databases (this is known as a synthetic identifier). In database terminology, the identifier is often referred to as the primary key. An `id` is required for all base classes modeled by Hibernate (see the `class` tag for more information).

NOTIONS OF IDENTITY

The Java Virtual Machine keeps track of objects using a identifier (loosely analogous to a handle). This is completely different from, and should not be confused with, the id expressed in the database.
    For more information on this topic, see Chapter 6.

The main purpose of an `id` tag is to specify the `column` and method to be used for generating a new identifier—a `generator` tag. For more information on the strategies available for generating identifiers, see the `generator` tag.

Used By
`class`

Contents
May only contain the following tags, in this order.

`meta`	Optional, one or more.
`column`	Optional, use this tag in lieu of the equivalent attributes.
`generator`	Required.

Optional Attributes

access (defaults to property) Possible values are `field`, `property`, and a fully qualified class name. See `hibernate-mapping` tag, `default-access` for more information on this attribute.

column (defaults to name attribute value) Specify the name of the primary key column.

length See the tag `property`, attribute `type`.

name   If specified, you can access the `id` as a named property (e.g. using `getId()` and `setId()` methods). If not present, use `net.sf.hibernate Session.getIdentifier(Object object)` to retrieve the identifier for an object loaded/created by the session. Normally, it's easiest to specify a name.

type   Specify the type (using a Hibernate type, as described in the type sidebar, `property` tag) for the unique identifier. Any basic type except `binary`, `blob`, and `clob` is allowed. Popular choices include `long` and `string`. For more information on possible types, see the tag `property`, attribute `type`. Make sure the type you choose is compatible with your choice of `generator`.

unsaved-value (optional, defaults to null)   Possible values include `any`, `none`, `null`, or an arbitrary constant value. Make sure that the default here is the same as the default value in your Java code for an object created with a no-argument constructor.

idbag

Before using an `idbag`, read the documentation for the use of a `bag`.

A normal many-to-many relationship is modeled using an association table. For example, let's say that you wish to link the `User` table with the `Beverage` table to indicate preferred beverages. To keep track of this link, you create an association table with two columns, `userID` and `beverageID`. The default implementation of `bag` does not include a mechanism for using an additional primary key ID column—you refer to records in the link table using the `userID` and `beverageID`. The `idbag` tag allows you to specify a link table with a primary key ID column using a `collection-id` tag, which in turn allows you to specify a `generator` tag.

In most respects, an `idbag` is treated the same as a `bag`. The advantage of `idbag` is faster updates and deletes. As of Hibernate version 2.1.2, the identity generator mechanism is not supported for `idbag`. In addition, as of Hibernate 2.1.2, there is no provision for easily obtaining the generated key.

Used By
`class`, `subclass`, `joined-subclass`, `component`, `dynamic-component`

Contents

`meta`	Optionally, one or more meta-tags.
`cache`	Optional, one tag only.

`collection-id`	Required, allows you to specify a generator for the primary key.
`key`	A single key tag must be specified.
`element	many-to-many	composite-element	many-to-any`	A single relationship tag must be specified.

Required Attributes

name   The name of the property. Use an initial lowercase character. For more information, see the `property` tag, `name` attribute.

Optional Attributes

access (defaults to property)   Possible values are `field`, `property`, and a fully qualified class name. See the tag `hibernate-mapping`, attribute `default-access` for more information.

batch-size (defaults to 1)   This allows you to specify the number of elements to be retrieved when data is retrieved via lazy instantiation.

cascade (defaults to none)   The possible values for this attribute are `none`, `all`, `save-update`, `delete`, `all-delete-orphan`, and `delete-orphan`. For more information, see the `map` tag, `cascade` attribute.

check (defaults to none)   Used only during schema generation/update. For more information, see the `check` attribute of the `column` tag.

lazy (defaults to false)   If set to `true`, the class won't actually load data from the database until specifically requested. For more information, see the `lazy` attribute of the `class` tag.

order-by (defaults to none)   Typically, this will be one or more `column_name asc` or `column_name desc` strings, expressed as SQL (not HQL).

outer-join (defaults to auto)   Possible values are `true`, `false`, or `auto`. For more information, see the tag `many-to-one`, attribute `outer-join`.

schema (defaults to none)   Used to specify the schema name. Overrides the `hibernate-mapping` setting (see the `schema` attribute of the `hibernate-mapping` tag for more information).

table (defaults to name value)   Use this attribute to specify the table the collection data this element maps against.

where (defaults to none)   Use this attribute to specify an arbitrary SQL `WHERE` condition to be used when retrieving or deleting data for the collection.

import

This tag serves three important functions—it allows you to import another `*.hbm.xml` class when you use a subclass directly inside of a `hibernate-mapping` file, it allows you to effectively "rename" a class, and it also allows you to refer to two classes differing only by package statement with a short name.

Superficially, this tag emulates the standard Java keyword `import` and serves as an important mechanism for linking persistent classes. Interestingly, the rename attribute allows you to change the imported class name to another value.

For example, let's say you'd like to refer to the class `com.example.SampleObject` in this mapping file, but you want to refer to it as `SampleObject` instead of by the fully qualified name.

A less common usage is when you have two classes with the same class name, distinguished only by package statement. For example, consider the two classes `com.example.ExampleObject` and `com.example.persistent.ExampleObject` (a terrible idea, by the way). You would like to be able to refer to these classes using a shorter syntax than the full class name in your queries, and you don't want to turn off the `auto-import="true"` in your hibernate-mapping. You therefore include the following import declarations in your hibernate-mapping:

```
<import class="com.example.ExampleObject" rename=
"BaseObject" />
<import class="com.example.persistent.ExampleObject"
rename="PersistObject" />
```

It's generally poor form to rely on package declarations to distinguish classes; if possible, try to avoid this situation.

Used By
`hibernate-mapping`

Contents
None.

Required Attributes

class   The original, fully qualified class name.

Optional Attributes

rename (defaults to the qualified name)   This optional attribute lets you specify a different class name (and is really needed only if you import two classes distinguished solely by package name).

index

Declares the type and column for a collection index. For more information, see the appropriate collection tag.

Used By
`map`, `list`, `array`, `primitive-array`

Contents
An `index` (much like a `property`) can optionally contain one or more `column` tags.

Optional Attributes

column   The name of the database column. Optional if specified with a column tag, but required if no column tag specified.

length   Used when Hibernate is asked to generate or update the schema. For more information, see the `property` tag, `length` attribute.

type (required for maps)   Required if an index is used in a `map`. For information on the `type` attribute, see the property tag, `type` attribute.

index-many-to-any

This tag allows you to use the `any` relationship as the index of a `map`. In effect, you're using a link to any other arbitrary object as the index of your map—an unusual and complex mapping.

For more information, see the `index` and `any` tags.

Used By
`map`

Contents

`column`	The first declared column is used as the discriminator (see the `discriminator` tag for more information).
`column`	At least one, and possibly more, additional `column` tags are used as foreign keys.

Required Attributes

id-type (required)   The type of the identifier (in other words, the type of the second and later columns).

Optional Attributes

meta-type (defaults to class)   The type of the discriminator (in other words, the type of the first column). For more information, see the `any` tag, `meta-type` attribute.

index-many-to-many

This tag allows you to specify an entity class to use as the key for a map. Normally, a `map` uses an ordinary index, which in turn is more or less analogous to a property. By specifying an index-many-to-many tag, you can instead use a foreign key as the index (and, in turn, obtain classes that map to this foreign key).

Used By
`map`

Contents
An `index-to-many-to-many` (much like a `property`) can optionally contain one or more `column` tags.

Required Attributes

class (required)   The fully qualified name of the target class.

Optional Attributes

column (required if no column tag)   The name of the database column. Optional if specified with a `column` tag, but required if no `column` tag is specified.

foreign-key (defaults to none)   Used only during schema export and update. For more information, see the `many-to-one` tag, `foreign-key` attribute.

joined-subclass

A `joined-subclass` is used to define a multiple-table object hierarchy in Hibernate. For more information, see Chapter 7.

If you wish to use a single table for your subclasses instead, see the tag `joined-subclass`. Note that you can't use both `subclass` and `joined-subclass` in the same `class` tag—you need to choose one strategy or the other.

You can declare subclasses in their own `*.hbm.xml` mapping file, directly inside the `hibernate-mapping` element. If you wish to do this, make sure that you specify the subclass's superclass using the `extends` attribute (see below).

Used By
`class`, `subclass`, `hibernate-mapping`

Contents
The following tags are allowed (or required):

`meta`	Optional, one or more.
`key`	Required to specify the primary key.
`property` | `many-to-one` | `one-to-one` | `component` | `dynamic-component` | `any` | `map` | `set` | `list` | `bag` | `idbag` | `array` | `primitive-array`	As many as required, in the order desired.
`joined-subclass`	You can nest additional `joined-subclasses` if desired.

Required Attributes

name   Specify the fully qualified class name of the subclass.

Optional Attributes

check (defaults to none)   For more information, see the `tag` column, attribute `check`.

dynamic-insert (defaults to false)   For more information, see the `class` tag, `dynamic-insert` attribute.

dynamic-update (defaults to false)   For more information, see the `class` tag, `dynamic-update` attribute.

extends (defaults to parent class/subclass)   For more information, see the `subclass` tag, `extends` attribute.

lazy (defaults to false)   For more information, see the `class` tag, `lazy` attribute.

persister (defaults to Hibernate internal)   For more information, see the `class` tag, `persister` attribute.

proxy (defaults to none)   For more information, see the `class` tag, `proxy` attribute.

schema (defaults to none)   For more information, see the `class` tag, `schema` attribute.

table (defaults to unqualified class name)   Use this to specify the table mapped to by this class. By default, this will be the unqualified class name. For example, if the name is specified as `com.example.Cat`, the default table name is `Cat`.

key

Use this to declare a foreign key for tags that require it. For more information, see the requiring tag.

Used By

`joined-subclass`, `map`, `set`, `bag`, `idbag`, `list`, `array`, `primitive-array`

Contents

A `key` (much like a `property`) can optionally contain one or more `column` tags.

Optional Attributes

column (required if no column tag)   The name of the database column. Optional if specified with a `column` tag instead, but required if no `column` tag specified.

foreign-key (defaults to none)   Used only during schema export and update. For more information, see the `many-to-one` tag, `foreign-key` attribute.

key-many-to-one

Used by the `composite-id` and `composite-index` tags. The `key-many-to-one` tag is used to specify a foreign key as an identifier in a `composite-id` or `composite-index`.

Note that this property is always set to `not-null`, and never to `cascade`.

Used By

`composite-id`, `composite-index`

Contents

`meta`	Zero, one, or more tags, as appropriate.
`column`	A `column` tag may be present in lieu of the `column` attributes. For certain situations (such as a complex custom value type), you may actually be mapping multiple columns to a single type, in which case you will be required to use multiple nested `column` tags. For more uses, see the `column` tag.

Required Attributes

name (required)   The name of the property. Use an initial lowercase character. For more information, see the `property` tag, `name` attribute.

Optional Attributes

access (defaults to property) Possible values are `field`, `property`, and a fully qualified class name. See the tag `hibernate-mapping`, attribute `default-access` for more information.

class The property type of the returned object. For more information, see the `many-to-one` tag, `class` attribute.

column (defaults to the name attribute) The name of the database column.

foreign-key (defaults to none) Used only during schema export and update. For more information, see the `many-to-one` tag, `foreign-key` attribute.

key-property

A `key-property` is used by the tags `composite-id` and `composite-index`. The `key-property` tags are used to specify the properties of the `composite-id` or `composite-index`.

Used By
`composite-id`, `composite-index`

Contents

meta	Zero, one, or more tags, as appropriate.
column	A `column` tag may be present in lieu of the `column` attribute. For certain situations (such as a complex custom value type), you may actually be mapping multiple columns to a single type, in which case you will be required to use multiple nested `column` tags. For more uses, see the `column` tag.

Required Attributes

name (required) The name of the property. Use an initial lowercase character. For more information, see the `property` tag, `name` attribute.

Optional Attributes

access (defaults to property) Possible values are `field`, `property`, and a fully qualified class name. See the tag `hibernate-mapping`, attribute `default-access` for more information.

column (defaults to the name attribute) The name of the database column.

length Used when Hibernate is asked to generate or update the schema. For more information, see the `property` tag, `length` attribute.

type   For information on the `type` attribute, see the `property` tag, `type` attribute.

list

A bag is one of the many ways to represent what in database terminology would be referred to as a foreign-key relationship. A Java programmer would think of this as a way to persist a `java.util.List`. The important distinction to remember is that a list is an ordered collection (also known as a sequence). The most interesting feature of a list (over, say, a bag; see Chapter 7 for more information) is the ability to specify precisely where in the list an element should be inserted. Additionally, elements can be accessed by an integer index. An index column is required in order to maintain this ordering.

Many developers expect to use a `java.util.List` (and therefore the `list` tag) when retrieving a collection from the database, but instead are retrieving the order from the database as part of a query, not as part of the data record. For example, the posts in a weblog might be retrieved by date, in which case the order is determined by date, not by the precise order as maintained by a list in the database. Because of this, for most common operations a sorted map, key, or set more accurately represents the desired model.

Used By
`class, subclass, joined-subclass, component, dynamic-component`

Contents

`meta`	Optionally, zero, one, or more meta-tags.
`cache`	Optional, one tag only.
`key`	A single key tag must be specified.
`index`	Required. This column contains sequential integers numbered from zero.
`element` | `one-to-many` | `many-to-many` | `composite-element` | `many-to-any`	A single relationship tag must be specified.

Required Attributes

name   The name of the property. Use an initial lowercase character. For more information, see the `property` tag, `name` attribute.

Optional Attributes

access (defaults to property)   Possible values are `field`, `property`, and a fully qualified class name. See the tag `hibernate-mapping`, attribute `default-access` for more information.

batch-size (defaults to 1)   This allows you to specify the number of elements to be retrieved when data is retrieved via lazy instantiation.

cascade (defaults to none)   The possible values for this attribute are `none`, `all`, `save-update`, `delete`, `all-delete-orphan`, and `delete-orphan`. For more information, see the `map` tag, `cascade` attribute.

check (defaults to none)   Used only during schema generation/update. For more information, see the `check` attribute of the `column` tag.

inverse (defaults to false)   If set to `true`, this association is marked as the many end of a one-to-many bi-directional relationship or one end of a bi-directional many-to-many relationship. For more information, see the `inverse` attribute, `map` tag.

lazy (defaults to false)   If set to `true`, the class won't actually load data from the database until specifically requested. For more information, see the `lazy` attribute of the `class` tag.

outer-join (defaults to auto)   Possible values are `true`, `false`, or `auto`. For more information, see the tag `many-to-one`, attribute `outer-join`.

schema (defaults to none)   Used to specify the schema name. Overrides the `hibernate-mapping` setting (see the `schema` attribute in `hibernate-mapping` for more information).

table (defaults to name value)   Use this attribute to specify the table for this collection.

where (defaults to none)   Use this attribute to specify an arbitrary SQL `WHERE` condition to be used when retrieving or deleting data for the collection.

many-to-any

A `many-to-any` tag allows you to define a polymorphic association to any table with the given type. While you use the `any` tag to declare this sort of foreign-key relationship in a `class`, `subclass`, etc., the `many-to-any` tag is used to declare a foreign-key-plus-discriminator relationship in a collection.

To better understand this tag, see the `many-to-one` and `any` tags.

Used By
map, set, bag, idbag, list, array

Contents

meta-value	Optionally, one or more meta-value tags may be present.
column	The first declared column is used as the discriminator (see the discriminator tag for more information).
column	At least one and possibly more additional column tags are used as foreign keys.

Required Attributes

id-type   The type of the identifier (in other words, the type of the second and later columns).

Optional Attributes

meta-type (defaults to class)   The type of the discriminator (in other words, the type of the first column). For more information, see the any tag, meta-type attribute.

many-to-many

This tag is used to describe a many-to-many relational model. It requires an association table (as specified by the collection tag's table attribute). This tag is used to identify the relevant foreign key of the association table. For more information on relationships, see Chapter 7.

You'll use this tag inside a collection tag (map, set, bag, idbag, list, array). The collection tag serves to identify how this relationship works, whereas the many-to-many tag serves to establish the column and class bindings.

Used By
map, set, bag, idbag, list, array

Contents

meta	Optionally, one or more meta-tags.
column	Can optionally contain one or more column tags (much like a property).

Required Attributes

class   The target class. There is no need (or ability) to specify an alternative target column—the primary key of the target class is automatically used.

Optional Attributes

column (required if there is no column tag)   The name of the database column. Optional if specified with a column tag, but required if no column tag is specified.

foreign-key (defaults to none)   Used only during schema export and update. For more information, see the `many-to-one` tag, `foreign-key` attribute.

outer-join (defaults to auto)   Possible values are `true`, `false`, or `auto`. For more information, see the tag `many-to-one`, attribute `outer-join`.

many-to-one

Defines a simple foreign-key association between two tables. For example, if you have a schema that defines a weblog with many associated posts, you would use the `many-to-one` tag to map the `Post.getWeblog()` method.

To define the other end of this relationship, use a collection, one of the `set`, `list`, `map`, `bag`, `array`, or `primitive-array` tags. For more information on relationships, see Chapter 7.

Used By

```
class, subclass, joined-subclass, composite-element,
nested-composite-element
```

Contents

meta	One or more tags, as appropriate.
column	A `column` tag may be present instead of the `column` attributes.

Required Attributes

name (required)   The name of the property. Use an initial lowercase character. For more information, see the `property` tag, `name` attribute.

Optional Attributes

access (defaults to property)   Possible values are `field`, `property`, and a fully qualified class name. See the tag `hibernate-mapping`, attribute `default-access` for more information.

cascade (defaults to none)   Possible values are `none`, `all`, `save-update`, or `delete`. Specifies operations that should be cascaded from the parent to the associated object. For example, let's say you load the post and the associated weblog (`cascade="save-update"`). Therefore, changes made to the associated weblog object will be made when the post is saved.

class   The property type of the returned object. The class property type is used to determine the target table. Using the weblog and posts example, if you have set the name of the weblog class to `com.example.Weblog`, you would set the class attribute of this end of the relationship to `com.example.Weblog` (for an example of this, see Chapter 2). Hibernate may auto-detect this association using reflection from the Java code, but it's often a good idea to set the class manually (for example, if you are relying on the `*.hbm.xml` file for code generation).

column (defaults to the name attribute)   The name of the database column.

foreign-key (defaults to none)   Used to specify foreign-key constraint generated for this association— Hibernate only uses this for generating and updating schema.

insert (defaults to true)   If set to `false`, this property/column will be ignored when a SQL `INSERT` is issued for this. This is only usable for properties of a class (not a component; see the component tag for more information).

not-null (defaults to false)   A `true`/`false` attribute. For more information, see the `property` tag, `not-null` attribute.

property-ref (defaults to none)   Normally, Hibernate will bind to the referenced table's primary key. On occasion, you may wish to define an association based on an alternative column. Generally speaking, this is a terrible design (if possible, you're usually better off adding a primary key instead), but you may need this feature for certain legacy data.

outer-join (defaults to auto)   Possible values are `true`, `false`, or `auto`. If set to `true` and the session configuration allows, `outer-join` fetching will always be used. If set to `auto` (and allowed by the session configuration), the association will be fetched by an `outer-join` if the associated class has no proxy. If set to `false`, an outer-join will never be used. For more information on joins, see Chapter 8.

unique (defaults to false)   A `true`/`false` attribute. For more information, see the `property` tag, `unique` attribute.

update (defaults to true)   If set to `false`, this property/column will be ignored when a SQL `UPDATE` is issued for this. This is only usable for properties of a class (not a component; see the `component` tag for more information).

map

A `map` is one of the many ways to represent what in database terminology would be referred to as a foreign key. A Java programmer would think of this as a way to persist a `java.util.Map` or, if a sorting order is specified, a `java.util.SortedMap`.

To be precise, a map is an object that maps keys to values (typically, name/value pairs, such as Java properties). A map cannot contain duplicate keys, and each key can map to at most one value. A sorted map will maintain the keys in order.

For more information on maps and other collection tags, see Chapter 7.

Used By

`class, subclass, joined-subclass, component, dynamic-component`

Contents

`meta`	Optionally, one or more meta-tags.
`cache`	Optional, one only.
`key`	A single `key` tag must be specified.
`index	composite-index	index-many-to-many	index-many-to-any`	A single index key must be specified.
`element	one-to-many	many-to-many	composite-element	many-to-any`	A single relationship tag must be specified.

Required Attributes

name   The name of the property. Use an initial lowercase character. For more information, see the `property` tag, name attribute.

Optional Attributes

access (defaults to property)   Possible values are `field`, `property`, and a fully qualified class name. See the tag `hibernate-mapping`, attribute `default-access` for more information.

batch-size (defaults to 1)   This allows you to specify the number of elements to be retrieved when data is retrieved via lazy instantiation.

cascade (defaults to none)   The possible values for this attribute are `none`, `all`, `save-update`, `delete`, `all-delete-orphan`, and `delete-orphan`. This attribute allows you to perform certain operations automatically as the total graph of objects is manipulated. This allows you to perform a broad suite of functionality very quickly, at the risk of significant possible unintended consequences.

For example, you might wish to delete all of the posts associated with a weblog automatically when the weblog is deleted (as shown in Chapter 2). Unfortunately, this carries two risks. First, unless you are very careful, you risk inadvertently deleting data (for example, if you later switch to a model in which a weblog might have multiple authors, but neglect to properly update your mapping). Second, Hibernate will issue individual DELETE statements for each deleted child (in order to ensure that all proper triggers, etc., are called), which may be far less efficient than explicit bulk deletes (see Chapter 8 for more information on this topic).

check (defaults to none)   Used only during schema generation/update. For more information, see the check attribute of the column tag.

inverse (defaults to false)   If set to true, this association is marked as the many end of a one-to-many bi-directional relationship or one end of a bi-directional many-to-many relationship.

The rule of thumb is that one end of a bi-directional relationship should be marked as inverse="true". For a one-to-many relationship, this will always be the collection tag (map, set, bag, etc.). For a many-to-many relationship, the end of the relationship containing the least amount of data should generally be marked inverse="true".

Changes made to the inverse end of an association are not persisted automatically. This means that you will want to issue a explicit Session.save() on both ends of an association to ensure that changes are properly saved.

Mapping one end of an association with inverse="true" doesn't affect the operation of cascading operations.

Here's a simple way to remember the meaning of inverse: if inverse is set to true, the association should be considered read-only (excluding cascading operations); changes to the association must be made to the owning, that is, non-inverse, or inverse=false, side.

lazy (defaults to false)   If set to true, the class won't actually load data from the database until specifically requested. For more information, see the lazy attribute of the class tag.

order-by (defaults to none)   Typically, this will be one or more column_name asc or column_name desc strings, expressed as SQL (not HQL).

outer-join (defaults to auto)   Possible values are true, false, or auto. For more information, see the tag many-to-one, attribute outer-join.

schema (defaults to none)   Used to specify the schema name. Overrides the hibernate-mapping setting (see the schema attribute of the hibernate-mapping tag for more information).

table (defaults to name value)   Use this attribute to specify the table for the collection data.

sort (defaults to unsorted)   This attribute may be set to `unsorted`, `natural` or the fully qualified class name of an implementation of `java.util.Comparator`.

where (defaults to none)   Use this attribute to specify an arbitrary SQL `WHERE` condition to be used when retrieving or deleting data for the collection.

meta

This tag is used primarily by code generators to hold values that are not directly related to object/relational bindings. Keep in mind that these tags are considered inherited. For example, if you specify `<meta attribute="interface">com.example.BusinessObject</meta>` in your `hibernate-mapping`, all the classes and subclasses declared in that mapping will implement the `com.example.BusinessObject` interface.

Used By
`hibernate-mapping, class, subclass, joined-subclass, id, composite-id, version, timestamp, property, many-to-one, one-to-one, key-property, key-many-to-one, any, component, map, set, bag, idbag, list, array, primitive-array, many-to-many, collection-id`

Contents
Arbitrary text, typically a name/value pair relationship between the attribute and the tag content. The following `meta` values are expected by Hibernate and the various Hibernate tools.

Attribute	Description
`class-description`	The contents of this `meta` tag are automatically added as `javadoc` descriptions for the generated class(es).
`field-description`	Contents are added to the `javadoc` for the generated fields/ properties.
`interface`	Set to `true` to generate an interface instead of a class.
`implements`	Use this to specify a specific interface for the class to implement.
`extends`	Use to specify a class the class should extend. Ignored for subclasses.
`generated-class`	Use this to override the name of the generated class.
`scope-class`	Sets the scope for class (e.g., `public`, `protected`, `private`).
`scope-set`	Sets the scope for generated set method (e.g., `public`, `protected`, `private`). Defaults to public.

scope-get	Sets the scope for generated set method (e.g., public, protected, private). Defaults to public.
scope-field	Sets the scope for the generated field (e.g., public, protected, private). Defaults to public.
use-in-tostring	If set to true, this property will be included in the generated toString() – method. For example, you might want to include the name field of a user object in the toString() method to aid in debugging. By default, only the id is included.
bound	Adds propertyChangeListener support for a property. For more information, see the JavaBean specifications.
constrained	Adds both bound and vetoChangeListener support for a property. For more information, see the JavaBean specifications.
gen-property	If set to false, this property will not be generated. Normally, you won't have any reason to use it (if you don't need the property to be generated, just don't declare it).
property-type	Overrides the default type of property. If you are using the any tag, you can use this to specify a type to be generated instead of simply Object. Setting the property-type is a useful way to increase the compile-time type checking of your application.
finder OR finder-method	Allows you to indicate that the code generator should generate methods to easily retrieve objects by property. For example, you may wish to add a method to easily retrieve an object by the id, or a user record by e-mail address. As of version 2.0.2 of the Hibernate Extensions download, you must use the term finder, but future releases may require the use of the term finder-method.
session-method	If you are using finder-method code generation to find objects, this optional meta tag will allow you to specify how the generated finder methods should obtain a Session.

Required Attributes

attribute   Expected values are shown above. You can define your own meta attribute/value pairs for your own purposes.

Optional Attributes

inherit (defaults to true)   Meta-tags are, by default, inherited to lower declarations. For example, if you declare <meta attribute="scope-set">private</a> in your hibernate-mapping, then all the set methods in all of the classes nested in the hibernate-mapping will be declared private. You can override this if needed. If you declare a particular property's meta scope-set tag to be public, that will override the hibernate-mapping and class declaration.

meta-value

The `meta-value` tag is used by the `any` and `many-to-any` tags to map discriminator values to classes. For example, let's say that you are using the `any` tag, and you have set the `meta-type` attribute of the tag to `string`. This means that we are using a `string` column to track the type of the type of reference being stored. For Hibernate to map these references to objects, the meta-value tag is used to bind a given constant to a specific Java class.

The `meta-value` tag is essentially analogous to the `discriminator-value` attribute of the `subclass` tag.

Used By
`any, many-to-any`

Contents
There are no nested tags present in a `meta-value`.

Required Attributes

class   The fully qualified name of a class. For record that matches the value attribute, Hibernate will return objects of this class.

value   The value of the discriminator as stored in the database.

nested-composite-element

The only use of a `nested-composite-element` is to specify a `composite-element` that in turn contains `components`. See `composite-element` for more information.

Used By
`map, set, bag, idbag, list, array`

Contents

`parent`	Optionally, a parent tag may be specified to provide a property to retrieve the owning collection. For more information, see the component and parent tags.
`property | many-to-one | any | nested-composite-element`	One or more of these may be specified.

Required Attributes

class   The fully qualified name of the class to be used to wrap the properties.

name   The property name to be used.

Optional Attributes

access (defaults to property)   Possible values are `field`, `property`, and a fully qualified class name. See the tag `hibernate-mapping`, attribute `default-access` for more information.

one-to-many

A `one-to-many` association is used to describe a foreign-key relationship. This is the "other end" of a `many-to-one` relationship; you may wish to read the `many-to-one` documentation as well. For more information on relationships, see Chapter 7.

Consider a weblog that contains many posts (where each post belongs to only one weblog, but a weblog can have zero, one, or more posts, as shown in Chapter 2). To obtain the posts from a weblog, you need to first use a collection tag as a property of the weblog class (using the `map`, `set`, `bag`, `list`, or `array` tag). You would then put the `one-to-many` tag inside the collection tag.

Put another way, a `class` tag is used to declare the base class (weblog). A collection tag is used to describe how the association should be managed. Then a `one-to-many` tag is used to specify the target class (posts).

Note that Hibernate does not support bi-directional `one-to-many` associations with an indexed collection (`list`, `map`, or `array`) as the many end.

For more information on relationships, see Chapter 7.

Used By
`map`, `set`, `bag`, `list`, `array`

Contents
None.

Required Attributes

class   The target class. Using the weblogs and posts example given above, note that there is no need (or ability) to specify an alternate target column—the primary key of the target class is automatically used.

one-to-one

Declares a `one-to-one` association between two entities. These come in two flavors. Either two different tables share the same primary key, or there is an ordinary foreign-key relationship. If you have two tables sharing the same primary key, you will want to set the `generator` class to `foreign` (see the `generator` tag and Chapter 6 for more information). For more information on relationships, see Chapter 7.

Used By

`class`, `subclass`, `joined-subclass`, `composite-element`, `nested-composite-element`

Contents

The only contents are zero, one, or more `meta` tags, as appropriate.

Required Attributes

name   The name of the property. Use an initial lowercase character. For more information, see the `property` tag, `name` attribute.

Optional Attributes

access (defaults to property)   Possible values are `field`, `property`, and a fully qualified class name. See the tag `hibernate-mapping`, attribute `default-access` for more information.

cascade (defaults to none)   Possible values are `none`, `all`, `save-update`, or `delete`. For more information, see the `many-to-one` tag, `class` attribute.

class   The property type of the returned object. For more information, see the `many-to-one` tag, `class` attribute.

constrained (defaults to false)   If set to `true`, specifies that a foreign-key constraint on the primary key of the mapped table references the table of the associated class. This option affects the order in which `Session.save()` and `Session.delete()` are cascaded. It is also used by Hibernate's schema export.

foreign-key (defaults to none)   Used only during schema export and update. For more information, see the `many-to-one` tag, `foreign-key` attribute.

outer-join (defaults to auto)   Possible values are `true`, `false`, or `auto`. For more information, see the `many-to-one` tag, `outer-join` attribute.

property-ref (defaults to none)   Normally, Hibernate will bind to the referenced table's primary key. If you are using a foreign-key relationship to associate two tables, you will use this attribute to make the relationship bi-directional.

param

A name/value pair, only used to configure a generator. See the `generator` tag and Chapter 6 for more information.

Used By
`generator`

Contents
The contents of the `param` tag are the value that you wish to set, dependent on the generator being used.

Required Attributes

name   Used to set the name of parameter you wish to set.

parent

The only use of the `parent` tag is to provide a `component`, `composite-element`, or `nested-composite-element` with a property pointing back to the owning class. For more information, see the `component` tag.

Used By
`component`, `composite-element`, `nested-composite-element`

Contents
None.

Required Attributes

name   The name of the property. Use an initial lowercase character. For more information, see the `property` tag, name attribute.

primitive-array

A primitive array is used to model an array of primitive Java language types (for example, an array of `long`, instead of `java.lang.Long`). For more information on arrays, see the `array` tag.

Used By
`class`, `subclass`, `joined-subclass`, `component`, `dynamic-component`

Contents

`meta`	Optionally, one or more meta-tags.
`cache`	Optional, one only.
`key`	A single key tag must be specified.
`index`	Required. This column contains sequential integers numbered from zero.
`element`	A single relationship tag must be specified. This is much more strict than the options available for a normal `array`.

Required Attributes

name (required)   The name of the property. Use an initial lowercase character. For more information, see the `property` tag, `name` attribute.

Optional Attributes

access (defaults to property)   Possible values are `field`, `property`, and a fully qualified class name. See the tag `hibernate-mapping`, attribute `default-access` for more information.

batch-size (defaults to 1)   This allows you to specify the number of elements to be retrieved when data is retrieved via lazy instantiation.

check (defaults to none)   Used only during schema generation/update. For more information, see the `check` attribute of the `column` tag.

outer-join (defaults to auto)   Possible values are `true`, `false`, or `auto`. For more information, see the tag `many-to-one`, attribute `outer-join`.

schema (defaults to none)   Used to specify the schema name. Overrides the `hibernate-mapping` setting (see the `schema` attribute of the `hibernate-mapping` tag for more information).

table (defaults to name value)   Use this attribute to specify the table for the collection data.

where (defaults to none)   Use this attribute to specify an arbitrary SQL `WHERE` condition to be used when retrieving or deleting data for the collection.

property

Simply put, a property is used to map a JavaBean-style property to a single table column. Optionally, Hibernate can access a variable directly.

Used By

`class`, `subclass`, `joined-subclass`, `component`, `dynamic-component`, `composite-element`, `nested-composite-element`

Contents

`meta`	One or more tags, as appropriate.
`column`	A `column` tag may be present instead of the `column` attributes. For certain situations (such as a complex custom value type), you may actually be mapping multiple columns to a single type, in which case you will be required to use multiple nested `column` tags. For more uses, see the `column` tag.

Required Attributes

name   The name of the property. Use an initial lowercase character. If you are generating Java source from your `*.hbm.xml` file, Hibernate will generate methods keeping with the JavaBean property standard (unless overridden by the `access` property).

Optional Attributes

access (defaults to property)   Possible values are `field`, `property`, and a fully qualified class name. See the tag `hibernate-mapping`, attribute `default-access` for more information.

column (defaults to the name attribute)   The name of the database column.

formula (defaults to none)   Use this to specify a SQL expression for this property. For example, you might specify database-specific formatting or other rules. This is only usable for properties of a `class` (not a `component` tag).

insert (defaults to true)   If set to `false`, this property/column will be ignored when a SQL `INSERT` is issued for this. This is only usable for properties of a class (not a `component` tag).

length (defaults to 255)   Used when Hibernate is asked to generate or update the schema. Typically, this is used to specify the length attribute of a character data field. A Hibernate-generated Java source does not include any special handlers for worrying about the length of a string, so you'll only see length-related errors at runtime from the database (if at all).

not-null (defaults to false)   A `true/false` attribute. If this value is set to `true`, values of `null` may not be stored in the database for this property. Only used when Hibernate is asked to generate or update the schema.

type   The type attribute can be set according to the following rules, as described in the sidebar Hibernate-Supported Data Types.

unique (defaults to false) A `true`/`false` attribute. Allows you to specify a constraint in the database. Only used when Hibernate is asked to generate or update the schema.

update (defaults to true) If set to `false`, this property/column will be ignored when a SQL `UPDATE` is issued for the owning class. This is only usable for properties of a `class` (not a `component` tag).

Hibernate-Supported Data Types

Hibernate supports a wide variety of data types. While the effort to understand and support all of these different data types can be confusing, it's important to understand the types and their implications.

Hibernate supports a number of basic types. It uses these type identifications to specify data types in a vendor-independent fashion. Hibernate basic types map to the Java object versions of the basic types because these types are "nullable."

To understand the notion of a nullable property, first imagine a Java class with a field declared as `long myPrimitiveLong`. The value of `myPrimitiveLong` could be zero, it could be −1, but it can't be null. The value of `java.lang.Long myObjectLong`, however, can be set to null (e.g. `myObjectLong = null`). This is an important distinction when you are working with a database in which specified columns may prohibit null values.

On occasion, Hibernate may attempt to "guess" the data type of a property (it's usually best to specify a specific Hibernate type when possible). If Hibernate is not given a Hibernate type, it will first attempt to use a basic Java type, an implementation of `net.sf.hibernate.PersistentEnum`, and finally a `Serializable` Java class.

Therefore, you should expect to see either a basic Hibernate type, a Java primitive, or a fully qualified Java class name specified as the type attribute. A fully qualified class will refer either to a primitive "wrapper" or an implementation of `net.sf.hibernate.PersistentEnum`, `java.io.Serializable`, `net.sf.hibernate.UserType` or `net.sf.hibernate.CompositeUserType`.

More information on these types is given below.

Hibernate Types

Hibernate types are represented in Java code by constants defined in `net.sf.hibernate.Hibernate`. For example, `Hibernate.STRING` refers to the string type.

These are the default Hibernate types, with their mapping to the appropriate vendor-specific SQL column types, and comments.

boolean, yes_no, true_false	Alternative encodings for a Java boolean or java.lang.Boolean.
byte	–128 to 127, inclusive.
short	–32768 to 32767, inclusive.
integer	–2147483648 to 2147483647, inclusive.
long	–9223372036854775808 to 9223372036854775807, inclusive.
char	From '\u0000' to '\uffff' inclusive, i.e., from 0 to 65535.
float	Single-precision 32-bit format number.
double	64-bit double-precision number.
string	A type mapping from java.lang.String to VARCHAR (on Oracle, this type maps to VARCHAR2).
date, time, timestamp	Type mappings from java.util.Date and its subclasses to SQL types DATE, TIME and TIMESTAMP (or the vendor equivalent).
calendar, calendar_date	Type mappings from java.util.Calendar to SQL types TIMESTAMP and DATE (or vendor equivalent).
big_decimal	A type mapping from java.math.BigDecimal to NUMERIC (on Oracle, maps to NUMBER).
locale, timezone, currency	Type mappings from java.util.Locale, java.util.TimeZone and java.util.Currency to VARCHAR (or Oracle VARCHAR2). Instances of Locale and Currency are mapped to their ISO codes. Instances of TimeZone are mapped to their ID. Note that java.util.Currency was introduced in Java 2 SDK 1.4.
class	A type mapping from java.lang.Class to VARCHAR (or Oracle VARCHAR2). A Class is mapped to its fully qualified name.
binary	Maps byte arrays to an appropriate SQL binary type.
text	Maps lengthy Java strings to a SQL CLOB or TEXT type.
serializable	Maps Serializable Java types to an appropriate SQL binary type. You may also indicate the Hibernate type serializable with the name of a serializable Java class or interface that does not default to a basic type or implement PersistentEnum.
clob, blob	Type mappings for the JDBC classes java.sql.Clob and java.sql.Blob. These types may be inconvenient for some applications, because the blob or clob object may not be reused outside of a transaction. (Furthermore, driver support is patchy and inconsistent.)

Java Basic Types

In addition to the Hibernate types listed above, you can also refer to a type by a Java class that corresponds to a Java primitive or the corresponding object version (e.g., long and java.util.Long).

Java SQL Types

You can also use the `java.sql.*` types for expressing data types not included by the standard Java types but commonly used when working with a database. One of these is `java.sql.Date`, `java.sql.Blob`.

net.sf.hibernate.PersistentEnum

You can write a class that implements the Hibernate interface `net.sf.hibernate.PersistentEnum`. There are only two methods, `toInt()` and `fromInt()`. The value of the code is limited to an `int`. Writing your own class allows Hibernate to call into your code to make the mapping between the `int` and the relevant data.

Serializable Java Class

A serialized Java class can be stored in the database as a binary object. You should be comfortable working with `Serializable` objects (start with the Java 2 SDK documentation for `java.io.Serializable`).

Custom Value Type

A custom value type implements either the `net.sf.hibernate.UserType` or `net.sf.hibernate.CompositeUserType` interface. For more information, see the javadoc for these interfaces.

---

query

You may wish to remove HQL strings from your Java code and instead store them in your `*.hbm.xml` files (much as you might use a properties file to externalize message strings).

You can declare a query in a `*.hbm.xml` file by name, with the contents of the tag containing the actual query. For example, you can put the following tag in your `*.hbm.xml` file:

```
<query name="com.example.Cat.by.name.and.minimum.weight"><![CDATA[
    from com.example. Cat as cat
        where cat.name = ?
        and cat.weight > ?
] ]></query>
```

In your Java code, you would therefore use the following to run this query:

```
net.sf.hibernate.Query myQuery =
    mySession.
        getNamedQuery
        ("com.example.Cat.by.name.and.minimum.weight");
myQuery.setString(0, "Bob");
```

```
myQuery.setInt(1, 5);
List cats = myQuery.list();
```

While externalizing your HQL statements using a query tag may be useful, you will almost certainly want to externalize native SQL statements using the `sql-query` tag.

Used By
`hibernate-mapping`

Contents
The contents of a query are raw character data, to be executed the same as any other HQL query. Use CDATA wrappers (as shown above) to wrap your HQL to avoid confusing the XML parser.

Required Attributes

name   The name of the query. All queries are loaded into a single name/value pair namespace, so you may wish to develop a strategy for keeping queries organized.

return

The `return` tag is only used when nested inside a `sql-query` tag. It is used to specify the class which should be used for data returned from the `sql-query`. For more information, see `sql-query`.

Used By
`sql-query`

Contents
None.

Required Attributes

alias   The native SQL term (see `sql-query` for more information).

class   The class to be returned (see `sql-query` for more information).

set

A `set` is one of the many ways to represent what in database terminology would be referred to as a foreign key—it is probably the most typical, natural mapping for a foreign key. A Java programmer would think of this as a way to persist a `java.util.Set` or, if a sorting order is specified, a `java.util.Sorted-Set`.

To be precise, a set is a collection that contains no duplicate elements (note that a set has no notion of a key; you are merely working directly with the elements). More formally, sets contain no pair of elements `e1` and `e2` such that `e1.equals(e2)`, and at most one `null` element. A sorted set will maintain the elements in order.

For more information (and a comparison with other collection types), see Chapter 7.

Used By

`class`, `subclass`, `joined-subclass`, `component`, `dynamic-component`

Contents

`meta`	Optionally, one or more meta-tags.
`cache`	Optional, one only.
`key`	A single key tag must be specified.
`element	one-to-many	many-to-many	composite-element	many-to-any`	A single relationship tag must be specified.

Required Attributes

name (required)   The name of the property. Use an initial lowercase character. For more information, see the `property` tag, `name` attribute.

Optional Attributes

access (defaults to property)   Possible values are `field`, `property`, and a fully qualified class name. See the tag `hibernate-mapping`, attribute `default-access` for more information.

batch-size (defaults to 1)   This allows you to specify the number of elements to be retrieved when data is retrieved via lazy instantiation.

cascade (defaults to none)   The possible values for this attribute are `none`, `all`, `save-update`, `delete`, `all-delete-orphan`, and `delete-orphan`. For more information, see the `map` tag, `cascade` attribute.

check (defaults to none)   Used only during schema generation/update. For more information, see the `check` attribute of the `column` tag.

lazy (defaults to false)   If set to `true`, the class won't actually load data from the database until specifically requested. For more information, see the `lazy` attribute of the `class` tag.

order-by (defaults to none)   Typically, this will be one or more `column_name` `asc` or `column_name` `desc` strings, expressed as SQL (not HQL).

outer-join (defaults to auto)   Possible values are `true`, `false`, or `auto`. For more information, see the tag `many-to-one`, attribute `outer-join`.

schema (defaults to none)   Used to specify the schema name. Overrides the `hibernate-mapping` setting (see the `schema` attribute in `hibernate-mapping` for more information).

sort (defaults to unsorted)   This attribute may be set to `unsorted`, `natural` or the fully qualified class name of an implementation of `java.util.Comparator`.

table (defaults to name value)   Use this attribute to specify the table the collection data should be retrieved from.

where (defaults to none)   Use this attribute to specify an arbitrary SQL `WHERE` condition to be used when retrieving or deleting data for the collection.

sql-query

Defines a named SQL query in the `*.hbm.xml` file. It's a good idea to externalize your native SQL queries, if possible, to aid in migrating your application to new or updated databases.

Hibernate requires you to wrap references to aliases in your native SQL in braces. So, instead of writing `SELECT cat.* FROM CAT AS cat WHERE ROWNUM<10`, you must write `SELECT {cat.*} FROM CAT AS {cat} WHERE ROWNUM<10`.

Your native SQL queries may contain named and positional parameters, just like HQL. You will want to use a `return` tag to specify the class to which the returned data should be mapped, and you'll want to specify the referenced table using the `synchronize` tag if you wish to use a cache (see the `cache` tag for more information on using a `cache` with Hibernate).

For more information on using a `sql-query` (including an example of the code used to retrieve and execute a `sql-query`), see the tag `query`.

Used By
`hibernate-mapping`

Contents

You can use `return` and `synchronize` tags in a `sql-query`, as well as the query itself.

Required Attributes

name   See the `query` tag, `name` attribute for more information.

subclass

A subclass is used to define a single-table object hierarchy in Hibernate. For more information, see Chapter 7. You can declare subclasses in their own `*.hbm.xml` file directly inside the hibernate-mapping. If you wish to do this, make sure that you specify the subclass's superclass using the `extends` attribute (see below).

Used By

`class`, `subclass`, `hibernate-mapping`

Contents

Only the following tags may be present. Note that you can include a subclass inside another subclass, allowing for potentially very deep hierarchies.

`meta`	Optional, one or more.
`property` | `many-to-one` | `one-to-one` | `component` | `dynamic-component` | `any` | `map` | `set` | `list` | `bag` | `idbag` | `array` | `primitive-array`	May be included in any order.
`subclass`	Optional, one or more.

Required Attributes

name   Use this attribute to specify the fully qualified class name. Note that this class is expected to extend or implement the parent class or subclass.

Optional Attributes

discriminator-value (defaults to unqualified class name)   You might decide that the full class name for the discriminator column is inefficient. If so, you might, for example, set the `discriminator-value` attribute for `com.example.Animal` to A, `com.example.Bird` to B, and `com.example.Cat` to C. Then the contents of the discriminator column, as shown above, would merely be A, C, and B.

For more information, see the `class` tag, `discriminator-value` attribute.

dynamic-insert (defaults to false)   A `true`/`false` attribute. For more information, see the `class` tag, `dynamic-update` attribute.

dynamic-update (defaults to false)   A `true`/`false` attribute. For more information, see the `class` tag, `dynamic-update` attribute.

extends (defaults to super-declaration)   This attribute allows you to declare a subclass in an independent `*.hbm.xml` file. For example, you might wish to declare `com.example.Animal`, `com.example.Bird` and `com.example.Cat` in their own `*.hbm.xml` files. You would therefore set `extends="com.example.Animal"` for the subclass declaration of `com.example.Bird` and `com.example.Cat`.

If you make use of this feature, be sure to declare the parent classes first when importing your `*.hbm.xml` files (in other words, make sure that Hibernate has loaded the `Animal.hbm.xml` file before loading the `Bird.hbm.xml` and `Cat.hbm.xml` files).

lazy (defaults to false)   A `true`/`false` attribute. For more information, see the `class` tag, `lazy` attribute.

persister (defaults to Hibernate internal)   For more information, see the `class` tag, `persister` attribute.

proxy (defaults to none)   For more information, see the `class` tag, `proxy` attribute.

synchronize

The `synchronize` tag is only used when nested inside a `sql-query` tag. It is used to indicate the table that should be considered when you attempt to cache the result set (for example, if `sql-query` retrieves data from the `Cat` table, you'd want to use this tag to specify the `Cat` table so the cache will know to invalidate the results if the `Cat` table is altered).

See the `sql-query` tag for more information.

Used By
`sql-query`

Contents
There are no contents.

Required Attributes

Table   The database table referred to by the native SQL query.

timestamp

If you wish to use optimistic locking, you need to specify either a `timestamp` tag or a `version` tag to indicate the record version. You can access the `timestamp` property just as you would access any other property.

A `timestamp` tag is **not** used to store arbitrary time and data in a record, only in conjunction with optimistic locking. For more information on optimistic locking, see the tag `class`, attribute optimistic-locking and Chapter 9. If you wish to store timestamp data, such as a user's birthday, use the `property` tag instead.

Used By
`class`

Contents
You may optionally include one or more `meta` tags.

Required Attributes

name   The name of the version property.

Optional Attributes

access (defaults to property)   Possible values are `field`, `property`, and a fully qualified class name. See the tag `hibernate-mapping`, attribute `default-access` for more information.

column (defaults to the value of the name attribute)   The column name holding the version data.

unsaved-value (defaults to undefined)   Possible values are `null`, `negative`, and `undefined`. The value used to distinguish a newly created or unloaded object from an object previously loaded. The default, `undefined`, means that the identifier property is used instead (see the tag `id` for more information).

version

If you wish to use optimistic locking, you need to specify either a `version` tag or a `timestamp` tag to indicate the record version. You can access a version property just as you would access any other property.

For more information on optimistic locking, see the `timestamp` tag and Chapter 9.

Used By
```
class
```

Contents
You may optionally include one or more `meta` tags.

Required Attributes

name   The name of the version property.

Optional Attributes

access (defaults to property)   Possible values are `field`, `property`, and a fully qualified class name. See the tag `hibernate-mapping`, attribute `default-access` for more information.

column (defaults to the value of the name attribute)   The column name holding the version data.

type (defaults to integer)   The type of the column. The only supported types for this attribute when used with this tag are `long`, `integer`, `short`, `timestamp`, and `calendar`. For more information, see the tag `property`, attribute `type`.

unsaved-value (defaults to undefined)   Possible values are `null`, `negative`, and `undefined`. The value used to distinguish a newly created or unloaded object from an object previously loaded. The default, `undefined`, means that the identifier property is used instead (see the tag id for more information).

Persistent Objects

Once you've described your persistence with Hibernate `*.hbm.xml` files and the corresponding Java sources, the basic mechanism for creating, updating, finding, and deleting objects is the Session class. This will be discussed in depth in the first part of the chapter.

Hibernate makes an important distinction between **transient** objects and **persistent** objects. A transient object is not associated with a particular session. A persistent object is associated with a session. This can be a subtle (and confusing) distinction when working with Hibernate, but it's important to keep in mind that the objects you are working with may not represent the correct state of affairs as represented in the database outside the context of a session.

The notion of persistent and transient objects is intertwined with the notion of object identity. The review of the session interface will be followed by an in-depth look at the various notions of identity. As long as you stick to a single thread per `net.sf.hibernate.Session` object, Hibernate will largely take care of identity automatically, but it can be confusing if you encounter problems related to identity (in particular, if you make use of composite identifiers).

Finally, the life-cycle methods provided by Hibernate will be reviewed. These methods allow the receipt of events at various points in an object's existence. Sample code for a simple object is shown, and can be used as the base for your own laboratory experiments with object identity.

Sessions

The core of database operations in Hibernate is the lightweight, not-thread-safe `net.sf.hibernate.Session` object. `Session` objects are obtained from instances of the heavyweight, thread-safe `net.sf.hibernate.Session Factory`. A `SessionFactory` is obtained from a `Configuration`, in turn a heavy, expensive-to-create, one-time use class. Typically, you will use a singleton pattern to obtain a `SessionFactory`, and the logic for initializing the `SessionFactory` will include the use of a `Configuration` object. For more details on the relationship between `Configuration`, `Session Factory`, `Session`, transactions, and the ordering of statements within a particular session, see Chapter 9.

`Session` object are lightweight and not-thread-safe, and typically are created and disposed of frequently.

Setting up the Configuration

A `Configuration` object is created once, typically as part of the launching process of your application. The primary task of a `Configuration` object is to load and process the various `*.hbm.xml` files, binding them to the relevant persistent code, and returning an appropriately configured `SessionFactory`.

The list of methods in Table 6.1 is not complete. For a complete list, refer to the Hibernate javadoc (`Hibernate_install_dir   \doc\api\index .html`). The summary shown in Table 6.1 illustrates the range of options available for storing configuration data.

Table 6.1. Adding Mapping Files

`addClass()`	Uses the class name and package statement to load the `*.hbm.xml`.
`addDirectory()`	Loads all of the `*.hbm.xml` files from a particular directory.
`addDocument()`	Adds a mapping as already loaded by a DOM object.
`addFile()`	Reads the mapping from a particular file (may have an extension other than `*.hbm.xml`).
`addInputStream()`	Reads the mapping from a supplied `java.io.InputStream`.
`addJar()`	Reads the `*.hbm.xml` file from a specified JAR file.
`addUrl()`	Reads the mapping file from a specified URL.
`addXML()`	Reads the mapping as passed by an arbitrary String (useful for dynamic mapping generation, perhaps by a Hibernate-enabled tool).
`configure()`	Reads the mapping files and properties as specified by a `hibernate.cfg.xml` file.
`configure(File)`	Reads mapping files and properties as specified by a specific file (as per a `hibernate.cfg.xml` file).
`configure(String)`	Reads mapping files and properties as specified by a resource path (as per `hibernate.cfg.xml` file).
`configure(URL)`	Reads mapping files and properties as specified by a URL resource (as per `hibernate.cfg.xml` file).

If you are using a `hibernate.cfg.xml` (or one of the `configure()` methods), you will define the connectivity properties in that file. Otherwise, these properties may be set at runtime using a `java.util.Properties` object via `Configuration.addProperties()`, `Configuration .setProperties()`, or individually using `Configuration.set Property()`.

Alternatively, the connectivity may be configured using a `hibernate .properties` file placed on the class path.

Tables 6.3 through 6.6 describe additional options for the configuration of Hibernate.

Listing 6.1   Sample Minimal Properties File

```
hibernate.connection.driver_class=com.mysql.jdbc.Driver
hibernate.connection.url=jdbc:mysql://localhost/hibernate
hibernate.connection.username=root
hibernate.connection.password=
hibernate.dialect=net.sf.hibernate.dialect.MySQLDialect
hibernate.show_sql=true
```

If you wish to use Hibernate (perhaps in conjunction with a pooling driver, as described in Chapter 10) to manage obtaining and releasing connections, you will want to set the properties as shown in Table 6.2.

If you wish to use Hibernate in the context of an application server, you will probably rely on the application server's built-in JNDI-based datasource mechanism for managing connections. Table 6.3 shows the properties that must be set to allow Hibernate to connect to JNDI datasources.

Hibernate also offers a wide variety of configurable options, as shown in Table 6.4. You can use them to provide additional database connectivity options or to set performance options.

Table 6.2.   JDBC Connectivity Configuration Properties

Property Name	Purpose
`hibernate.connection.driver_class`	JDBC driver class
`hibernate.connection.url`	JDBC URL
`hibernate.connection.username`	Database user account
`hibernate.connection.password`	Database user password
`hibernate.connection.pool_size`	Maximum number of pooled connections

Table 6.3.   JNDI Datasource Connectivity Configuration Properties

Property Name	Purpose
`hibernate.connection.datasource`	datasource JNDI name
`hibernate.jndi.url`	URL of the JNDI provider (optional)
`hibernate.jndi.class`	class of the JNDI `InitialContext Factory` (optional)
`hibernate.connection.username`	database user (optional)
`hibernate.connection.password`	database user password (optional)
`hibernate.jndi.<propertyName>`	Pass the property `<propertyName>` to the JNDI `InitialContext Factory` (optional)

Typically, Hibernate is able to automatically detect the proper SQL dialect to use based on the JDBC driver. You may wish to manually set the SQL dialect, either to ensure the proper dialect or for schema management (as described in Chapter 11). Table 6.5 shows the possible values for `hibernate.dialect`.

Similarly, Hibernate offers support for JTA to manage your transactions. Table 6.6 shows the supported JTA transaction managers.

Obtaining the Session

Listing 6.2 shows an example of the use of the `Configuration` object to obtain a `Session`.

Listing 6.2   Typical Configuration Initialization

```
Configuration myConfiguration = new Configuration();

myConfiguration.addClass(Exam.class);
myConfiguration.addClass(Examresult.class);
myConfiguration.addClass(Course.class);
myConfiguration.addClass(Student.class);

// Sets up the session factory (used in the rest
// of the application).
sessionFactory = myConfiguration.buildSessionFactory();
```

Once a `SessionFactory` has been obtained, you will store this object somewhere (typically in a `static` variable) and use it throughout the rest of your application.

Table 6.4. Miscellaneous Optional Hibernate Configuration Properties

Property Name	Purpose	Value
`hibernate.dialect`	The class name of a Hibernate `Dialect` enables certain platform-dependent features.	`full.classname.of.Dialect` (see Table 6.5)
`hibernate.default_schema`	Qualify unqualified table names with the given schema/table space in generated SQL.	`SCHEMA_NAME`
`hibernate. session_factory_name`	Bind this name to the `SessionFactory`.	`jndi/composite/name`
`hibernate.use_outer_join`	Enables outer join fetching. For more information on outer joins, see Chapter 8.	`true	false`
`hibernate.max_fetch_depth`	Set a maximum "depth" for the outer join fetch tree. For more information on outer joins, see Chapter 8.	recommended values between 0 and 3
`hibernate.jdbc.fetch_size`	A nonzero value determines the JDBC fetch size (calls `Statement.setFetchSize()`).	
`hibernate.jdbc.batch_size`	A nonzero value enables use of JDBC2 batch updates by Hibernate.	recommended values between 5 and 30
`hibernate.jdbc. use_scrollable_resultset`	Enables use of JDBC2 scrollable result sets by Hibernate. This property is only necessary when using user-supplied connections. In all other instances Hibernate uses connection metadata.	`true	false`
`hibernate.jdbc. use_streams_for_binary`	Use streams when writing / reading binary or serializable types to/from JDBC. System-level property.	`true	false`
`hibernate.cglib. use_reflection_optimizer`	Enables use of CGLIB instead of runtime reflection (system-level property, default is to use CGLIB where possible). Defaults to true. Setting this to false can sometimes be useful when troubleshooting.	`true	false`

(continued)

201

Table 6.4. Miscellaneous Optional Hibernate Configuration Properties (*continued*)

Property Name	Purpose	Value
`hibernate.connection` `isolation`	Set the JDBC transaction isolation level (optional)	`1`, `2`, `4`, `8` (as defined by `java` `.sql.Connection`)
`hibernate.connection.` `<propertyName>`	Pass the JDBC property `<propertyName>` to `DriverManager.` `getConnection()`.	
`hibernate.connection.` `provider_class`	Class name of a custom `ConnectionProvider`.	Fully qualified class name of an implementation of `net.sf.hibernate.` `connection.` `ConnectionProvider`
`hibernate.cache.` `provider_class`	Class name of a custom `CacheProvider`. See Chapter 10 for more information.	Fully qualified class name of an implementation of `net.sf.hibernate.` `cache.CacheProvider`
`hibernate.cache.` `use_minimal_puts`	Optimize second-level cache operation to minimize writes, at the cost of more frequent reads (useful for clustered caches). See Chapter 10 for more information.	`true`|`false`
`hibernate.cache.` `use_query_cache`	Enable the query cache.	`true`|`false`
`hibernate.cache.` `region_prefix`	Prefix to use for second-level cache region names.	`prefix`

Property	Description	Value
`hibernate.transaction.factory_class`	Class name of a `TransactionFactory` to use with Hibernate Transaction API.	Use JDBC Transactions: `net.sf.hibernate.transaction.JDBCTransactionFactory` To use JTA Transactions `net.sf.hibernate.transaction.JTATransactionFactory`
`jta.UserTransaction`	JNDI name used by `JTATransactionFactory` to obtain the JTA `UserTransaction`	`jndi/composite/name`
`hibernate.transaction.manager_lookup_class`	Class name of a `TransactionManager Lookup`—required when JVM-level caching is enabled in a JTA environment	A value from Table 6.6 or a custom implementation of `net.sf.hibernate.transaction.Transaction ManagerLookup`
`hibernate.query.substitutions`	Mapping from tokens in Hibernate queries to SQL tokens (tokens might be function or literal names, for example)	`hqlLiteral=SQL_LITERAL, hqlFunction=SQLFUNC`
`hibernate.show_sql`	Write all SQL statements to console (a minimal alternative to the use of the logging functionality as described in Chapter 10)	`true	false`
`hibernate.hbm2ddl.auto`	Automatically export schema DDL.	`update	create	create-drop`

Table 6.5.   Supported SQL Dialects

Database	Dialect
DB2	`net.sf.hibernate.dialect.DB2Dialect`
DB2400	`net.sf.hibernate.dialect.DB2400Dialect`
Firebird	`net.sf.hibernate.dialect.FirebirdDialect`
FrontBase	`net.sf.hibernate.dialect` `.FrontBaseDialect`
Generic	`net.sf.hibernate.dialect.GenericDialect`
HypersonicSQL	`net.sf.hibernate.dialect.HSQLDialect`
Informix	`net.sf.hibernate.dialect.InformixDialect`
Ingres	`net.sf.hibernate.dialect.IngresDialect`
Interbase	`net.sf.hibernate.dialect` `.InterbaseDialect`
Mckoi SQL	`net.sf.hibernate.dialect.MckoiDialect`
Microsoft SQL Server	`net.sf.hibernate.dialect` `.SQLServerDialect`
MySQL	`net.sf.hibernate.dialect.MySQLDialect`
Oracle 9	`net.sf.hibernate.dialect.Oracle9Dialect`
Oracle	`net.sf.hibernate.dialect.OracleDialect`
Pointbase	`net.sf.hibernate.dialect` `.PointbaseDialect`
PostgreSQL	`net.sf.hibernate.dialect` `.PostgreSQLDialect`
Progress	`net.sf.hibernate.dialect.ProgressDialect`
SAP DB	`net.sf.hibernate.dialect.SAPDBDialect`
Sybase Anywhere	`net.sf.hibernate.dialect` `.SybaseAnywhereDialect`
Sybase 11.9.2	`net.sf.hibernate.dialect` `.Sybase11_9_2Dialect`
Sybase	`net.sf.hibernate.dialect.SybaseDialect`

Table 6.6.   Supported JTA Transaction Managers

Application Server	Transaction Factory
JBoss	`net.sf.hibernate.transaction.JBoss` `TransactionManagerLookup`
Weblogic	`net.sf.hibernate.transaction.Weblogic` `TransactionManagerLookup`

Table 6.6. Supported JTA Transaction Managers (*continued*)

Application Server	Transaction Factory
WebSphere	`net.sf.hibernate.transaction.WebSphere` `TransactionManagerLookup`
Orion	`net.sf.hibernate.transaction.Orion` `TransactionManagerLookup`
Resin	`net.sf.hibernate.transaction.Resin` `TransactionManagerLookup`
JOTM	`net.sf.hibernate.transaction.JOTM` `TransactionManagerLookup`
JOnAS	`net.sf.hibernate.transaction.JOnAS` `TransactionManagerLookup`
JRun4	`net.sf.hibernate.transaction.` `JRun4TransactionManagerLookup`
Borland ES*	`net.sf.hibernate.transaction` `.BESTransactionManagerLookup`
JNDI*	`net.sf.hibernate.transaction` `.JNDITransactionManagerLookup`
Sun ONE Application Server 7*	`net.sf.hibernate.transaction.Sun` `ONETransactionManagerLookup`

*Available in Hibernate 2.1.5

Most commonly, `openSession()is` the only method of a `Session-Factory` that you will use. The no-argument version will use the mechanism as described by the `Configuration` properties to connect to the database (usually the preferred mechanism).

Once you have obtained a session, you have access to a variety of options for manipulating data, as shown in Figure 6.2.

Generally speaking, the methods of a session are concerned with the traditional create, retrieve, update, and delete operations.

TRANSACTIONS

You'll want to wrap calls to the session using method `beginTransaction()` and then calling `Transaction.commit()` when finished. Note that Hibernate will sometimes not actually flush SQL statements to the transaction until after the transaction is committed, which can on occasion lead to

(continues)

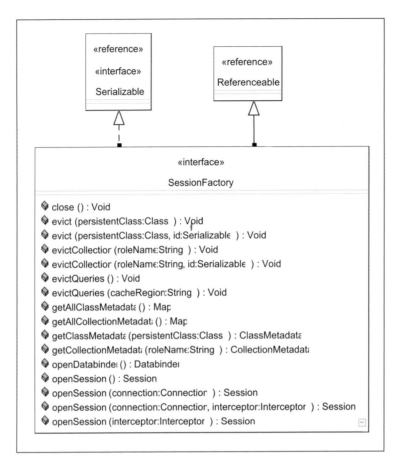

Figure 6.1. SessionFactory

unwanted reordering of the SQL execution. For more information on flushing statements as part of a transaction, see Chapter 9.

In other words, Hibernate may not execute the SQL in the order in which you issue the commands in the session. To avoid this, use the `session.flush()` when executing statements to ensure the proper order of execution (see Chapter 9 for more information).

As shown in examples throughout this book, make sure that you are using try/catch/finally blocks to properly commit or roll back transactions as needed and that sessions are closed properly.

Figure 6.2. Session

Creating Objects

Creating objects in Hibernate is straightforward. Simply allocate the persistent objects using `new`, set the properties, and then use `Session.save()`.

A complication may arise when you are creating objects with collections, however. The important thing to remember is that collection elements added to a parent where the collection is set to `inverse="true"` are not persisted automatically—you must manually save them and add them to the `inverse="false"` end of the relationship to persist them.

Unfortunately, Hibernate does not allow both sides of a collection to be set to `inverse="false"`. This means that you must think carefully about your needs in order to decide which side of an association to map as `inverse="false"`. To complicate matters somewhat, this is also true when objects are deleted—it's easy to manually delete the associations, as long as the proper side of the relationship is used. You can work around this when working with the "wrong end" of a bi-directional association by using the outer-join-as-inverse-of-inner technique described in Chapter 8.

Session methods that are useful when you are saving objects are shown in Table 6.7.

Finding Objects

Hibernate offers a wide variety of options for retrieving objects from the database, including HQL, the Criteria API, and using SQL directly (or even mixing different strategies). For more information, see Chapter 8.

The various methods available for retrieving objects via HQL (as described in Chapter 8) are shown in Table 6.8. These methods are routinely expected to return no results (for example, a query for the number of students in a class may legitimately return no students if there are none enrolled). If you wish to view the inability to retrieve an object as an application failure use `load()`, described under Refreshing Objects below, instead of `get()`.

Some of these methods return a `net.sf.hibernate.Query` object instead of an immediate set of results. The `net.sf.hibernate.Query` object can be used to bind parameters and configure other aspects of the query before execution. The advantages of using an intermediate `Query` object include:

- Selecting a portion of the results (using `setMaxResults()` and `setFirstResult()`)
- Required to use named query parameters
- Retrieve the results as `ScrollableResults`

Table 6.7. Object Creation

`save(Object object)`	Saves the object, and sets the id to the generated identifier.
`save(Object object, Serializable id)`	Saves the object using the specified identifier. Useful if you use an alternative mechanism for managing identifiers (for example, if you are relying on your EJB container for identifiers).
`saveOrUpdate(Object object)`	Will save the object if no identifier is present, or update the object if the identifier is valid.
`saveOrUpdateCopy (Object object)`	Will generate a new object either way, and will make a copy of the object from the current version if one already exists.
`saveOrUpdateCopy(Object object, Serializable id)`	Will generate a new object with the specified identifier either way, and will make a copy of the object from the current version if one already exists.

Table 6.8. Finding Objects via HQL

`createQuery(String)`	Use to retrieve a Query object based on an HQL query.
`find(String)`	Returns a java.util.List containing the results of the HQL query.
`find(String query, Object[] values, Type[] types)`	Returns a java.util.List, using the values and types provided as bound parameters.
`find(String query, Object value, Type type)`	Returns a java.util.List, using the value and type provided as a bound parameter.
`get(Class, Serializable)`	Retrieves a single persistent object, or null if not present.
`get(Class, Serializable, LockMode)`	Retrieves a single persistent object with the specified lock mode. Not normally necessary—Hibernate manages lock modes automatically.
`getNamedQuery(String)`	Gets a query based on a query specified in the *.hbm.xml mapping file.
`iterate(String)`	Executes the query, returning the results lazily, loading each object with a new SELECT statement.
`iterate(String query, Object[] values, Type[] types)`	Executes the query, returning the results lazily, loading each object with a new SELECT statement. Values and types are used to set bound parameters.
`iterate(String query, Object value, Type type)`	Executes the query, returning the results lazily, loading each object with a new SELECT statement. Value and type are used to set a bound parameter.

You may notice that there are two seemingly similar methods for retrieving results: `find()` and `iterate()`. The `find()` method executes immediately, whereas `iterator()` executes on demand. Therefore, `find()` methods typically perform better than `iterator()` methods. If you fear you may retrieve too many results with `find()`, you would probably be better off using `create-Query()` to configure the returned results.

ONE POSSIBLE GOOD USE FOR ITERATE

Technically, the `iterate()` method returns only the object identifiers and a proxy, whereas the `find()` method performs a full retrieval. Thus the one time an `iterate()` could outperform a `find()` is if you are only interested in the returned primary keys, not the full objects.

In addition to HQL, Chapter 8 describes the use of both the Hibernate Criteria API and raw SQL to access data. Table 6.9 shows these methods.

Refreshing Objects

Sometimes, you know that an object exists, but only have part of the object's information. The most typical example would be a situation in which you know an object's identify reference but don't have the rest of the object information (this is shown in the sample application in Chapter 2). Given an identifier, the `load()` method can be used to retrieve the rest of the information about an object. The difference between a `load()` and a `get()` is that a `load()` will fail with an exception if the object is not found, whereas a `get()` will simply return `null`.

Within the context of a single session, you may expect that the mere act of updating or saving the object will modify the properties. For example, a trigger

Table 6.9. Finding Objects via Criteria and SQL

`createCriteria(Class)`	Pass in a persistent class to use as the base of the criteria, and then use additional methods to modify the query, as shown in Chapter 8.
`createSQLQuery(String sql, String[] returnAliases, Class[] returnClasses)`	Use to execute a query with multiple alias and classes, as shown in Chapter 8.
`createSQLQuery(String sql, String returnAlias, Class returnClass)`	Use to execute a query with a single alias and class, as shown in Chapter 8.

Table 6.10. Obtaining the Current Data

`load(Class clazz, Serializable id)`	Use to load an object at any time, given only an identifier.
`load(Object object, Serializable id)`	As load, with a specific identifier.
`load(Class clazz, Serializable id, LockMode lockMode)`	As load, with a specific identifier and lock mode.
`refresh(Object object)`	Only usable if the object has already been loaded by this session.
`refresh(Object obj, LockMode lockMode)`	Only usable if the object has already been loaded by this session

may modify the data written to a particular column when a record is saved. The `refresh()` method is used in the context of a single `Session` to retrieve these changes. In practice, you'll probably use the `load()` method much more frequently than the `refresh()` method. The `refresh()` method can also be used to reassociate objects across transactions with a session (converting a transient object to a persistent object). This is especially important if you wish to take advantage of cascading operations, because Hibernate may not recognize cascading associations if objects are not properly refreshed. For an example of this, see Listing 2.17, Deleting an Author.

Deleting Objects

Deleting an object is largely a simple matter of passing the object to the `session.delete()`. You can use HQL to identify a range of records for higher-performance bulk deletes.

Table 6.11. shows the methods available for deleting data.

Table 6.11. Deleting Data

`delete(Object object)`	Removes a persistent instance from the database.
`delete(String query)`	Deletes all objects returned by the HQL query.
`delete(String query, Object[] values, Type[] types)`	Deletes all objects returned by the HQL query.
`delete(String query, Object value, Type type)`	Deletes all objects returned by the HQL query.

Table 6.12.   Deleting Data

`update(Object object)`	Updates the persistent instance with the identifier of the given transient instance.
`update(Object object, Serializable id)`	Updates the persistent instance with the identifier as specified. Particularly useful if using EJB to manage identity.

Updating Objects

Much like creating an object, updating an object is a matter of simply modifying a persistent object and passing it to `Session.update()`. Table 6.12 shows the methods available for updating data.

Objects and Identity

Our applications so far have used several different mechanisms for determining whether two objects are to be considered equal. It's important to understand the different mechanisms for identity, especially concerning the difference between transient and persistent objects as defined by Hibernate.

What Is Identity?

The first form of identity is expressed in terms of the database key. For example, two records could be considered equal if they have the same primary key value.

The second form of identity is expressed in terms of the Java object reference. We can imagine a situation in which two Java objects contain the same data from the perspective of the developer but are different objects because they are stored in two different places in memory.

Finally, the third form of identity derives from a comparison of all of the data associated with the object. For example, consider an object containing student data. This object might be represented by a primary key (for example, 543), a JVM object reference (for example, 82340), or the values of the associated data (for example, the primary key, 543, the first name, and the last name).

If the student object were to change the value of the last-name property, neither the primary key nor the object reference would be changed, even though the object is clearly no longer equivalent.

Consider the following snippet of code and the different values that may be considered when evaluating equality:

	JVM	Primary Key	Data
Student myStudent = new Student();	45678	null	null
myStudent.setID(new Long(23));	45687	23	23+null
myStudent.setLastName ("Smith");	45687	23	23+Smith
Student altStudent = new Student();	09875	null	null
myStudent.setID(new Long(23));	09875	23	23+null
myStudent.setLastName ("Garod");	09875	23	23+Garod

Obviously, these different notions of equality can lead to radically different answers when one is trying to answer the question "Are these two objects equal?"

Hibernate expresses these two different notions of equality by taking advantage of the two different mechanisms for equality built into the Java language. The Java = and == operators rely on the object reference. All Java objects, on the other hand, descend from the base `java.lang.Object` class, which defines an `equals()` method. Therefore, Hibernate uses the `equals()` method to determine persistent identity, and the == method to determine JVM equality.

Let's look at a standard Hibernate `equals()` implementation, as shown in Listing 6.3. This is declared in a class called Message (as described in more detail later in this chapter). The first order of comparison in the snippet is by class instance. Then the objects are compared for equality by their primary-key value and nothing else (for more information on the Apache Jakarta Commons Lang project's EqualsBuilder class, see http://jakarta.apache.org/commons/lang/api/org/apache/commons/lang/builder/EqualsBuilder.html). Therefore, this object will rely on the notion of primary-key values for equality.

Listing 6.3 Sample Primary-Key Equality Method

```
public boolean equals(Object other)
{
    if (!(other instanceof Message))
        return false;
    Message castOther = (Message)other;
    return new EqualsBuilder()
        .append(this.getId(), castOther.getId())
        .isEquals();
}
```

Similarly, Listing 6.4 shows the matching implementation of `hashCode()`.

Listing 6.4   Sample Primary-Key Hash Method

```
    public int hashCode()
    {
        return new
HashCodeBuilder().append(getId()).toHashCode();
    }
```

The documentation for the Apache Jakarta Commons Lang HashCodeBuilder will be found at http://jakarta.apache.org/commons/lang/api/org/apache/commons/lang/builder/HashCodeBuilder.html. The `hashCode` is principally derived from the primary key id, as in the `equals()` method.

WHAT IS A HASH CODE?

`public int hashCode()` returns a hash code value for the object. This method is supported for the benefit of hashtables such as those provided by `java.util.Hashtable`.

The general contract of `hashCode` is:

- Whenever it is invoked on the same object more than once during an execution of a Java application, the hashCode method must consistently return the same integer, provided that no information used in equals comparisons on the object is modified. This integer need not remain consistent from one execution of an application to another execution of the same application.
- If two objects are equal according to the equals(Object) method, then calling the hashCode method on each of the two objects must produce the same integer result.
- If two objects are unequal according to the equals(java.lang.Object) method, then calling the hashCode method on each of the two objects need not produce distinct integer results. Be aware, however, that producing distinct integer results for unequal objects may improve the performance of a hashtable.
- As much as is reasonably practical, the hashCode method defined by class Object does return distinct integers for distinct objects. (This is typically implemented by converting the internal address of the object into an integer, but the JavaTM programming language does not require this implementation technique.)

—Documentation for the Java Object, hashCode method.

Identity within a Session

Hibernate has the very interesting capability of replacing instances that you pass to it with new instances as needed, in order to maintain internal consistency.

This means that you will always get back the same JVM object reference when you perform operations in the context of a single session. For example, consider the Hibernate pseudo-code shown in Listing 6.5.

Listing 6.5 Session Identity

```
hibernateSession = sessionFactory.openSession();
Student myStudent = hibernateSession.load(Student.class, new
Long(23));
...
Student altStudent = hibernateSession.load(Student.class, new
Long(23));
if(myStudent == altStudent)
        System.out.println("Students are equal!");
```

The snippet in Listing 6.5 will evaluate `myStudent == altStudent` to true, because Hibernate maintains the object reference as part of the open session.

Conversely, this state is not shared across sessions, and so if `myStudent` and `altStudent` were retrieved from different sessions, they may or may not evaluate to true, depending on the session, cache, thread, and other JVM details. All this means that you don't need to worry about object identity or concurrency as long as you don't share a session across threads (virtually never a good idea).

Later in this chapter, we will show how to use Hibernate object life-cycle methods to examine the issues of identity in more detail.

Generating Identity (Primary Keys)

The terms *identity* and *primary key* have different meanings, but they are often used interchangeably when working with Hibernate. Object identity refers to the more general notion of identity—a unique value that can be used to retrieve a unique object.

Generally speaking, when a record is stored in a database, it is given a primary key as the main indicator of its identity. As a safeguard against possible changes to the application, this primary key typically has no particular business value or association with other data in the record.

WARNING

It bears repeating: you are strongly encouraged to *not* use a primary key with a business value. Avoiding the use of business values is sometimes trickier than might be expected. For example, you may think that a social security number (a standard U.S. government identifier) would serve as a reasonable primary key number. Unfortunately, in this age of identity theft, it's possible for people to change their social security numbers (and thereby the value used for key relationships). Therefore, whenever possible use a synthetic, internal-to-the-application-only value for primary keys.

In certain instances, however, object identity is not managed by a primary key, but by another mechanism. For example, the records in a collection table may be referred to by a composite key (the fusion of the two collected foreign keys), with no primary key required.

There are several built-in strategies available for primary key generation. Hibernate controls the configuration of identity generation for standard primary keys using the `generator` tag in the `*.hbm.xml` mapping file (see the `generator` tag in Chapter 5 for more information). Hibernate allows you to specify a custom Java class that implements the interface `net.sf .hibernate.id.IdentifierGenerator` for identity generation, but it also includes a large suite of built-in generation classes.

Built-In Hibernate Generators

Hibernate includes many built-in implementations of `net.sf.hibernate .id.IdentifierGenerator` that allow you to easily support a wide variety of possible key generators. You can refer to these built-in generators either by their fully qualified class names or by their "shortcut" names.

If you are working with an existing database, you'll want to select the generator that matches the current key generation strategy.

* `increment`
  Generates in-process (i.e., within this JVM instance only) identifiers of type `long`, `short`, or `int`. Only guaranteed to be unique when no other process is inserting data into the same table. Do not use in a cluster.

* `identity`
  Use when working with an identity column in DB2, MySQL, MS SQL Server, Sybase, or HypersonicSQL. The returned identifier is of type `long`, `short`, or `int`.

* `sequence` (`net.sf.hibernate.id.SequenceGenerator`)
  Use when working with a sequence column in DB2, PostgreSQL, Oracle, SAP DB, McKoi, or a generator in Interbase. The returned identifier is of type `long`, `short`, or `int`.

* `hilo` (`net.sf.hibernate.id.TableHiLoGenerator`)

Uses a particular hi/lo table to keep manage identifier generation. Whereas a simple table generator hits the database every time an identifier is requested, the hi/lo strategy minimizes database access by requesting possible identifiers in blocks. The size of the block of possible identifiers reserved is specified by the required `<param name="max_lo">100</param>` tag.

You can use `<param nam="table">mytable</param>` tag to override the default table name (`hibernate_unique_key`), and `<param nam="column">mycolumn</param>` to override the default column name (`next`) if desired.

The hi/lo algorithm generates identifiers that are unique only for a particular database. This generator requires a new database transaction to retrieve the identifier, so do not use it with connections managed by JTA or with a user-supplied connection.

- `seqhilo` (`net.sf.hibernate.id.SequenceHiLoGenerator`)

  Similar to the hi/lo algorithm, but uses an underlying sequence to generate identifiers of type `long`, `short`, or `int`, given a named database sequence. In addition to the `<param name="max_lo">100</param>`, you will also need to identify the sequence using a `<param name="sequence">hi_value</param>` tag.

- `uuid.hex` (`net.sf.hibernate.id.UUIDHexGenerator`)

  Uses a 128-bit UUID algorithm to generate identifiers of type string, unique within a network. The UUID is encoded as a 32-character-long string of hexadecimal digits. The UUIDs are based on IP address, startup time of the JVM (accurate to a quarter-second), system time, and a counter value (unique in the JVM). You can pass in a `<param name="separator">-</param>` tag to configure a separator character. Use this class if you want human-readable UUID values.

- `uuid.string` (`net.sf.hibernate.id.UUIDStringGenerator`)

  Uses the same UUID algorithm as `uuid.hex`, only instead of encoding as a 32-character-long string of hex digits, uses a 16-character string of ASCII characters (including unprintable, non-human-readable characters). Do not use with PostgreSQL or if you want a human to be able to reasonably view or edit the key.

- `native` (assigned in `net.sf.hibernate.id. Identifier Generator`)

  Automatically chooses either `identity`, `sequence`, or `hilo` depending upon the capabilities of the target database.

- `assigned(net.sf.hibernate.id.Assigned)`

  Lets the **application** assign an identifier to the object before `Session.save()` is called. This generator is especially important for use in one-to-one relationships (see the `one-to-one` tag in Chapter 5 for more information). Due to its inherent nature, entities that use this generator cannot be saved via the `Session.saveOrUpdate()` method. Instead you have to explicitly specify to Hibernate whether the object should be saved or updated by calling either `Session.save()` or `Session.update()`. If you are using this strategy, be very careful to assign proper identifiers (especially if you also rely on cascading object updates).

- `foreign(net.sf.hibernate.id.ForeignGenerator)`
- Uses the identifier of another associated object. Generally used in conjunction with a one-to-one primary-key association. Requires a `<param name="property">target_key</param>`.

Composite Identity

Most objects will rely on a built-in generator for key generation. Some objects, however (in particular, those used in collection tables) may rely on composite keys. An example of this is shown in the ownership table in Chapter 3. Listing 6.6 shows the description of the ownership table as given by MySQL. Note that the table has two primary keys. In the discussion that follows, we will assume that the most popular use of composite keys is for collection tables (of course this may not be true for certain applications), and therefore we will discuss them in that context.

Listing 6.6   Composite Identity Example

```
mysql> desc ownership;
+-------------+------------+------+-----+---------+-------+
| Field       | Type       | Null | Key | Default | Extra |
+-------------+------------+------+-----+---------+-------+
| owner_id    | bigint(20) |      | PRI | 0       |       |
| artifact_id | bigint(20) |      | PRI | 0       |       |
+-------------+------------+------+-----+---------+-------+
```

On reflection, you will realize that this makes it difficult to work individual records outside the context of the related objects. Although this is largely a non-issue, it makes working with composite identity records more difficult as you develop certain complex relationships. If you are content to allow Hibernate to manage your collections, and do not impose any additional fields beyond those

Hibernate requires for the collection (for example, `index` columns as needed, but no additional data fields), you may never need to deal with composite identity directly.

Putting this in the context of the example application shown in Chapter 3, you will note that there is no class-level declaration of the ownership table. Instead, all references to the ownership table are made via collection-tag bindings. Listing 6.7 shows one side of this binding from the `Artifact.hbm.xml` file. A similar (but inverted) binding exists in the `Owner.hbm.xml` file.

Listing 6.7 One Side of a Collection

```
<set name="owners" table="ownership" lazy="false"
inverse="true" cascade="none" sort="unsorted">
<key column="artifact_id"/>
<many-to-many class="com.cascadetg.ch03.Owner"
column="owner_id" outer-join="auto"/>
</set>
```

Thus, even though this application uses a table with composite identity, there is no need to explicitly deal with the composite-identity as such; Hibernate takes care of this for us.

In certain situations, particularly when working with a legacy database schema, you won't have the luxury of a pure collection table. In situations in which you have a collection table with additional data, you are often best off representing the collection table as an independent class (an example of which is shown in Chapter 4). In this case, the table identity may need to be modeled using a composite identity tag, such as `composite-element`, `composite-id`, or `composite-index`. These tags, described in Chapter 5, are used in combination with nested property tags to declare the columns used to manage the composite identifiers.

It's very important to correctly implement the `Object.equals()` and `Object.hashCode()` methods to correctly handle composite identity. The default methods, as shown in Listing 6.3 and Listing 6.4, should include all of the property values required to correctly map the composite identity, not just the `getId()` methods as shown.

Unsaved Value

Hibernate offers a feature that allows you to perform a save-or-update with a single method call (as shown in Table 6.7). In other words, let's say that you wish to either update an object (if it exists) or create it (if it doesn't). In order to know whether an object has been created (at least from the perspective of the application running in the JVM), Hibernate will inspect certain values to see if they have been set.

The most immediate and obvious example is the primary key (or id) of the object. For example, perhaps you are using a `java.lang.Long` to track the primary key of an object. If this field is set to `null`, then Hibernate knows that the object has not been saved in the database. Similarly, if the value is not `null`, then Hibernate knows that the object has a primary key and therefore must exist in the database (because `null` is the unsaved value).

This use of a `null` is an important reason to use the object version of a value (e.g., `java.lang.Long`) instead of the primitive form (e.g., `long`). While null values are sometimes simulated with a primitive (e.g., 0 or -1), this is a fragile and non-standard approach. Normally, this is the most significant impact of the notion of unsaved value, but as you develop complex data models or cope with certain legacy data models, you may find other reasons to change the notion of an unsaved value.

Life-Cycle Methods

Now that we have looked in depth at the various notions of identity, we can take advantage of the life-cycle methods built in to Hibernate to experiment with the various available systems.

There are two main interfaces of life-cycle interest, one for general notifications and one for validation. Let's start by looking at an example of life-cycle application. Figure 6.3 shows a persistent Java object, a simple message. Note the implementation of the `net.sf.hibernate.Lifecycle` and `net.sf.hibernate.Validatable` interfaces. These are used to flag that this class is interested both in events relating to the object's life cycle (e.g., creation, saving, updating, destruction) and in events providing an opportunity to validate the state of the object before certain operations (in particular, saving or updating the object).

As you review the life-cycle methods shown below, keep in mind that the life-cycle events correspond to the terminology used at the start of this chapter. For example, the update event corresponds to when a transient object is rendered persistent, and not to all instances when a given persistent object is updated. Similarly, the validation methods are called when appropriate from a persistence perspective. Do **not** use these life-cycle methods to manage your business logic—the terminology and events are only relevant from a persistence model perspective.

The code for the message object, as shown in Listing 6.8 (with white space trimmed) is based on XDoclet (described in Chapter 3). In particular, note the methods implementing the various life-cycle interfaces. This class doesn't do anything very interesting (beyond echoing the fact of notification), but it's easy to envision possible uses.

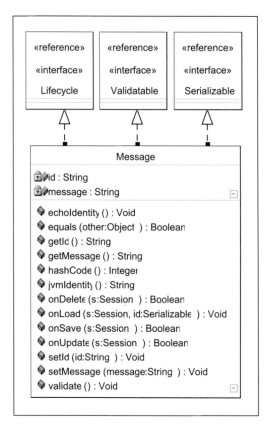

Figure 6.3.   Message

Listing 6.8   Object Life-Cycle Example

```
package com.cascadetg.ch06;

import java.io.Serializable;

import net.sf.hibernate.CallbackException;
import net.sf.hibernate.Lifecycle;
import net.sf.hibernate.Session;
import net.sf.hibernate.Validatable;
import net.sf.hibernate.ValidationFailure;

import org.apache.commons.lang.builder.HashCodeBuilder;
import org.apache.commons.lang.builder.EqualsBuilder;

/**
 * @author Will Iverson
```

Listing 6.8   Object Life-Cycle Example (*continued*)

```
 * @hibernate.class
 * @since 1.0
 */

public class Message
     implements Lifecycle, Validatable, Serializable
{

     String message;

     /**
      * @hibernate.property
      * @return Returns the message.
      */
     public String getMessage() { return message; }

     /**
      * @param comments
      * The comments to set.
      */
     public void setMessage(String message)
     { this.message = message; }
     String id;
     /**
      * @hibernate.id generator-class="uuid.hex"
      * Xhibernate.id generator-class="native"
      * Xhibernate.id generator-class="increment"
      *
      * @return Returns the id.
      */
     public String getId() { return id; }

     /**
      * @param id
      * The id to set.
      */
     public void setId(String id) { this.id = id; }

     /* see
net.sf.hibernate.Lifecycle#onSave(net.sf.hibernate.Session)
     */
     public boolean onSave(Session s) throws CallbackException
     {
         echoIdentity();
         System.out.println("saved.");
         return Lifecycle.NO_VETO;
```

Listing 6.8   Object Life-Cycle Example (*continued*)

```
    }
    /* see net.sf.hibernate.Lifecycle#onUpdate(
        net.sf.hibernate.Session)
    */
    public boolean onUpdate(Session s) throws CallbackException
    {
        echoIdentity();
        System.out.println("updated.");
        return Lifecycle.NO_VETO;
    }

    /* see net.sf.hibernate.Lifecycle#onDelete(
        net.sf.hibernate.Session)
    */
    public boolean onDelete(Session s) throws CallbackException
    {
        echoIdentity();
        System.out.println("deleted.");
        return Lifecycle.NO_VETO;
    }
    /* see net.sf.hibernate.Lifecycle#onLoad(
        net.sf.hibernate.Session,
          java.io.Serializable)
    */
    public void onLoad(Session s, Serializable id)
    {
        echoIdentity();
        System.out.println("loaded.");
    }

    /* see net.sf.hibernate.Validatable#validate()
     */
    public void validate() throws ValidationFailure
    {
        echoIdentity();
        System.out.println("validated.");
    }

    /** Standard Hibernate equality override */
    public boolean equals(Object other)
    {
        if (!(other instanceof Message))
            return false;
        Message castOther = (Message)other;
        return new EqualsBuilder()
```

(*continues*)

Listing 6.8   Object Life-Cycle Example (*continued*)

```
                    .append(this.getId(), castOther.getId())
                    .isEquals();
    }

    /** Standard Hibernate hash override. */
    public int hashCode()
    { return new
      HashCodeBuilder().append(getId()).toHashCode(); }

    /** Not certain to work on all JVMs */
    public String jvmIdentity() { return super.toString(); }

    public void echoIdentity()
    {
        System.out.print("JVM:" + this.jvmIdentity());
        System.out.print(", KEY:" + this.getId());
        System.out.print(" HASH:" + this.hashCode() + " ");
    }

}
```

Executing the build file for this class, a `*.hbm.xml` file is generated by XDoclet, as shown in Listing 6.9 (white space edited).

Listing 6.9   Message Mapping

```xml
<?xml version="1.0"?>

<!DOCTYPE hibernate-mapping PUBLIC
    "-//Hibernate/Hibernate Mapping DTD 2.0//EN"
    "http://hibernate.sourceforge.net/hibernate-mapping-2.0.dtd">

<hibernate-mapping>
    <class name="com.cascadetg.ch06.Message"
        dynamic-update="false"
        dynamic-insert="false" >

        <id name="id" column="id" type="java.lang.String" >
            <generator class="uuid.hex">
            </generator>
        </id>

        <property name="message" type="java.lang.String"
```

Listing 6.9   Message Mapping (*continued*)

```
                   update="true" insert="true" column="message" />

        <!--
            To add non XDoclet property mappings, create a
            file named hibernate-properties-Message.xml
            containing the additional properties and place
            it in your merge dir.
        -->

    </class>

</hibernate-mapping>
```

Given the Java object and the mapping file, a simple test harness can be used to exercise the object (as shown in Listing 6.10). You'll notice that this class echoes the results of various object identity, validation, and life-cycle features of Hibernate.

Listing 6.10   Testing Life Cycles, Validation, and Identity

```
package com.cascadetg.ch06;

/** Various Hibernate-related imports */
import net.sf.hibernate.*;
import net.sf.hibernate.cfg.*;
import net.sf.hibernate.tool.hbm2ddl.SchemaUpdate;

public class MessageTest
{
    public static void main(String[] args)
    {
        initialization();
        createMessage();
        loadMessage();
        updateMessage();
//      deleteMessage();
    }


    /** We use this session factory to create our sessions */
    public static SessionFactory sessionFactory;

    /** Loads the Hibernate configuration information,
     * sets up the database and the Hibernate session factory.
```

(*continues*)

Listing 6.10   Testing Life Cycles, Validation, and Identity (*continued*)

```
    */
public static void initialization()
{
    //System.setErr(System.out);
    System.out.println("initialization");
    try
    {
        Configuration myConfiguration = new Configuration();

        myConfiguration.addClass(Message.class);

        // This is the code that updates the database to
        // the current schema.
        new SchemaUpdate(myConfiguration).execute(true,
            true);

        // Sets up the session factory (used in the rest
        // of the application).
        sessionFactory =
            myConfiguration.buildSessionFactory();

    } catch (Exception e)
    {
        e.printStackTrace();
    }
}

static String savedMessageID = null;

public static void loadMessage()
{
    System.out.println();
    System.out.println("loadMessage");

    Session hibernateSession = null;
    Transaction myTransaction = null;
    try
    {
        hibernateSession = sessionFactory.openSession();
        myTransaction = hibernateSession.beginTransaction();

        Message newMessage = new Message();
        newMessage.echoIdentity();
        System.out.println("pre-set");
```

Listing 6.10 Testing Life Cycles, Validation, and Identity (*continued*)

```
            newMessage.setId(savedMessageID);
            newMessage.echoIdentity();
            System.out.println("pre-load");

            // This object is not "owned" by Hibernate,
            // so the onUpdate() method IS called.
            hibernateSession.load(
                Message.class,
                newMessage.getId());

            hibernateSession.flush();
            myTransaction.commit();

            newMessage.echoIdentity();
            System.out.println("post-load");

        } catch (Exception e)
        {
            e.printStackTrace();
            try
            {
                myTransaction.rollback();
            } catch (Exception e2)
            {
                // Silent failure of transaction rollback
            }
        } finally
        {
            try
            {
                hibernateSession.close();
            } catch (Exception e2)
            {
                // Silent failure of session close
            }
        }

    }

    public static void updateMessage()
    {
        System.out.println();
        System.out.println("updateMessage");

        Session hibernateSession = null;
        Transaction myTransaction = null;
```

(*continues*)

Listing 6.10   Testing Life Cycles, Validation, and Identity (*continued*)

```
        try
        {
            hibernateSession = sessionFactory.openSession();
            myTransaction = hibernateSession.beginTransaction();

            Message newMessage = new Message();
            newMessage.setId(savedMessageID);
            newMessage.setMessage("updated");

            // This object is not "owned" by Hibernate,
            // so the onUpdate() method IS called.
            hibernateSession.update(newMessage);

            hibernateSession.flush();

            newMessage.setMessage("indigo");
            hibernateSession.save(newMessage);

            hibernateSession.flush();
            myTransaction.commit();
        } catch (Exception e)
        {
            e.printStackTrace();
            try
            {
                myTransaction.rollback();
            } catch (Exception e2)
            {
                // Silent failure of transaction rollback
            }
        } finally
        {
            try
            {
                hibernateSession.close();
            } catch (Exception e2)
            {
                // Silent failure of session close
            }
        }

    }

    public static void deleteMessage()
    {
```

Listing 6.10   Testing Life Cycles, Validation, and Identity (*continued*)

```
        System.out.println();
        System.out.println("deleteMessage");

        Session hibernateSession = null;
        Transaction myTransaction = null;
        try
        {
            hibernateSession = sessionFactory.openSession();
            myTransaction = hibernateSession.beginTransaction();

            Message newMessage = new Message();
            newMessage.setId(savedMessageID);

            hibernateSession.delete(newMessage);

            hibernateSession.flush();
            myTransaction.commit();
        } catch (Exception e)
        {
            e.printStackTrace();
            try
            {
                myTransaction.rollback();
            } catch (Exception e2)
            {
                // Silent failure of transaction rollback
            }
        } finally
        {
            try
            {
                hibernateSession.close();
            } catch (Exception e2)
            {
                // Silent failure of session close
            }
        }

    }

    public static void createMessage()
    {
        System.out.println();
        System.out.println("createMessage");
```

Listing 6.10   Testing Life Cycles, Validation, and Identity (*continued*)

```
Session hibernateSession = null;
Transaction myTransaction = null;
try
{
    hibernateSession = sessionFactory.openSession();
    myTransaction = hibernateSession.beginTransaction();

    Message myMessage = new Message();
    myMessage.setMessage("foo");

    hibernateSession.save(myMessage);

    hibernateSession.flush();
    myTransaction.commit();

    System.out.println(
        "New message id: " + myMessage.getId());

    myTransaction = hibernateSession.beginTransaction();

    // This object is already "owned" by Hibernate,
    // so the onUpdate() method is NOT called.
    myMessage.setMessage("bar");
    hibernateSession.update(myMessage);

    hibernateSession.flush();
    myTransaction.commit();

    // Save the message ID for later use.
    savedMessageID = myMessage.getId();

} catch (Exception e)
{
    e.printStackTrace();
    try
    {
        myTransaction.rollback();
    } catch (Exception e2)
    {
        // Silent failure of transaction rollback
    }
} finally
{
    try
    {
        hibernateSession.close();
```

Listing 6.10 Testing Life Cycles, Validation, and Identity (*continued*)

```
                } catch (Exception e2)
                {
                    // Silent failure of session close
                }
            }
        }
    }
```

When run, the application produces output similar to that shown in Listing 6.11. You may wish to compare the values below to the results of the application as run on your system to verify aspects of identity as described earlier in the chapter. In addition, note the various validation and life-cycle method notifications, and compare the messages echoed to the state of the objects as they correspond to the source shown in Listing 6.9 and Listing 6.10. Finally, you may wish to change the identity and generator values of the Message object to see how different systems implement identity.

Listing 6.11 Results of the Identity Test Suite

```
initialization

createMessage
JVM:com.cascadetg.ch06.Message@484861a2,
KEY:8a8092dcfbf4fd0100fbf4fd05eb0001 HASH:1212703138 saved.
JVM:com.cascadetg.ch06.Message@484861a2,
KEY:8a8092dcfbf4fd0100fbf4fd05eb0001 HASH:1212703138 validated.
New message id: 8a8092dcfbf4fd0100fbf4fd05eb0001
JVM:com.cascadetg.ch06.Message@484861a2,
KEY:8a8092dcfbf4fd0100fbf4fd05eb0001 HASH:1212703138 validated.

loadMessage
JVM:com.cascadetg.ch06.Message@275, KEY:null HASH:629 pre-set
JVM:com.cascadetg.ch06.Message@484861a2,
KEY:8a8092dcfbf4fd0100fbf4fd05eb0001 HASH:1212703138 pre-load
JVM:com.cascadetg.ch06.Message@484861a2,
KEY:8a8092dcfbf4fd0100fbf4fd05eb0001 HASH:1212703138 loaded.
JVM:com.cascadetg.ch06.Message@484861a2,
KEY:8a8092dcfbf4fd0100fbf4fd05eb0001 HASH:1212703138 post-load

updateMessage
JVM:com.cascadetg.ch06.Message@484861a2,
KEY:8a8092dcfbf4fd0100fbf4fd05eb0001 HASH:1212703138 updated.
```

Listing 6.11   Results of the Identity Test Suite (*continued*)

```
JVM:com.cascadetg.ch06.Message@484861a2,
KEY:8a8092dcfbf4fd0100fbf4fd05eb0001 HASH:1212703138 validated.
JVM:com.cascadetg.ch06.Message@484861a2,
KEY:8a8092dcfbf4fd0100fbf4fd05eb0001 HASH:1212703138 validated.
```

CHAPTER 7

Relationships

Object/relational mapping highlights the confusion arising from the fact that experts in the object-oriented world and the relational world use different concepts and terminology. For example, a Java developer may speak in terms of a collection and classes, whereas a database guru will talk of things in terms of foreign keys and joins. In this chapter, we'll try to explain and reconcile these terms.

The discussion in this chapter breaks the different types of relationships into a few basic categories.

- *Database Relationships:* How relationships are viewed from a database perspective. Regardless of the type of relationship you choose, it will (obviously) be stored in the database somehow.

- *Java Collection Relationships:* How groups of objects can relate to one other. Governs the precise behavior of a database relationship from the Java application's perspective. All collection tags (described in Chapter 5) require a nested database relationship tag.

- *Java Class Relationships:* The expression of a Java class hierarchy in a database. An example of this is shown in Chapter 3.

The chapter concludes with a discussion of bi-directional collection relationships and the notion of an "any" relationship, one of the more advanced uses of Hibernate that combines aspects of Java class relationships with collection behavior.

TIP

Hibernate uses many terms in ways that differ from what a Java developer might expect. For example, the Java terms *component, class, association, subclass,* and *collection* also refer to specific Hibernate functionality or mapping tags. If a reference to a concept is confusing, make sure that you understand whether the context is a database, Java, or Hibernate.

Database Relationships

There are a few basic mechanisms for tracking relationships between tables in a database. The many-to-one and one-to-many relationships are used to model the simplest versions of a foreign key, and should be considered your default (especially if you are modeling legacy data). The next stage, using Hibernate to manage collection tables using the many-to-many relationship, should be considered a somewhat more advanced technique (but not necessarily—don't fall into the trap of trying to jam an incompatible model into a many-to-many relationship). Finally, a one-to-one model can be useful in certain situations.

Many-to-One

The name many-to-one simply refers to another object (in Java terms) or a foreign key (in database terms).

The `many-to-one` and `one-to-many` terms describe two sides of the same relationship. In Figure 7.1, the many-to-one relationship is used to describe the relationship from the perspective of the `Parts` table.

One-to-Many

The one-to-many relationship is used to model a collection (in Java terms) or the referred table of a foreign-key relationship (in database terms). The precise behavior of a one-to-many collection is determined by the type of collection (as described below, under the heading Java Collection Relationships).

A one-to-many relationship is generally modeled by a table with a foreign key. In Figure 7.1, for instance, a one-to-many relationship is described by the `CarModel` table. The one-to-many model is used to represent the relationship from the perspective of the target table.

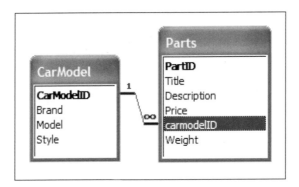

Figure 7.1. Basic Foreign-Key Relationship

This relationship is modeled in the `CarModel` mapping file, but note that the `CarModel` table does not actually contain any data referring to the `Parts` table. The only notion of the relationship that is expressed in the database comes from the addition of a foreign key (as shown in Chapter 4). Putting this in parent/child terms, the relationship is modeled on the parent, but technically the data is stored in the child.

If the one-to-many relationship is part of a bi-directional relationship (in other words, if you can navigate using your Java code from the `CarModel` object to `Parts` and back), you will probably wish to set the `inverse="true"` attribute for the collection tag used to wrap the relationship. For more information on bi-directional relationships, see the section at the end of this chapter.

Many-to-Many

A many-to-many relationship is used to model a collection (in Java terms) or a collection table (in database terms). In a many-to-many relationship, neither the parent nor the child table contains data about the relationship. Instead this information is stored in a collection table. Figure 7.2 shows a collection table, `CarModelOrders`.

Because there is no additional information in the `CarModelOrders` collection table, using a many-to-many relationship allows Hibernate to effectively "hide" the `CarModelOrders` table. Since `CarModelOrders` is present in the mapping files for `CarModels` and `Orders`, there is no need to make a separate mapping file for it.

Hibernate expects a many-to-many relationship to be mapped as a simple collection table, meaning that no additional data is stored in the table. You may

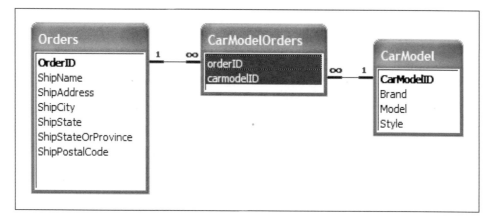

Figure 7.2. Collection Table

occasionally wish to store a many-to-many mapping that also contains additional information. Since this table would no longer be a pure binding, it should be modeled with a new class and many-to-one/one-to-many relationships, as shown in Chapter 4.

If the many-to-many relationship is part of a bi-directional relationship (i.e., you can expect to navigate using your Java code from `CarModel` to `Orders` and back), you must set the `inverse="true"` attribute on one side of the relationship. For more information on bi-directional relationships, see the section at the end of this chapter.

One-to-One

A one-to-one relationship models two tables that are logically "glued" together in some fashion. For example, an existing human resources database might have a table used to represent employees and another table to represent employee medical records. The table for employees is available to all human resources staff, whereas the medical record table is only accessible via a special administrative connection to maintain high security. You would therefore use one-to-one mapping in the administrative application to manage this relationship.

You will need to use the assigned generator for one side of your one-to-one relationship. See Chapter 6 for more information.

Java Collection Relationships

A collection is a group of objects related to another group of objects by aggregation. For example, a weblog has a collection of posts. Depending on the type of collection, this may mean a one-to-one, many-to-one, one-to-many, or many-to-many relationship. In other words, to represent a Java collection, you will first need to choose the underlying database relationship (as described above).

Most developers assume that an ordinary foreign-key-based, one-to-many relationship is best modeled with a `java.util.List`. However, the precise index of a relationship is actually not included as a foreign key. For example, consider a weblog with a relationship to a number of posts. While you may retrieve the posts in order (for example, sorted by date), the precise index of the post as part of the relationship *is not part of the database record.* Instead, the result set (and ordering) is an artifact of the runtime results as retrieved by the query.

> *Array:* An ordinary, pure Java array. Keep in mind that an array is a primitive, and therefore must be loaded entirely by the owning class (i.e., it cannot be specified as lazy; see tag class, attribute lazy in Chapter 5 for more information).

Bag: An unordered collection that may contain duplicate elements.

List: An ordered collection (also known as a sequence). The user of this interface has precise control over where in the list each element is inserted. The user can access elements by their integer index (position in the list), and search for elements in the list.

Map: An object that maps keys to values. A map cannot contain duplicate keys; each key can map to at most one value. A sorted map will maintain the keys in order.

Primitive Array: An array of Java primitive types. Like an array, loaded entirely by the owning class and cannot be lazily loaded.

Set: A collection that contains no duplicate elements. More formally, sets contain no pair of elements `e1` and `e2` such that `e1.equals(e2)`, and at most one `null` element. A sorted set will maintain the elements in order.

Several of these collection types enforce rules regarding duplicates. The rules for identity (used to handle duplicates) are described in more detail in Chapter 6.

Table 7.1 compares the different features of the collection types. The implementation column is provided for reference if you are unsure which implementation to use when creating a new collection of the appropriate type; technically, you can use any implementation of the interface shown. You should only work with these collections using the interface shown, and never rely on the underlying implementation, because Hibernate will sometimes change the underlying implementation class (for example, as part of the ability of Hibernate to manage lazy-loaded relationships).

For more information on the various built-in JDK 1.4 collections and alternative interfaces, see http://java.sun.com/j2se/1.4.2/docs/guide/collections/reference.html.

Interface: The expected Java interface for this collection type.

Implementation: A suggested Java implementation.

Duplicates: Are duplicate elements allowed?

Keys: Are elements accessible by a key value (e.g. ,`java.util.Hashtable`)?

Indexed: Does a column in the database maintain the order of the elements?

Lazy: Can the parent object be loaded without loading the collection data?

Ordered: Are the results returned as a sorted collection?

Table 7.1. Collection Features

	Interface	Implementation	Duplicates	Keys	Indexed	Lazy	Ordered
Array	`Object[]`	`Object[]`	Yes	No	Yes	No	Yes
Bag	`java.util.List`	`java.util.ArrayList`	Yes	No	No	Yes	No
List	`java.util.List`	`java.util.ArrayList`	Yes	No	Yes	Yes	Yes
Map	`java.util.Map`	`java.util.HashMap` `java.util.SortedMap`	No	Yes	No	Yes	Optional
Primitive Array	`primitive[]`	n/a	Yes	No	Yes	No	Yes
Set	`java.util.Set`	`java.util.HashSet` `java.util.SortedSet`	No	No	No	No	Optional

Table 7.2. Relative Collection Performance

	Keys	Indexed	Lazy	Insert	Update	Delete
Array	No	Yes	No	Medium	Medium	Medium
Bag	No	No	Yes	High	Poor	Poor
List	No	Yes	Yes	Medium	High	Medium
Map	Yes	No	Yes	Medium	High	Medium
Primitive Array	No	Yes	No	Medium	Medium	Medium
Set	No	No	No	Medium	High	Medium

The feature set shown in Table 7.1 has both functional implications and performance implications. Table 7.2 shows a rough guide to the relative performance of the different collection types.

Java Class Relationships

The Java class relationships in Hibernate boil down to two main types, subclasses and components.

A subclass refers to an object-oriented programmer's typical view of a class hierarchy. In the object-oriented view, a dog could be modeled as a subclass of mammal. From a database developer's perspective, subclasses are a way for a Java developer to logically group several different types of records that might be stored in a given table.

A component is a way to nest data within a particular class. For example, a `Person` class might use a nested component to store the person's address. This is simply a Java developer's tool for managing a table with many columns.

> **TIP**
>
> If you are designing an application top-down, you will probably want to use the discriminator column strategy described in subclasses rather than the joined subclass strategy. This is likely to be the first strategy supported by EJB 3.0, but joined subclasses may not be available until EJB 3.1.

Subclasses

Consider an application that wishes to persist objects of the type `com.example.Animal`, `com.example.Cat`, and `com.example.Bird` to a single table (`Cat` and `Bird`, of course, extend `Animal`). `Animal` records have the properties `name` and `weight`. `Cat` entries have the additional properties

Table 7.3.   Single Table Subclasses

Id	Discriminator	Name	Weight	Color	Teeth	Wingspan
1	com.example.Animal	Bob	10	null	null	null
2	com.example.Cat	Ashe	8	gray	26	null
3	com.example.Bird	Mika	2	blue	null	10

color and teeth, and Bird records the additional properties color and wingspan. A column (called a **discriminator**) is present in the single table used to keep track of all three classes. The Animal, Cat, and Bird records would be tracked in the database as shown in Table 7.3.

Because color is common to both com.example.Cat and com.example.Bird, it is not repeated. Note that columns not used by an object are set to null—for example, com.example.Cat has no wingspan, and therefore that value is set to null. Make sure that the columns used by your subclass **do not** define properties with the attribute not-null="true". Otherwise, an attempt to save a Cat may fail with an error indicating that there is no wingspan.

The *.hbm.xml mapping to corresponding to the table in Table 7.3 is shown in Listing 7.1.

Listing 7.1   Subclass Mapping

```
<hibernate-mapping>
    <class name="com.example.Animal">
        <id name="id" type="long" column="ID">
        <generator class="native"/></id>
        <discriminator column="discriminator"
        type="string"/>
        <property name="name" type="string" />
        <property name="weight" type="integer" />
        <subclass name="com.example.Cat">
            <property name="color" type="string"
            column="color"/>
            <property name="teeth" type="integer"
            column="teeth" />
        </subclass>
        <subclass name="com.example.Bird">
            <property name="color" type="string"
            column="color"/>
            <property name="wingspan" type="integer"
            column="wingspan" />
        </subclass>
    </class>
</hibernate-mapping>
```

e subclass declarations in Listing 7.1 do not specify an id tag (or
r version tag). These must be declared in the base class.

ish to use multiple tables for your subclasses instead of a single table,
ctually be using a joined-subclass relationship. You can't use both a sub-
a joined subclass in the same class tag; you have to choose one strategy
other.

Joined Subclasses

A joined subclass is used to define a multiple-table object hierarchy in Hibernate.
For example, let's say we wish to persist objects of the type
com.example.Animal, com.example.Cat, and com.example.Bird
to three tables, one per class (Cat and Bird, of course, extend Animal).
Instead of using a discriminator column (as per a normal subclass), the application will use a JOIN statement to mesh the tables together as needed (hence the
name "joined subclass"). Animal records have the properties name and
weight. Cat records define the additional properties color and teeth,
Bird records the additional properties color and wingspan. So our Animal, Cat, and Bird records could be tracked using three tables, as shown
Tables 7.4, 7.5, and 7.6.

Table 7.4. Animal Base Class

Id	Name	Weight
1	Bob	10
2	Ashe	8
3	Mika	2

Table 7.5. Cat Joined Subclass

Id	Color	Teeth
2	Gray	26

Table 7.6. Bird Joined Subclass

Id	Color	Wingspan
3	Blue	10

In this case, the primary key values are used to keep track of the appropriate class— no discriminator is required.

The *.hbm.xml mapping corresponding to Table 7.4, Table 7.5, and Table 7.6 would be as shown in Listing 7.2.

Listing 7.2   Joined Subclass Mapping

```
<hibernate-mapping>
      <class name="com.example.Animal" table="Animal">
            <id name="id" type="long" column="ID">
                  <generator class="native"/></id>
            <property name="name" type="string" />
            <property name="weight" type="integer" />
            <joined-subclass name="com.example.Cat"
            table="Cat">
                  <key column="ID" />
                  <property name="color" type="string"
                  column="color"/>
                  <property name="teeth" type="integer"
                  column="teeth" />
            </subclass>
            <subclass name="com.example.Bird" table="Bird">
                  <key column="ID" />
                  <property name="color" type="string"
                  column="color"/>
                  <property name="wingspan" type="integer"
                  column="wingspan" />
            </subclass>
      </class>
</hibernate-mapping>
```

Note that the subclasses specify a key tag pointing back to the id property of com.example.Animal. As a reminder: you can't use both subclass and joined subclass in the same class tag—you'll need to choose one strategy or the other.

Components

In Hibernate terminology, a component refers to the notion of breaking up a table into pieces. For example, many User tables grow rather large because they contain information about several different aspects of the user. With some applications, it may be easier to map these aspects separately using components instead of a single monolithic user class.

The use of a component allows for certain interesting features. For example, setting a component to null is the same as setting all of the subvalues to null.

Continuing the example of a `User` table, you could invalidate all of the user's address fields with a single call—simply setting the address component to `null`—instead of naming the individual components.

You might even map multiple sequences but bind them to the same component, allowing your Java application to reuse an object to apply data in multiple places. For example, consider the mapping shown in Listing 7.3.

TIP

The use of components generally boils down to a question of the number of columns in a given table. For example, a user table with 50 columns might be an excellent candidate for the use of components. Generally speaking, I find components to be most useful when I am dealing with a legacy system, and I am more likely to model logical components with a one-to-one relationship for new development (especially if I have a core subset of the columns that will be used much more frequently than the rest).

Listing 7.3 Example Component Mapping

```xml
<?xml version="1.0"?>
<!DOCTYPE hibernate-mapping SYSTEM "C:\devenv\hibernate-
2.1.2\src\net\sf\hibernate\hibernate-mapping-2.0.dtd">
<hibernate-mapping>
  <class name="com.cascadetg.ch07.ComponentExample"
      table="componentexample">
    <id name="id" column="ID" type="string" unsaved-
    value="null">
      <generator class="uuid.hex"/>
    </id>
    <property name="name" column="name"
      type="string" length="50" not-null="true"/>
      <component name="homeAddress"
          class="com.cascadetg.ch07.AddressComponent">
        <property name="street" column="home_street"
        type="char" />
        <property name="city" column="home_city" type="char" />
      </component>
      <component
          name="workAddress"
          class="com.cascadetg.ch07.AddressComponent">
          <property name="street" column="work_street"
          type="string" />
          <property name="city" column="work_city"
          type="string" />
      </component>
  </class>
</hibernate-mapping>
```

The mapping file shown in Listing 7.3 would only have a single table (com-ponentexample), but would correspond to two Java classes (`Component Example` and `AddressComponent`). The columns of the `component example` table would be `id`, `name`, `home_street`, `home  city`, `work_street`, and `work city`.

Given this mapping, it would then be possible to set both the home and work address information using the same object, as shown in Listing 7.4.

Listing 7.4   Using Components

```
hibernateSession = sessionFactory.openSession();
myTransaction = hibernateSession.beginTransaction();

ComponentExample myMessage = new ComponentExample();
myMessage.setName("foo");

AddressComponent myAddressComponent = new AddressComponent();
myAddressComponent.setStreet("123 Anywhere");
myAddressComponent.setCity("Universal City");

myMessage.setHomeAddress(myAddressComponent);
myMessage.setWorkAddress(myAddressComponent);

hibernateSession.save(myMessage);

myTransaction.commit();
```

A component is used to break up a single monolithic table, whereas a one-to-one mapping is used to associate two different tables.

Any-Based Relationships

A relationship based on the concept of an any endpoint (for example, one-to-any or any-to-any) allows you to map a relationship from one table to more than one other table.

For example, let's say that you have three tables, a `House` table, an `Auto` table, and a `Transaction` table. The application wishes to record transactions in which a person has bought or sold either a car or a house. Figure 7.3 shows this relationship as expressed in the database.

As shown in Figure 7.3, by using an any relationship, you store a reference in each `Transaction` with an `reference` identifier and a `discriminator` indicating the proper target table.

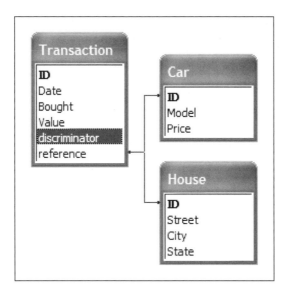

Figure 7.3. Any Relationship

For more information and some examples of different types of relationships, see http://www.xylax.net/hibernate/, which provides a list of mapping types, with explanations in terms of both the database schema and the Java code.

Bi-directional Relationships

Many of the relationships you will wish to model using Hibernate will be bi-directional. For example, given an author, you will wish to know the posts written by that author, and given a post, you will wish to know the author. As you use the various collection tags to model these bi-directional relationships, you will encounter one of the more confusing aspects of Hibernate: the `inverse` attribute.

Simply put, `inverse="false"` defines the side of a bi-directional relationship responsible for maintaining the association. The collection mapping with the `inverse="false"` attribute (the default value) is responsible for the appropriate SQL query (`INSERT`, `UPDATE`, or `DELETE`). If the `inverse="false"` attribute is set on a one-to-many relationship, the column of the target will be updated. If `inverse="false"` is set on a many-to-many association, the association table will be updated.

Conversely, Hibernates ignores changes made to the association set to `inverse="true"`.

This can be somewhat confusing, but once you understand that the `inverse="false"` side is responsible for managing a relationship, there are just a few simple guidelines to follow.

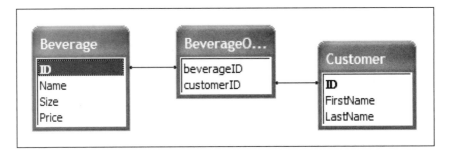

Figure 7.4.   Choosing the Inverse Side

If you are using a one-to-many/many-to-one bi-directional relationship, the many-to-one side will be responsible for managing the relationship (and therefore the one-to-many side should be set to `inverse="true"`). For example, in the example shown in Chapter 2, the `Author` side of the bi-directional relationship is set to `inverse="true"`. This means that Hibernate ignores changes to the `Author` object's set of posts. For performance reasons, this is virtually always the correct model.

The choice of `inverse="true"` and `inverse="false"` is really only complex in a bi-directional many-to-many relationship (i.e., when Hibernate handles a collection table is handled under the covers). In this situation, the rule of thumb is that `inverse="false"` should be set for the side of the relationship with the smallest number of elements changed the most frequently. For example, consider the relationship shown in Figure 7.4.

Assuming that the list of beverages (i.e., the `Beverage` table) is relatively small and static, but that the customers are numerous and place many orders, you should model this many-to-many relationship by setting the mapping of the `Beverage` collection to `inverse="true"` and the `Customer` side to `inverse="false"`.

Queries

Hibernate supports a wide variety of options for retrieving objects from a database. These include the Hibernate Query Language (HQL), the Criteria API, and ordinary Structured Query Language (SQL).

In this chapter, we will take a look at each of these three retrieval mechanisms, and conclude with a mechanism for storing HQL and SQL queries directly in your `*.hbm.xml` mapping files.

HQL

The first thing you should know about HQL is that it is exclusively a query language. Unlike SQL, which offers statements of different forms for `SELECT`, `UPDATE`, `DELETE`, and `INSERT`, HQL is designed exclusively for retrieval. As a result, the syntax is most similar to the `SELECT` statement. There is no such thing as HQL for updating or inserting data, and the exact same HQL can be used for both `SELECT` and `DELETE` operations.

Some of the examples in Chapter 3 and Chapter 4 give an introduction to the use of HQL, and the methods for executing HQL are shown in Chapter 6. Nonetheless, HQL is most easily explored in the context of the Hibern8 IDE, a simple tool for executing HQL statements on the fly in a graphical environment.

Using Hibern8 IDE

The Hibern8 IDE is distributed with the Hibernate Extensions package. To use it, simply launch it using the command `java net.sf.hibern8ide.Hibern8IDE` (found in the `hibern8ide.jar`), with the class path set to include the various required Hibernate and Hibernate Extensions libraries as well as the persistent classes used by your application. Launching Hibern8 IDE will display the interface shown in Figure 8.1.

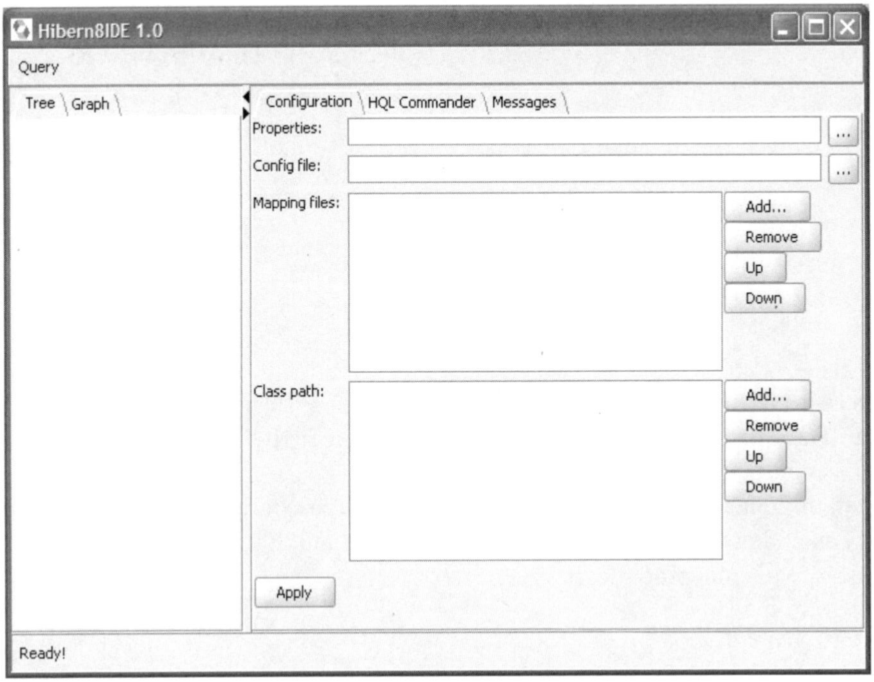

Figure 8.1.   Starting Hibern8 IDE

To establish the Hibernate configuration, click on the `...`   button next to either the `Properties` field (to select a `hibernate.properties` file) or the `Config File` field (to select a `hibernate.cfg.xml` file).

Click the Add button to add one or more `*.hbm.xml` mapping files. After adding all of the needed files, click the Apply button.

Using the `hibernate.properties` and `*.hbm.xml` files and classes from Chapter 3, Hibern8 IDE will look as shown in Figure 8.2.

Clicking on the HQL Commander tab, you can drag and drop objects or object properties from the left-side object display to the HQL entry field so that Hibern8 IDE can automatically generate HQL for you. Pressing control-enter will cause Hibern8 IDE to execute the HQL and display the results. Figure 8.3 shows an example of retrieving the `artifact.id` values.

Hibern8 IDE allows you to inspect the values of returned results, tunneling in through the returned object hierarchy. Figure 8.4 shows an example of this, allowing you to see in detail the objects returned by a request.

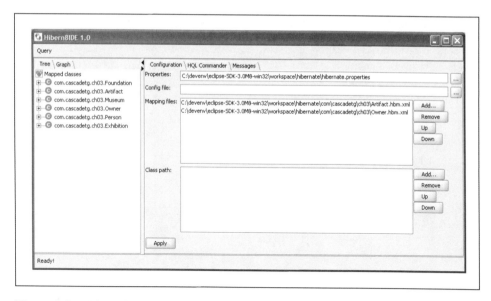

Figure 8.2. Hibern8 IDE Configured

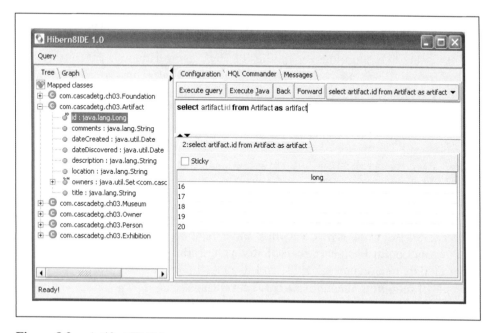

Figure 8.3. Artifact ID Values

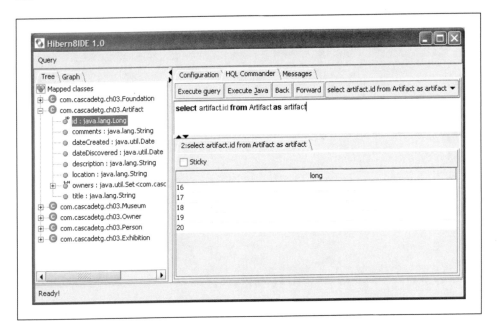

Figure 8.4.   Inspecting Hibern8 IDE Results

As described in Chapter 9, you can use Hibern8 in conjunction with a tool like IronTrack SQL to easily monitor the SQL generated by a given HQL statement. This can be very useful as you experiment with HQL using Hibern8.

It is easy to explore the capabilities of HQL using Hibern8, but to truly take advantage of Hibernate you need to understand the structure of HQL in more detail. You are encouraged to work through this reference in conjunction with Hibern8 and the various mapping files in the rest of the book to fully understand HQL.

HQL Reference

```
[select] from [where] [group by] [having] [order by];
```

This section serves as a road map for understanding the HQL syntax. It can be used to diagram a HQL statement, much as you diagram a sentence in English (circling the noun, the verb, etc.).

A HQL command is composed of several clauses, as shown above. The `from` clause is the only portion of a query that is mandatory. For example, the simple command `from com.cascadetg.ch03.Owner` will return all of the `owner` table records as `Owner` objects.

The `select` clause is used to limit the returned data to specific properties or to control the format for the returned data. It will be used to return either an aggregate value (e.g., the number of records returned) or a subset of the data (e.g., just the first name of the student objects).

The `from` clause is used to widen the returned data to additional classes. The tables used are as determined by the class mappings (defined by your `*.hbm.xml` files). HQL requires at least one class to form the basis of the query. If you wish to use more than one table, you may have to use join statements (described below) to control how the tables are returned.

The `where`, `group by`, and `having` clauses are used to cull the data returned. You can use a combination of logical expressions and Boolean expressions to compose your `where` clause. In addition, you can use collection commands to work with collections in your where statements.

The `order by` clause is used to sort the returned data.

Notation Reference

The clauses given below are expected to be formatted with a particular set of tokens. The format of this HQL guide is based on the notation shown in Table 8.1.

This reference uses uppercase to indicate HQL terms, but in actual use HQL terms are case-insensitive.

Obviously, HQL uses some of the symbols shown in Table 8.1. Parentheses, for example, are used to indicate precedence in HQL queries as well as in the notation. Therefore, the tokens in Table 8.2 should be translated to these terms when writing actual HQL queries.

Note that the path elements are case-sensitive. For example, `select owner from Owner as owner` and `SELECT owner FROM Owner AS owner` are equivalent, whereas `SELECT FROM OWNER` is invalid (because `OWNER` doesn't match the case of the name Owner given in the mapping file).

Table 8.1 HQL Grammar Notation

`[ ... ]`	Indicates an optional term.
`( ... )`	Indicates a grouping of terms.
`...	...`	Indicates that one side or the other of the | is expected.
`*`	Indicates that zero, one, or many terms are expected.
`?`	Indicates that zero or one terms expected.
`UPPERCASE`	Used to indicate an expected token.
`lowercase`	Used to indicate additional text, as specified by another clause or some other text.

Table 8.2   HQL Grammar Symbols

Notation	Symbol
COMMA	,
OPEN	(
CLOSE	)
OPEN_BRACKET	[
CLOSE_BRACKET	]
CONCAT	||
PLUS	+
MINUS	–
DIV	/
STAR	*
path	An identifier to a particular class or property

Select

```
SELECT DISTINCT? selectedPropertiesList | ( NEW className OPEN
selectedPropertiesList CLOSE );
```

The optional `distinct` keyword can be used to reduce the result set to unique results (no result is returned more than once). This can be useful when you wish to limit the results. For example, the statement `select student.id from Student as student, Student as student2` returns the full product of every record in the `Student` table as matched with every other student record (literally, the records in the `student` table multiplied by the records in the `student` table). The `distinct` keyword can be used to limit these results back to the individual student records. For example, the statement `select distinct student.id from Student as student, Student as student2` will return the same results as a `from Student`.

If one or more properties (`selectedProperties`) are specified, the query will return them as mapped to objects. For example, the HQL `select owner.id, owner.name from com.cascadetg.ch03.Owner as owner` will return a set of `java.lang.Long` and `java.lang.String` objects.

Instead of specifying that the properties should be returned as a set of different objects, you may wish to use the `new className` statement instead. This will return an arbitrary class, calling the constructor as the result of a query. For example, the HQL command `select new java.lang.StringBuffer (owner.name) from Owner as owner` returns a set of `java.lang.StringBuffer` objects, initialized with the `owner.name` property.

Selected Properties List

```
( path | aggregate ) ( COMMA path | aggregate )*
```

The properties returned by a SELECT statement can be either a set of properties or an aggregate function. For example, the HQL `select max(result .score), min(result.score) from Examresult as result` is valid, as is `select result from Examresult as result`. The statement `select result, max(result.score), min(result.score) from Examresult as result`, however, is NOT valid.

Aggregate

```
COUNT OPEN path CLOSE
SUM OPEN path CLOSE
AVG OPEN path CLOSE
MAX OPEN path CLOSE
MIN OPEN path CLOSE
COUNT OPEN STAR CLOSE
COUNT OPEN DISTINCT | ALL path CLOSE
```

The aggregate functions are used to return statistical data on a set of records rather than the records themselves.

- `avg(path)` calculates the mean average value.
- `count(*)` returns the number of items in a group, including null values and duplicates.
- `count(ALL path)` returns the number of non-null values.
- `count(DISTINCT path)` returns the number of unique, non-null values.
- `max(path)` finds the maximum value.
- `min(path)` finds the minimum value.
- `sum(path)` adds the values specified.

Collection Properties

```
( OPEN query CLOSE ) | ( 'elements'|'indices' OPEN path CLOSE )
```

Collections have several special properties in addition to the obvious properties that are dependent on the type of collection. All collections can refer to the `elements` property, which is simply a result of all the possible objects.

For example, `select student.examresults.elements.score from com.cascadetg.ch04.Student as student` returns the `score` values from the `examresult` table as `java.lang.Integer`, where `examresult.studentID` is bound to a valid `student.id`.

As another example, `select student.examresults.elements from com.cascadetg.ch04.Student as student` returns the set of examresult records, bound as `com.cascadetg.ch04.Examresult`.

Table 8.3 shows the various collection properties.

You can extend the path of a collection past the `elements` property. For example, the statement `select student.examresults.elements.score from Student as student` returns the scores of the student as `java.lang.Integer` objects.

From

```
FROM className AS? identifier (  ( COMMA className AS? identifier
) | ( joinType classname AS? identifier ) )*
```

The `from` clause is used to identify the source of the data to be returned. The tables are specified by the `classname` (`com.cascadetg.ch04.Student`, or just by `Student` if the `auto-import` attribute of the `hibernate-mapping` tag is set to true as described in Chapter 5.

An identifier must be assigned to the class for queries that need to refer to a class property. For example, `com.cascadetg.ch04.Student` is typically assigned an identifier such as `student`. This identifier is required in order to refer to the class in other clauses of the query. For example, `select first-`

Table 8.3   Collection Properties

Property	Meaning
elements	The objects in the collection.
indices	The index values of the collection (only available if the collection is indexed; see Chapter 7).
size	The size of the collection. Useful if you wish to know the number of associated objects without fetching the entire collection.
maxIndex	The maximum index value (only available if the collection is indexed).
minIndex	The minimum index value (only available if the collection is indexed).
maxElement	The element corresponding to the maximum index value (only available if the collection is indexed).
minElement	The element corresponding to the maximum index value (only available if the collection is indexed).
index [...]	Used to find elements in an indexed collection. The expression inside the [ ] tokens is evaluated to determine the resulting elements against the index.

```
mysql> select * from student;
+----+-----------+----------+-------------+
| ID | firstName | lastName | idString    |
+----+-----------+----------+-------------+
|  1 | Bob       | Smith    | 123-45-6789 |
|  2 | John      | Stevens  | 456-78-9012 |
|  3 | Betty     | Almara   | 098-76-5432 |
+----+-----------+----------+-------------+
3 rows in set (0.00 sec)
```

Figure 8.5. Student Data

`Name from Student` is invalid HQL; the valid statement would be `select student.firstName from Student as student`.

The identifier is particularly useful when you are writing a complex query that needs to refer to the same table with two different meanings; for example, if you wish to join a class against itself.

The `AS` token is optional, but some prefer it to enhance readability. The statements `select owner from Owner as owner` and `select owner from Owner owner` are equivalent.

The values of the `joinType` token are as shown below.

Join Types

```
( ( 'left'|'right' 'outer'? ) | 'full' | 'inner' )? JOIN FETCH?
```

The join syntax is used to control the product of the result of joining two tables together. To consider the results of the various types of join, let's start with a bit of data as shown in Figures 8.5 and 8.6.

```
mysql> select * from examresult;
+----+-------+-----------+--------+
| ID | score | studentID | examID |
+----+-------+-----------+--------+
|  1 |    85 |         1 |      1 |
|  2 |    89 |         2 |      1 |
|  4 |    75 |         1 |      2 |
|  5 |    83 |         2 |      2 |
+----+-------+-----------+--------+
4 rows in set (0.01 sec)
```

Figure 8.6. Exam Result Data

Looking at the data, we see that there are three students, but only students 1 and 2 have actually taken any exams. Joins allow us to glue together the data items from Figure 8.5 and Figure 8.6 in different ways to obtain different results (the heart of the notion of a relational database).

WARNING

Some databases do not support all of the various forms of join supported by Hibernate. Try to avoid being too clever with your joins if possible. Even if the join works, make sure that it performs well. See Chapter 10 for more information on managing performance.

Inner Join

From basic SQL, we know that the query `select result, student from Student as student, Examresult as result` will result in a multiplied set of returned data, as shown in Figure 8.7. This is what is referred to as an inner join.

A `where` clause is used to cull the data down. The statement `select result, student from Student as student, Examresult as result where result.student=student` restricts our query to the students who have taken exams, as shown in Figure 8.8.

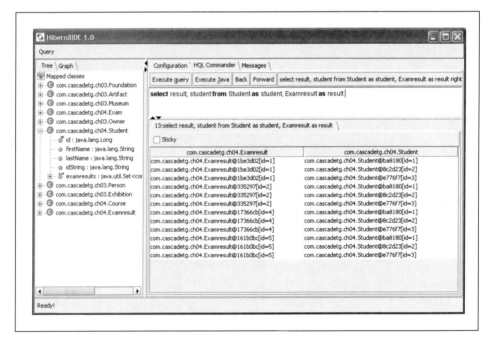

Figure 8.7.   Unrestricted Inner Join Results

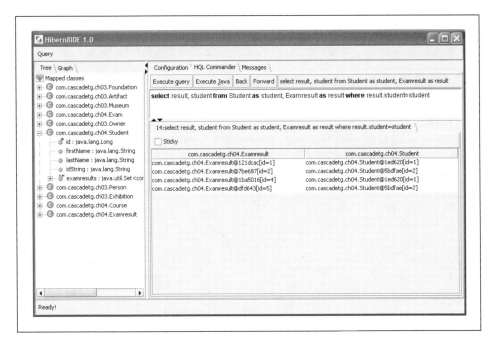

Figure 8.8. Bound Inner Join Results

Inner joins are the most basic form of join, and the easiest to understand.

Left/Right Joins

Now, imagine that we wish to retrieve all of the students even if they haven't taken a test—in other words, return the records even of a student for whom there are no `examresult` records. We have to use an outer join to retrieve all of the records. Outer joins come in two flavors, right join and left join. The use of the right or left term depends on the table you wish to use as the "master" table.

The statement `select result, student from Student as student, Examresult as result right join result.student joinedstudent where student=joinedstudent` returns all the students, including the student with a null examresult as shown in Figure 8.9.

The join is performed and retrieves all of the records from the student table, even though the record may not be present in the right table (the student table). In effect, you are asking for all records from the right table, in this case student, even if there are no corresponding entries present in the `examresult` table.

Conversely, using the left join statement instead, as in `select result, student from Student as student, Examresult as result left join result.student joinedstudent where student= joinedstudent` returns the joined records from the perspective of the

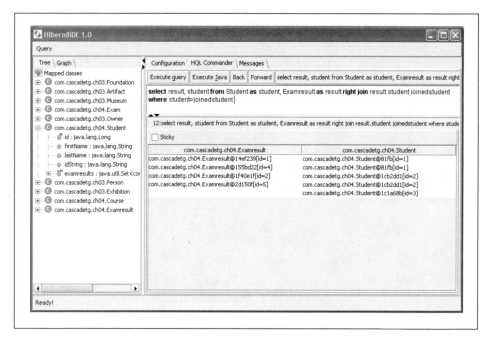

Figure 8.9.   Right Outer Join

examresult table (the left table), as shown in Figure 8.10. In effect, you are asking for all of the records in the examresult table, even if not present in the student table. As there are no records in the examresult table that do not point to a student (that would be a foreign-key violation), you simply get the exam results.

Full Joins

A full join will return all records from both tables, regardless of any matches between the tables. Note that this command is not supported on all databases (in particular, MySQL doesn't offer support for the full join command).

Outer as Inverse of Inner

It's worth pointing out that you may be specifically seeking the records that do not match a regular join. For example, you may only be interested in the students who haven't taken an exam. To perform this query, you can use the `is null` modifier, as in `select result, student from Student as student, Examresult as result right join result.student joinedstudent where student=joinedstudent and result is null`, which produces the results shown in Figure 8.11.

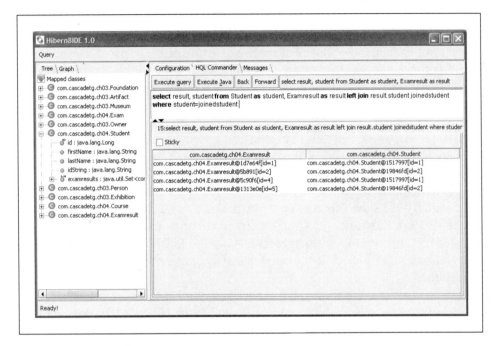

Figure 8.10.   Left Outer Join

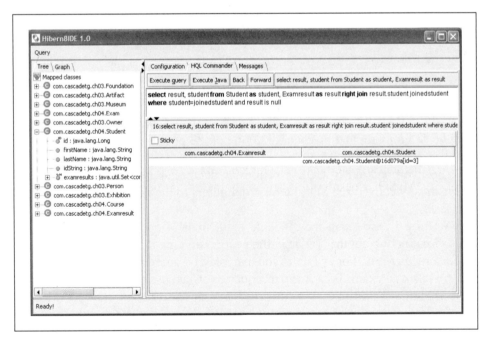

Figure 8.11.   Using an Outer Join to Obtain the Inverse of an Inner Join

Fetch Joins

The fetch join is a useful shortcut used to fetch parent and child objects in a single select. For example, the statement `select student from Student as student left join fetch student.examresults` returns all of the students and their `Examresult` objects, regardless of whether the `student` has any associated exam results. If there are any `examresults`, they are already loaded into `Examresult` objects, associated with the `Student` object (accessible via the `Student.getExamresults()` method. If you know that you will be reading the exam results of the student objects, but have the exam result relationship set to lazy by default, this is an excellent way to retrieve all of the needed data in a single statement.

Similarly, the statement `select distinct student from Student as student inner join fetch student.examresults` retrieves the student objects with an exam record. As in the left join fetch, the `Student` and `Examresult` objects are loaded, but only students with an `Examresult` are returned.

The `fetch` statement may only be used as an inner join or a left outer join.

As of the release of Hibernate Extensions-2.1, the Hibern8 IDE does not support the fetch statement. To test fetch joins, you'll need to use the HQL in your own sample code.

Where

```
WHERE expression
```

The `where` clause is used to cull the set of returned rows.

A huge variety of possible expressions, some of them database-dependent, are allowed in a WHERE clause. Regardless of the expression, parentheses ( ) are used to indicate grouping and precedence. Some of the possible elements in a `where` clause are shown in Table 8.4.

The interpretation of SQL functions is database-dependent. Hibernate will automatically convert the SQL literal ' delimiters to the proper characters for the database.

A `where` expression may include mathematical operations, logical operations, boolean operations, or a quantified expression (in SQL terms, a subselect).

Logical Operations

Two logical operations are commonly used in a `where` statement.

The `and` operator requires both sides to evaluate to true, otherwise it evaluates to false.

Table 8.4   Where Operations

Element	Examples
Mathematical operators	`+, -, *, /`
Binary comparison operators	`=, >=, <=, <>, !=, like`
Logical operations	`and, or`
String concatenation	`||`
JDBC IN parameters	`?`
Named parameters	`:name, :start_date, :x1`
SQL scalar functions	`upper(), lower()`
SQL literals	`'foo', 69, '1970-01-01 10:00:01.0'`
Java public static final constants	`java.lang.Integer.MAX_VALUE`

The `or` operator evaluates both sides. If either side evaluates to true, it will return true; otherwise it evaluates to false.

For example, the statement `select student from Student as student where student.id=1 or student.id=3` will return two records, with an id of 1 and 2.

Boolean Operations

Table 8.5 lists the boolean operations supported by the majority of databases.

When using the like and ilike statements, the % (percent) character is used as a multiple-character wildcard, and the _ (underscore) character is used to indicate a single character. For example, the statement `select student.firstName from Student as student where firstName like '_ob'` returns the value Bob. The statement `select student.firstName from Student as student where firstName like 'B%'` returns Bob and Betty.

The tokens #, ~, !#, !~, =>, =<, !<, and !> are reserved by Hibernate as boolean operators but have no meaning in standard SQL. The meaning of these tokens (if any) is database-dependent. Consult your database manual for more information.

Quantified Expression

```
'exists' | ( expression 'in' ) | ( expression OPERATION 'any' |
'some' ) collection
```

Valid options for `OPERATION` are `like`, =, <, >, <>, !=, ^=, <=, and >=.

Table 8.5 Boolean Operations

Operator	Meaning	Inverse
`!=`	Is not equal	`=`
`<`	Less than	`>=`
`<=`	Less than or equal	`>`
`<>`	Is not equal	`=`
`=`	Equals	`!= or <>`
`>`	Greater than	`<=`
`>=`	Greater than or equal	`<`
`between`	Inclusive query (used with the and operator). For example, `select student from Student as student where id between 1 and 3` will return students 1, 2, and 3.	`not between`
`ilike (case-insensitive)`	Case-insensitive like (not supported on all databases).	`not ilike`
`in`	Used to limit in conjunction with a collection. Alternatively, used in statements like select student from `Student as student where first Name in` ('Bob', 'John').	`not in`
`is`	Used for queries such as `is null` or `is not null`	`is not`
`is not`	Used as part of the `is not null`	`is`
`like`	Like	`not like`
`not between`	Reverse of between	`between`
`not ilike (case-insensitive)`	Reverse of ilike	`llike`
`not in`	Reverse of in	`in`
`not like`	Reverse of like	`like`

A qualified expression is an HQL mechanism for expressing a SQL subselect of a collection. A subselect describes using the results of a `SELECT` statement as part of the `WHERE` clause of another statement—in effect, a nested select. The subselect must return a single column, which is compared against an expression using an operation. The evaluation of this operation determines whether the resulting record should be returned. A subselect is described by the term `any`, `some`, `all`, `exists`, or `not exists`.

any	`some` or `any` returns true when the comparison specified is true for any of the values returned by the subselect (typically a collection column). Imagine a subselect that returns the numbers 1 through 10. Therefore, the statement `5 < any` (subselect expression) would evaluate to true.

some	Synonym for any.
all	Returns true when the comparison specified is true for all pairs (scalar_expression, x) where x is a value in the single-column set; otherwise returns false. Imagine a subselect that returns the numbers 1 through 10. Therefore, the statement 5 < any (subselect expression) would evaluate to false, because some of the results of the subselect are greater than or equal to 5.
exists	Returns true if the subselect matches elements from the select.
not exists	Reverse of exists.

Parameter Binding

When working with a WHERE clause, you may be tempted to include constants directly in the string. For example, you may wish to use a string such as select student from Student as student where firstName='Bob'. Instead, you are advised (and in some instances required) to use parameter binding. HQL supports two styles of parameter binding, JDBC and named. JDBC uses the ? character to indicate bindings, and named uses the : character to preface a named parameter substitution.

Use the Session and Query classes to set parameters, as described in Chapter 6. Listing 8.1 shows an example of the use of a named parameter.

Listing 8.1   Named Parameter Binding

```
Query myQuery = hibernateSession.
 createQuery("from Student as student where student.firstName =
  :name");
myQuery.setString("name", "Bob");
Iterator students = myQuery.iterate();
```

Listing 8.2 shows an example of the use of a JDBC-style bound parameter. *Note that the parameters are set based on an index of 0, not 1.*

Listing 8.2   JDBC Parameter Binding

```
Query myQuery = hibernateSession.
 createQuery("from Student as student where student.firstName =
  ?");
myQuery.setString(0, "Bob");
Iterator students = myQuery.iterate();
```

Group By

```
GROUP BY path ( COMMA path )*
```

The command `GROUP BY` is used to restrict the results to a single result per table. This command is useful in a variety of situations, such as when you are using aggregate functions. For example, the command `select   student, max(result.score) from Student as student, Examresult as result where student=result.student group by student` returns a set of students and the corresponding `java.lang.Integer` value for each student's high score.

Having

```
HAVING expression
```

A `HAVING` clause is used in the same way as a `WHERE` clause except for one key difference. `WHERE` selects rows before the groups and aggregates are calculated, whereas `HAVING` selects rows after the groups and aggregates have been calculated.

In practice, there is no reason to use a `HAVING` clause unless the `HAVING` clause has an aggregate function (otherwise, it's equivalent to a `WHERE` clause). Unfortunately, certain databases (such as MySQL) don't support an aggregate in the `HAVING` clause. For those databases, `HAVING` and `WHERE` are the same.

Order By

```
ORDER_BY selectedPropertiesList (ASC | DESC)?
```

The `order  by` command allows you to specify the order in which the data should be returned, as performed by the database. By default, the values are sorted in ascending (ASC) order. This order can be reversed using the DESC token.

As an example, the statement `select student from Student as student order by student.firstName` returns the students sorted by first name, starting with the letter A, whereas the statement `select student from Student as student order by student.firstName desc` returns the students starting with the letter Z.

The ordering is performed by the database, and the precise results are dependent on its sorting mechanisms.

Criteria Queries

Hibernate supports the Criteria API, an object-based query mechanism that constructs a query from a set of objects. The Criteria API is perhaps best understood in the context of an ordinary HQL statement, as described earlier in this chapter.

HQL Clause	Criteria Equivalent[s]
`select`	Not available
`from`	`Criteria criteria = session.create` `Criteria(Student.class);`
`from joins`	`Criteria.setFetchMode()` for associations.
`where`	`net.sf.hibernate.expression.Expression` to obtain built-in `net.sf.hibernate.expression.Criterion`
`group by`	Not available
`having`	Not available
`order by`	`Criteria.addOrder()` to add `net.sf.hibernate` `.expression.Order`

The Criteria interface, as shown in Figure 8.12, is returned by a simple `Session.createCriteria()` call.

Normally, you will use the `Expression` factory, as shown in Figure 8.13, to obtain a criterion that you wish to apply.

Figure 8.14 shows the hierarchy of built-in criteria. Normally, you won't instantiate these directly, and instead will use the built-in Expression factory.

The code shown in Listing 8.3 returns the same result set as the HQL `select student.firstName from Student as student where student.firstName like 'B%'`.

Listing 8.3 Criteria Query

```
Criteria myQuery =
        hibernateSession.createCriteria(Student.class);
myQuery.add(Expression.like("firstName", "B%"));
```

Method Chaining

In addition to the standard method execution shown in Listing 8.3, the Criteria API supports the notion of method chaining. Simply put, most of the methods on the Criteria interface return the calling object (i.e., they conclude with the statement

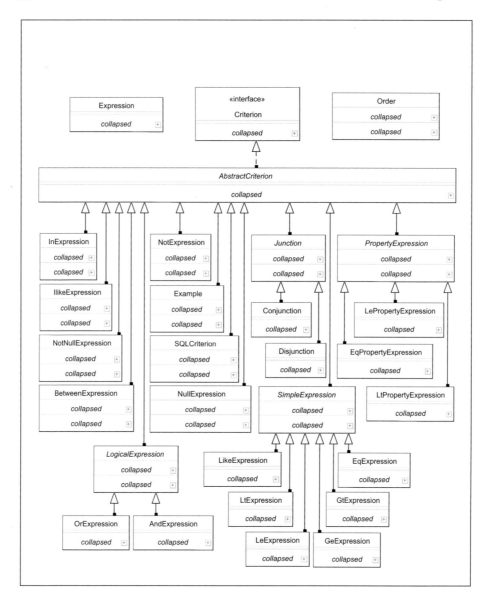

Figure 8.12.   Criteria Interface

Figure 8.13. Expression Factory

`return this`). This allows you to rewrite the code shown in Listing 8.3 as shown in Listing 8.4.

Listing 8.4 Chained Criteria Query

```
Criteria myQuery =
    hibernateSession.createCriteria(Student.class).add(
        Expression.like("firstName", "B%"));
```

As can be seen, this may lead to different (but equivalent) ways of expressing more complex statements. For example, the code shown in Listing 8.5 is equivalent to the code in Listing 8.6.

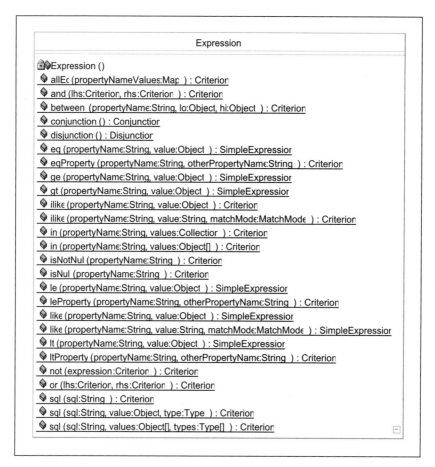

Expression
Expression ()
allEq (propertyNameValues:Map) : Criterion
and (lhs:Criterion, rhs:Criterion) : Criterion
between (propertyName:String, lo:Object, hi:Object) : Criterion
conjunction () : Conjunction
disjunction () : Disjunction
eq (propertyName:String, value:Object) : SimpleExpression
eqProperty (propertyName:String, otherPropertyName:String) : Criterion
ge (propertyName:String, value:Object) : SimpleExpression
gt (propertyName:String, value:Object) : SimpleExpression
ilike (propertyName:String, value:Object) : Criterion
ilike (propertyName:String, value:String, matchMode:MatchMode) : Criterion
in (propertyName:String, values:Collection) : Criterion
in (propertyName:String, values:Object[]) : Criterion
isNotNull (propertyName:String) : Criterion
isNull (propertyName:String) : Criterion
le (propertyName:String, value:Object) : SimpleExpression
leProperty (propertyName:String, otherPropertyName:String) : Criterion
like (propertyName:String, value:Object) : SimpleExpression
like (propertyName:String, value:String, matchMode:MatchMode) : SimpleExpression
lt (propertyName:String, value:Object) : SimpleExpression
ltProperty (propertyName:String, otherPropertyName:String) : Criterion
not (expression:Criterion) : Criterion
or (lhs:Criterion, rhs:Criterion) : Criterion
sql (sql:String) : Criterion
sql (sql:String, value:Object, type:Type) : Criterion
sql (sql:String, values:Object[], types:Type[]) : Criterion

Figure 8.14. Built-in Criteria Hierarchy

Listing 8.5 Complex Criteria

```
Criteria myQuery =
                hibernateSession.createCriteria(Student.class);
myQuery.add(Expression.like("firstName", "B%"));
myQuery.add(Expression.like("lastName", "S%"));
myQuery.setFetchMode("examresults", FetchMode.EAGER);
myQuery.setMaxResults(10);
myQuery.setTimeout(1000);
```

Listing 8.6 Complex Criteria with Method Chaining

```
Criteria myQuery =
    hibernateSession
        .createCriteria(Student.class)
        .add(Expression.like("firstName", "B%"))
        .add(Expression.like("lastName", "S%"))
        .setFetchMode("examresults", FetchMode.EAGER)
        .setMaxResults(10)
        .setTimeout(1000);
```

In certain instances, the more verbose method shown in Listing 8.5 is easier to understand and debug, but the choice of syntax is largely a matter of style.

Easily Override Lazy Settings

One helpful use of the Criteria API is the ability to easily override a `lazy="true"` setting in a Hibernate mapping with the use of the `setFetchMode()` method. For example, as shown in Listing 8.6, the method `setFetchMode()` overrides the `lazy="true"` setting in the Student mapping of the `examresults` collection.

Put another way, the `setFetchMode()` is a convenient way to express an HQL join statement.

Native SQL Queries

In addition to HQL and Criteria, Hibernate allows you to retrieve data from the database using native SQL. Describing SQL would go beyond the scope of this text, but it should be noted here that Hibernate requires aliases to be used when working with native SQL. The aliases are used to bind the SQL to the returned objects. Listing 8.7 shows an example of the execution of a native SQL statement binding to the return objects.

Listing 8.7 Executing Native SQL

```
session.createSQLQuery("SELECT {student.*} FROM student AS
{student}
WHERE ID<10", "student", Student.class).list();
```

If you simply wish to execute raw SQL against the database (and not retrieve a set of objects bound to a query), you will probably need to query the session for the underlying JDBC connection. An example of the use of raw SQL execution from a Hibernate session can be found in Listing 2.7 (the `setInnoDB()` method).

Keep in mind that SQL statements mixed with other statements may not execute in the order desired unless you use the `Session.flush()` method. For more on this, see Chapter 9.

The full scope and theory of SQL is beyond the scope of this book (especially considering the wide variety of proprietary extensions). Consult your database documentation or another text on SQL for more information on native SQL queries.

CHAPTER **9**

Transactions

This chapter explains transactions and a somewhat related topic, locking. Both of these features require database support, but are critical for ensuring data integrity.

Introduction to Transactions

A transaction is a mechanism for grouping a set of statements together as a unit. A transaction should be atomic, consistent, independent, and durable (ACID). Depending on the application, this capability can be extremely important.

As an example of the importance of a transaction's ACID properties, consider the elements of a bank transaction. Let's say that you wish to move money from a checking account into a savings account, using the conceptual tasks:

- Verify that checking account has more than $100.
- Remove $100 from checking account.
- Add $100 to savings account.

These three statements should be thought of as comprising one transaction, and therefore a failure in any of the three steps means that all of them should be ignored. For example, a failure to add $100 to the savings account means that the $100 should not be removed from the checking account.

This leads to a key aspect of any transaction. A transaction can be started and then either committed if there are no problems or rolled back if there is a problem. A transaction that is rolled back should have no impact on the data in the database.

Hibernate supports transactions, but does not actually provide the transaction implementation. Typically, this functionality is provided by the underlying database. To enable this functionality, the `hibernate.transaction.factory_class.` property should be set to `net.sf.hibernate.transaction.JDBCTransactionFactory`. Before relying on JDBC transactions, you should check your database's documentation for more information about transaction support.

JTA SUPPORT

In addition to JDBC transactions, Hibernate also supports the use of JTA. To use JTA, set the `hibernate.transaction.factory_class` to `net.sf.hibernate.transaction.JTATransactionFactory`. You will also need to set the JTA transaction manager to the appropriate provider, as described in Chapter 6, Table 6.6.

As a general guide, your environment may require the use of JTA if you are accessing multiple databases or have complex transactions spanning multiple systems (for example, distributed objects using EJB), but it may add significant overhead if you are not.

For more information on JTA, see your application server's documentation.

Sessions, Transactions, and Flushing

Hibernate uses several terms to describe the logical phases of database interaction. Figure 9.1 illustrates the relationship between a session, a transaction, and a flush.

A session is a lightweight object, representing a JDBC connection.

A transaction represents an ACID unit of work (with the precise meaning dependent on the underlying database and/or transaction manager).

A flush statement may be used to indicate a specific ordering of the execution of a set of SQL. Certain session methods will cause a flush to occur automatically:

- Certain calls to `Session.find()` or `Session.iterate()`
- `net.sf.hibernate.Transaction.commit()`
- `net.sf.hibernate.Session.flush()`

Unless a `Session.flush()` statement is used to override the statement ordering, Hibernate will execute SQL statements in the following order:

1. Entity insertions

2. Entity updates

3. Collection deletions

4. Collection element deletions, updates, and insertions

5. Collection insertions

6. Entity deletions

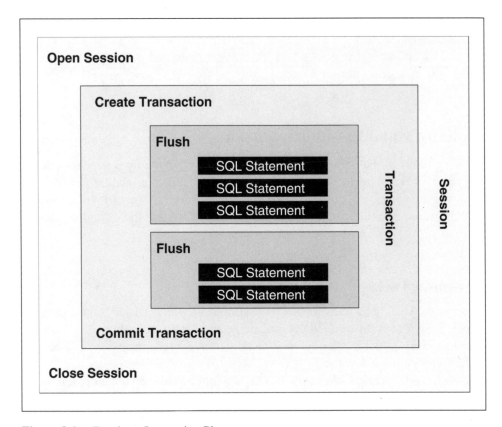

Figure 9.1. Database Interaction Phases

Within each of these broad operational types, the SQL is executed in the same order in which the method calls are made. For example, consider the following operations:

- `Session.update(object1);`
- `Session.delete(object2);`
- `Session.update(object3);`

When Hibernate translates these operations into SQL, it will first issue SQL to UPDATE the `object1` and `object3` records, and then DELETE the `object2` record.

Under certain circumstances, Hibernate may optimize the generated SQL. In most cases this is the most desirable (and best-performing) behavior, but there are situations (for example, if you have certain database triggers) in which it might be preferable to use a `Session.flush()` statement to ensure the proper execution of statements.

An exception is that the `Session.save()` method is called when objects using `native` generator are inserted.

Optimistic and Pessimistic Locking

Locking refers to the notion that changes to a record made by one person should not overwrite changes made by someone else. Strategies for dealing with this fall into two categories. Pessimistic locking assumes that every record will be subject to contention; optimistic locking assumes that conflicts are the exception, not the rule.

Pessimistic Locks

Pessimistic locking is used to denote a system in which an individual user can check out a record. It is called pessimistic because it assumes the worst-case scenario in every possible transaction—namely, that every transaction will conflict unless a strict monitor is used.

With a pessimistic lock, users may or may not be able to view or edit a record until the lock is released. To support this style of lock, the database must support pessimistic locking. Obtaining and releasing of locks on specific rows of a table can be managed with the `net.sf.hibernate.LockMode` class in conjunction with certain methods of `Session`. For example, you can use the method `session.load(object, type, LockMode.UPGRADE)` for explicit pessimistic locking. While pessimistic locking can be useful in some circumstances the application must take great care to avoid locking objects for an unnecessarily long time. In addition, care must be taken to release every lock at the right time, or else the record will become unavailable for a lengthy period.

Optimistic Locks

Optimistic locking refers to the notion that "checking out" an object and applying changes are two independent steps. For example, consider the post system described in Chapter 2. A single record is used to store a post. A user at work downloads the original version of the post into his or her Swing client and makes some changes, thereby creating version two of the post. The user leaves for home without saving the changes. At home, the user opens the same post, makes a different set of changes, and then saves the post data. This becomes version three.

The next morning, the user returns to the Swing client and clicks "save post" on version two of the document.

VERSION CONTROL LOCKING

If you have ever used a version control system, you've seen one of these two strategies in action. For example, Microsoft Visual SourceSafe uses a pessimistic system in which locks are explicitly managed by the developer (but conflicts are impossible), and CVS uses an optimistic system with no locks (but occasionally requiring merges to deal with conflicts).

If the developer had chosen pessimistic locking, the record would have been locked when checked out by the Swing client, and the user would not have been able to save the changes at home (generally speaking, pessimistic locking is easier for the developer, but frustrating for users). Optimistic locking, in contrast, refers to the fact that we "optimistically" assume that no changes are made between when the record is read and when the record is updated. This is only a problem if a "secret" change is made (in the example above, version two).

The user experience for resolving an optimistic conflict will vary depending on the application. In the example given above, when the user clicks "save post" for version three, we probably would like to notify the user that the record has been updated since the last viewing. Ideally, we'd want to let the user compare versions and select the preferred version (as shown in Chapter 2). If the application is an elaborate one, it may even provide a mechanism for merging changes. Listing 9.1 shows an excerpt of the code given in Chapter 2. Note how the `net.sf.hibernate.StaleObjectStateException` is caught to manage the pessimistic conflict.

Listing 9.1 Handling an Optimistic Conflict

```
try
{
      hibernateSession = AppSession.getSession();
      myTransaction = hibernateSession.beginTransaction();

      myPost = new Post();
      myPost.setId(request.getParameter("postID"));
      myPost.setRevision(
            new Integer(
```

(continues)

Listing 9.1   Handling an Optimistic Conflict (*continued*)

```
                        request.getParameter("revision"))
                            .intValue());
        myPost.setTitle(request.getParameter("title"));
        myPost.setDate(new java.util.Date());
        myPost.setSummary(request.getParameter("summary"));
        myPost.setContent(request.getParameter("content"));

        Author myAuthor = new Author();
        myAuthor.setId(request.getParameter("authorID"));
        myPost.setAuthor(myAuthor);

        hibernateSession.update(myPost);

        myTransaction.commit();
        hibernateSession.close();

        redirect_page =
            redirect_page +
                request.getParameter("postID");
        done = true;
    }
    catch (net.sf.hibernate.StaleObjectStateException stale)
    {
        error =
        "This post was updated by another " +
        "transaction. You may either update " +
        "the existing data, or resubmit ";
        "your changes.";
        conflict=true;
    }
    catch (Exception e) {
        error = e.getMessage(); e.printStackTrace();
        try{ myTransaction.rollback(); }
        catch (Exception e2) {;}
    }
    finally
    {
        try{hibernateSession.close();}
        catch (Exception e) {;}
    }
```

Hibernate supports several different models for detecting this sort of versioning conflict (or optimistic locks). The *versioning* strategy uses a version column in the table. You can use either a `version` property tag or a `timestamp` property tag to indicate a version column for the class (see the appropriate tag for more information). When a record is updated, the versioning column is automatically updated as well. This versioning strategy is generally considered the best way to check for changes—both for performance and for compatibility with database access that occurs outside of Hibernate. For example, you can simply issue a SELECT to obtain a record by id, and include the version column in the WHERE clause to indicate the specific record you wish to UDPATE; a failure to update is an easy way to detect that the record is not properly synchronized. This is precisely the functionality as provided by the StaleObjectException. An example of the versioning strategy (and a user interface for managing conflicts) is shown in Chapter 2.

The *dirty* strategy only compares the columns that need to be updated. For example, let's say you load a Cat object, with a name ("Tom"), weight, and color. You change the name to "Bob" and want to save the change. Hibernate will verify that the current Cat name is "Tom" before updating the name to "Bob." This is computationally intensive compared to the versioning strategy, but can be useful in situations in which a version column is not feasible.

The *all* strategy compares all the columns, verifying that the entire Cat is as it was when loaded before saving. Using the Cat example in the preceding paragraph, Hibernate will verify that the name, weight, and color are as loaded before persisting the change to the name. While more secure than the dirty strategy, this strategy, too, is more computationally intensive.

Finally, the *none* strategy can be used to ignore optimistic locking. Updated columns are updated, period. This obviously performs better than any other strategy but is likely to lead to problems if you have more than a single user updating related records.

Generally speaking, I recommend using the versioning strategy to manage conflicts if at all possible. The pessimistic model, unless very carefully managed, can lead to more problems than it solves, and the dirty and all mechanisms are not very high-performance. Also, don't go overboard with versioning—the likelihood of contention is quite low if a resource is owned by only a single user.

CHAPTER **10**

Performance

When you begin experimenting with Hibernate, one of the first tasks you are likely to perform is the installation of a monitor to see the generated SQL. This is especially important if you want to understand how Hibernate generates SQL for such features as collections and lazy loading of data. This chapter describes how to gather performance metrics for the use of Hibernate in the field.

Finding and Solving Problems

Hibernate affords a basic SQL monitoring capability, but for real development you are best advised to use a tool with a bit more sophistication. By definition, every interaction between your application and the database is translated through a JDBC driver. A pass-through driver is used to analyze the data. The pass-through driver does not change the data, but records all of the interaction for analysis. In this section, we will look at the pass-through JDBC driver p6spy and the use of IronTrack SQL to understand the data it generates.

IronTrack SQL

IronTrack SQL is an open-source Apache-licensed tool that works in conjunction with the p6spy driver monitor. Using p6spy (included with IronTrack SQL), every interaction between the application and the database is logged. IronTrack SQL, in turn, allows you to view these generated logs (either at runtime via TCP/IP or by opening generated log files).

Configuring IronTrack SQL

IronTrack SQL can be downloaded free from http://www.irongrid.com/. You will obtain a file with a name such as `irontracksql-installer-1_0_172.jar`. Once you have saved this file to your system, you can install it

Figure 10.1.   Starting IronTrack SQL Installation

with the command `java   -jar   irontracksql-installer-1_0_`
`172.jar`. The installer will launch, presenting a language screen, as shown in
Figure 10.1.

You can accept the defaults throughout the installation, although you may
wish to specify a shorter, alternative destination path for the installation, as shown
in Figure 10.2, because you will be placing libraries present in the installation in
your application path.

If you are using an application server, the precise installation process for Iron-
Track SQL varies (see http://www.irongrid.com/documentation/). To use Iron-
Track with a standalone application, you will need to place the following files on
your class path:

```
ironeyesql.jar
p6spy.jar
```

Next, you will need to update your Hibernate.properties to point to the p6spy
driver (or whatever mechanism you are using to specify JDBC connectivity). You
will observe that the line with the default driver has been commented out with a #
character, not deleted. The log files generated by p6spy can become quite large

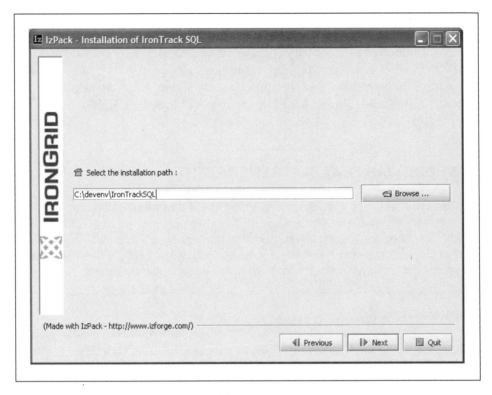

Figure 10.2. Alternative Installation Directory

(especially with full logging and stack trace tracking turned on). Therefore, you'll want to keep your standard driver class close at hand for when you wish to switch to production use. Listing 10.1 shows the Hibernate properties that should be set to make use of p6spy.

Listing 10.1 Configuring p6spy Properties

```
#hibernate.connection.driver_class=com.mysql.jdbc.Driver
hibernate.connection.driver_class=com.p6spy.engine.spy.
P6SpyDriver
hibernate.connection.url=jdbc:mysql://localhost/hibernate
hibernate.connection.username=root
hibernate.connection.password=
hibernate.dialect=net.sf.hibernate.dialect.MySQLDialect
hibernate.show_sql=false
```

Finally, you will need to place a `spy.properties` file in your class path (typically next to your `hibernate.properties`). This file is used to configure the logging produced by p6spy. You should start by copying the `spy.properties` file included with the IronTrack SQL distribution. The most important thing is to set the `spy.properties` to use the correct driver, as in `realdriver=com.mysql.jdbc.Driver`.

After changing these configuration options, simply run your application as you normally would. The default p6spy options will log every SQL statement to a log file (`spy.log`) in the application root directory.

WHERE WAS THAT SQL GENERATED?

p6spy will generate a stack trace pointing to the class that generated a SQL statement if you set `stacktrace=true` in the `spy.properties` file. This will slow your application down, because generating a stack trace is expensive, but it can be very helpful if you are working with a large, unfamiliar application and are having trouble tracking down a particular statement.

Using IronTrack SQL

If you are running your application in a long-lived environment (for example, in the context of an application server), you can use the IronTrack SQL graphical user interface to view your data at runtime via TCP/IP. Alternatively, you can simply load the generated `spy.log` file. This would be appropriate if your application runs and then terminates (as do several of the examples in this book) or, to cite another example, if you are unable to connect to the server via TCP/IP (perhaps due to a firewall installed on the server).

You may have a shortcut already created that can launch IronTrack SQL. If not, you can launch IronTrack SQL from the command line with the command `java -jar irontracksql.jar`. Once you've launched the IronTrack SQL interface, you can either connect to a running application via TCP/IP or you can import a generated log file. Figure 10.3 shows IronTrack SQL launched, with the Import... command selected.

To view the generated log files, you'll need to change the Files of Type option to `spy.log` files, as shown in Figure 10.4.

IronTrack allows you to sort and filter the loaded SQL statements. For example, Figure 10.5 shows the results of a run of the sample application shown in Chapter 3. As can be seen, the `ALTER TABLE` statements are relatively expensive, but so are our `INSERT` statements.

Clicking the Graphing tab on the IronTrack SQL main interface allows us to see a graph of the generated SQL statements. As shown in Figure 10.6, the load on the server can be viewed at different points in time (useful for identifying certain operations that may be highly performance intensive).

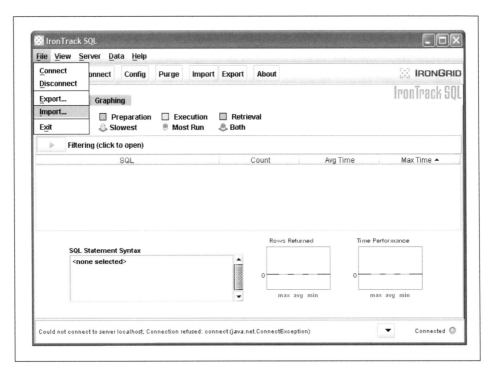

Figure 10.3. IronTrack SQL Import

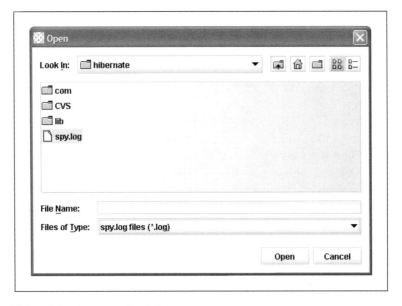

Figure 10.4. Selecting a spy.log File

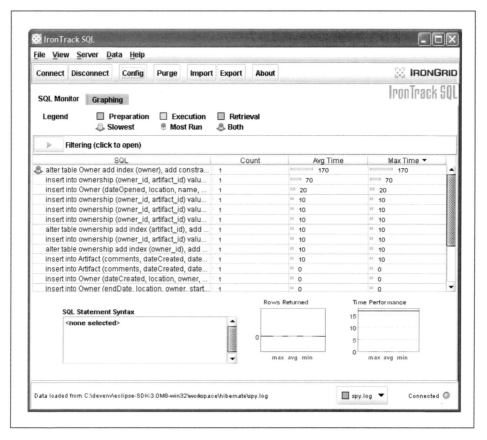

Figure 10.5.   Viewing SQL Statements

Queries

You may wish to use Hibern8 IDE and IronTrack SQL in conjunction to test the SQL generated by your HQL queries. Simply launch the Hibern8 IDE as described in Chapter 8, specifying `hibernate.properties` with the p6spy configuration, as shown in Listing 10.1.

After loading the first `*.hbm.xml` file, you can connect to the Hibern8 IDE instance with the IronTrack SQL monitor via TCP/IP. Assuming that you are using the default configuration values and are running your application on your local system, you will then be able to connect to the Hibern8 IDE instance and see real-time results of your HQL—both the generated SQL and the resulting timing information.

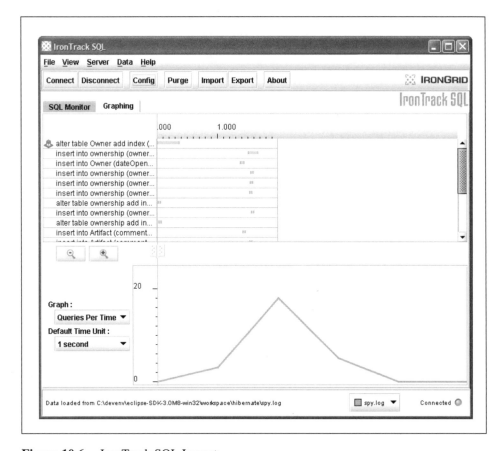

Figure 10.6. IronTrack SQL Import

When using Hibern8 IDE and IronTrack SQL in conjunction, you may obtain better results if you disable your cache and connection pool settings.

Two areas are of special interest in regard to query performance—lazy objects and collections.

Lazy Objects

When designing your application, you should generally default to `lazy="true"` whenever possible, and then tune your application to ensure that your queries return the object set as needed (see the `class` tag in Chapter 5 for more information).

As shown in Chapter 8, it's easy to write a query that uses the `fetch` outer join command to have Hibernate automatically load the child objects of a collection that has been marked `lazy="true"`. Thus the rule of thumb should be: only

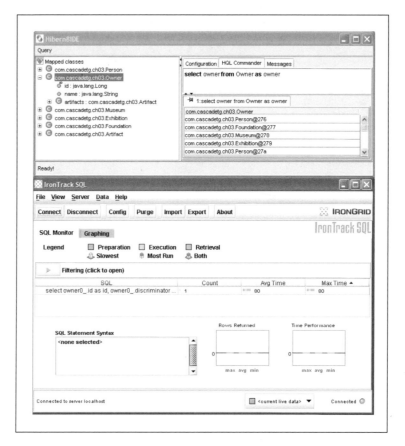

Figure 10.7.   Real-Time HQL Testing

use `lazy="false"` if you expect to actually need access to the collection on every possible read.

This is likely to be an area of some confusion when you start working with Hibernate. For example, given a teacher -> student relationship, if `lazy="false"`, loading the teacher will load the entire class. Similarly, if `lazy="true"` and the students aren't pre-fetched by a `fetch` statement (or the `Criteria.setFetchMode()`), iterating through the teacher's student list will generate a new SQL `SELECT` statement for each student.

Collections

Many of the performance issues pertaining to collections derive from the semantic collision between what most developers think of as a collection and the actual contracts of a collection. For example, duplicates are not allowed when you are inserting a value into a set, so when adding a new element, Hibernate needs to at least know the primary-key identifier(s). Similarly, for a map, the keys need to be loaded to ensure the proper ordering. The index values must be known for a list (and other indexed collections). The only collection that doesn't have any of these rules is bag, but it offers poor performance when loading data.

After reading the rules regarding collections, you may find that it would be better (or even required) to model your data with a class declared for the collection table, an example of which is shown in Chapter 4. In this case, instead of letting Hibernate to manage the collection for you behind the scenes using the collections contracts, you are free to implement your own queries and retrieval policies.

An area of special interest when working with collections is the extent to which outer joins (as described in Chapter 8) and lazy fetching are used to optimize performance. You can use the `lazy="true"` attribute (as described above and in Chapter 5) to reduce the amount of collection data returned and various outer joins to control the results more carefully, as described in Chapter 8.

Inserts

Bulk inserts of data are a type of operation best **not** performed by Hibernate. For example, a user may have 100,000 records that have to be imported into a single table. Don't use Hibernate for this sort of operation—use your database's built-in import tools instead. The built-in import will be faster than Hibernate (or, for that matter, handwritten JDBC).

If, for some reason, you do need to do a bulk import via Hibernate, take account of the following tips:

- Make sure the `hibernate.jdbc.batch_size` option (specified in your `hibernate.properties`, as described in Chapter 6) is turned on and set to a reasonably large value.

- Consider `Session.commit()` on to break up the transactional overhead. Presumably you will do this only if you are very confident that it will succeed.

- Make sure that you call `Session.close()` it or `Session.clear()` after each call to `Session.commit()`. Otherwise, Hibernate will attempt to maintain the inserted object in the session-level cache.

- Consider the `seqhilo` or `assigned` generator to optimize key generation.

Connection Pooling

Opening a connection to a database is generally much more expensive than executing an SQL statement. A connection pool is used to minimize the number of connections opened between application and database. It serves as a librarian, checking out connections to application code as needed. Much like a library, your application code needs to be strict about returning connections to the pool when complete, for if it does not do so, your application will run out of available connections.

STARVING A POOL

When using connection pooling, it is important to remember that a chunk of bad code that neglects to return connections can starve the rest of the application, causing it to eventually run out of connections and hang (potentially failing nowhere near the actual problem). To test for this, set the maximum connections in your pool to a small number (as low as 1), and use tools like p6spy and IronTrack SQL (described above) to look for statements that fail to close.

This problem can be avoided by **always** using a `finally` block to close your connection, as shown throughout this book.

Hibernate supports a variety of connection pooling mechanisms. If you are using an application server, you may wish to use the built-in pool (typically a connection is obtaining using JNDI). If you can't or don't wish to use your application server's built-in connection pool, Hibernate supports several other connection pools, as shown in Table 10.1.

STATEMENT CACHE

Certain connection pools, drivers, databases, and other portions of the system may provide an additional cache system, known as a statement cache. This cache stores a partially compiled version of a statement in order to increase performance. By reusing the parsed or precompiled statement, the application is able to trade an increase in memory usage for a boost in performance.

You should consider using a statement cache if one is available, but keep in mind that a statement cache is not the same thing as the other forms of caching described later in this chapter.

Table 10.1. Hibernate-Supported Connection Pools

c3p0	http://sourceforge.net/projects/c3p0	Distributed with Hibernate
Apache DBCP	http://jakarta.apache.org/commons/dbcp/	Apache Pool
Proxool	http://proxool.sourceforge.net/	JDBC Pooling Wrapper

The choice of a connection pool is up to you, but be sure to remember that a connection pool is necessary for every production use.

If you wish to use c3p0, the version distributed with Hibernate 2.1.2 (0.8.3) is out of date (and GPL is a problem if you wish to distribute a non-GPL application). If you wish to distribute an application that makes use of c3p0, make sure to download the latest (LGPL) release, `c3p0-0.8.4-test1` or later.

Because Hibernate ships with c3p0, configuration is a simple matter of adding a few Hibernate configuration properties to your `hibernate.properties` (or `hibernate.cfg.xml`) file. Listing 10.2 shows an example of the configuration of c3p0.

Listing 10.2 Sample Hibernate c3p0 Configuration

```
hibernate.connection.driver_class=com.mysql.jdbc.Driver
hibernate.connection.url=jdbc:mysql://localhost/hibernate
hibernate.connection.username=root
hibernate.connection.password=
hibernate.dialect=net.sf.hibernate.dialect.MySQLDialect
hibernate.show_sql=false

hibernate.c3p0.max_size=1
hibernate.c3p0.min_size=0
hibernate.c3p0.timeout=5000
hibernate.c3p0.max_statements=100
hibernate.c3p0.idle_test_period=300
hibernate.c3p0.acquire_increment=2
hibernate.c3p0.validate=false
```

The properties shown in Listing 10.2 are as described in Table 10.2.

If you prefer to use Apache DBCP, make sure that the Apache DBCP library is on your class path, and add the properties to your hibernate.properties file, as shown in Table 10.3.

Finally, if you wish to use Proxool as your connection pool provider, you will need to specify `hibernate.properties` values as shown in Table 10.4.

Table 10.2.   c3p0 Configuration Options

Property Meaning	Property	Example
Maximum number of database connections to open	`hibernate.c3p0.max_size`	15
Initial number of database connections	`hibernate.c3p0.min_size`	3
Maximum idle time for a connection (in seconds)	`hibernate.c3p0.timeout`	5000
Maximum size of c3p0 statement cache (0 to turn off)	`hibernate.c3p0.max_statements`	0
Number of connections in a clump acquired when pool is exhausted	`hibernate.c3p0.acquire_increment`	3
Idle time before a c3p0 pooled connection is validated (in seconds)	`hibernate.c3p0.idle_test_period`	300
Validate the connection on checkout. Recommend setting the `hibernate.c3p0.idle_test_period` property instead. Defaults to `false`	`hibernate.c3p0.validate`	`true | false`

Unlike c3p0 and DBCP, you will need to include additional configuration options as described at http://proxool.sourceforge.net/configure.html.

Caching

So you've got a performance problem, and you're pretty sure that it lies in a bottleneck between your database and your application server. You've used IronTrack SQL or some other tool to analyze the SQL sent between your application and the database, and you're pretty sure that there isn't much advantage to be squeezed from refining your queries. Instead, you feel certain that the problems are due to the amount of traffic between your application and the database. The solution in this case may be a cache. By storing the data in a cache instead of relying solely on the database, you may be able to significantly reduce the load on the database, and possibly to increase overall performance as well.

Understanding Caches

Generally speaking, anything you can do to minimize traffic between a database and an application server is probably a good thing. In theory, an application ought to be able to maintain a cache containing data already loaded from the database, and only hit the database when information has to be updated. When the database is hit, the changes may invalidate the cache.

Table 10.3. Apache DBCP Configuration Options

Property Meaning	Property	Example
Maximum number of checked-out database connections	`hibernate.dbcp` `.maxActive`	8
Maximum number of idle database connections for connection pool	`hibernate.dbcp` `.maxIdle`	8
Maximum idle time for connections in connection pool (expressed in ms). Set to -1 to turn off	`hibernate.dbcp.max` `Wait`	-1
Action to take in case of an exhausted DBCP connection pool. Set to 0 to fail, 1 to block until a connection is made available, or 2 to grow)	`hibernate.dbcp` `.whenExhaustedAction`	1
Validate connection when borrowing connection from pool (defaults to `true`)	`hibernate.dbcp.test` `OnBorrow`	true | false
Validate connection when returning connection to pool (optional, true, or false)	`hibernate.dbcp.test` `OnReturn`	true | false
Query to execute for connection validation (optional, requires either `hibernate.dbcp.testOn` `Borrow` or `hibernate.dbcp` `.testOnReturn`)	`hibernate.dbcp` `.validationQuery`	Valid SQL SELECT statement (e.g., SELECT 1+1)
Maximum number of checked-out statements	`hibernate.dbcp.ps` `.maxActive`	8
Maximum number of idle statements	`hibernate.dbcp.ps` `.maxIdle`	8
Maximum idle time for statements (in ms)	`hibernate.dbcp.ps` `.maxWait`	1000 * 60 * 30
Action to take in case of an exhausted statement pool. Set to 0 to fail, 1 to block until a statement is made available, or 2 to grow)	`hibernate.dbcp.ps` `.whenExhaustedAction`	1

FIRST-LEVEL AND SECOND-LEVEL CACHES

Hibernate actually implements a simple session-level cache, useful on a per-transaction basis. This cache is primarily used to optimize the SQL generated by Hibernate. It is sometimes referred to as a first-level Hibernate cache. For more information on the relationship between a session and the underlying SQL, see Chapter 9.

(continues)

Table 10.4.   Proxool Configuration Options

Property Meaning	Property	Example
Configure Proxool provider using an XML file	`hibernate.proxool.xml`	`/path/to/` `file.xml`
Configure the Proxool provider using a properties file `.properties`	`hibernate.proxool` `.properties`	`/path/` `to/proxool`
Configure the Proxool provider from an existing pool	`hibernate.proxool` `.existing_pool`	`true | false`
Proxool pool alias to use (required for `hibernate.proxool` `.existing_pool,` `hibernate.proxool` `.properties, hibernate` `.proxool.xml)`	`hibernate.proxool` `.pool_alias`	As set by Proxool configuration

> The JVM and distributed cache discussed in this section is referred to as a second-level cache in other sources. Since you will never need to configure the first-level cache, the discussion in the rest of this chapter will refer to the second-level cache simply as "the cache."

Let's start by looking at Hibernate without a cache, as shown in Figure 10.8. Data is transferred between Hibernate and the database, and transactions are managed by the database. Hibernate assumes that the data in memory should be refreshed on every access (a reasonable assumption, especially if Hibernate does not have exclusive access to the database).

Figure 10.9 shows Hibernate operating with a single JVM cache used to minimize traffic between Hibernate and the database. This will increase the perfor-

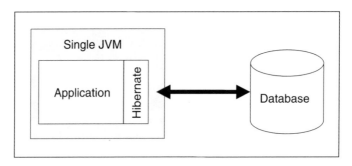

Figure 10.8.   Hibernate without a Cache

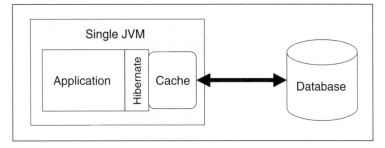

Figure 10.9. Hibernate with a Cache

mance of the application and minimize the load on the database, but at the cost of a bit more configuration complexity (described later in this chapter) and memory usage.

You may wonder how to use Hibernate to perform multithreaded object access and begin pondering strategies for sharing persistent objects across threads. The short answer is: don't! Instead, if you are interested in sharing object data across threads, simply use a cache, as shown in Figure 10.9. If you try to implement your own, the odds are good that you'll have to implement a complex, difficult-to-manage set of thread management, only to end up with cache and concurrency problems.

Figure 10.10 illustrates a problem that may arise when you use a cache. If your application does not have exclusive access to the database (a common situation in

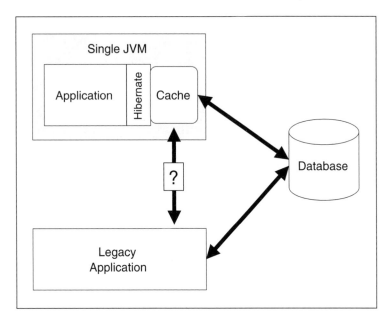

Figure 10.10. Hibernate and a Legacy System

an enterprise environment), your cache can easily become out of sync with the database. If a legacy application updates a record stored in the cache, there is no notification that the data is stale, and therefore the data in the cache will be incorrect.

MULTIPLE SESSIONFACTORY OBJECTS

A JVM cache, as described here, is actually a `SessionFactory`-level cache (see Chapter 9 for more information on the scope of a `Session Factory`). There is normally no reason not to share a `SessionFactory` instance throughout your JVM instance, but if for some reason your application uses more than one `SessionFactory`, you're effectively building a multiple JVM system, and therefore will need to use a distributed cache.

Similarly, if you have multiple JVMs running on a single physical system, that still counts as a distributed system.

Unfortunately, there is no ideal solution to the problem of distributed object cache in conjunction with a legacy system. If your Hibernate application has a read-only view of the database, you may be able to configure some cache system to periodically expire data.

If you are able to control all the access to a particular database instance, you may be able to use a distributed cache to ensure that the data traffic is properly synchronized. An example of this is shown in Figure 10.11. Take care when choosing a distributed cache to ensure that the overhead of the cache traffic does not overwhelm the advantages of the cached data.

As a final note, keep in mind that a distributed cache is only one of several possible solutions to a performance problem. Some databases, for example, support an internal distribution mechanism, allowing for the distribution complexity to be entirely subsumed by the database infrastructure (thereby letting the application continue to treat a multisystem database as a single data source).

Configuring a Cache

Applications that perform a large number of read operations in relation to the number of write operations generally benefit the most from the addition of a cache.

The type of cache that would be best depends on such factors as the use of JTA, transaction isolation-level requirements, and the use of clusters. Because of their broad possible needs and uses, Hibernate does not implement caches, but instead relies on a configurable third-party library.

Table 10.5. Supported Cache Environments

Cache	Type	URL
EHCache (Easy Hibernate Cache)	In Process	http://ehcache.sourceforge.net/
OSCache (Open Symphony)	In Process OR Cluster	http://www.opensymphony.com/oscache/
SwarmCache	Cluster	http://swarmcache.sourceforge.net/
JBoss TreeCache	Cluster	http://jboss.org/wiki/Wiki.jsp?page= JBossCache

Standard Caches

In addition to the open-source caches described above, you may wish to investigate Tangosol Coherence, a commercial cache. For more information, see http://hibernate.org/132.html and http://tangosol.com/.

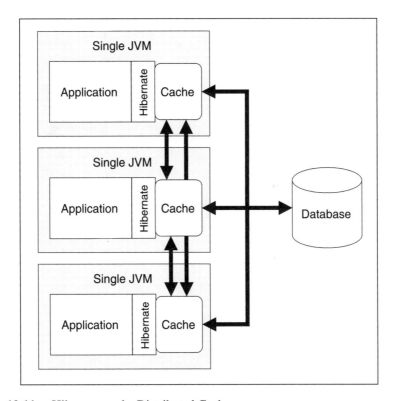

Figure 10.11. Hibernate and a Distributed Cache

Table 10.6 shows the proper setting for the `hibernate.cache` `.provider_class` property to be passed via the `hibernate.proper-` `ties` file to enable the use of a cache.

Each cache offers different capabilities in terms of memory and disk-based cache storage and a wide variety of possible configuration options.

Regardless of which cache you choose, you will need to tell Hibernate what sort of cache rules should be applied to your data. This is defined using the `cache` tag (as described in Chapter 5). You can place the `cache` tag in your `*.hbm.xml` files or in the `hibernate.cfg.xml` file. Alternatively, you can configure cache settings programmatically using the `Configuration` object. Table 10.7 shows the values allowed for the `usage` attribute of the `cache` tag.

Conceptually, you are using the options in Table 10.7 to set the per-table read-write options for your data.

Some providers do not support every cache option. Table 10.8 shows which options the various providers support.

JAVA TRANSACTION API (JTA)

According to Sun's documentation, JTA "specifies standard Java interfaces between a transaction manager and the parties involved in a distributed transaction system: the resource manager, the application server, and the transactional applications." In other words, JTA provides for transactions that span multiple application servers—a powerful capability for scaling. Covering JTA is beyond the scope of this text (see http://java.sun.com/products/jta/), but you may wish to consult Chapter 9 for more information on transactions.

Table 10.6. Specifying a Cache

Cache	Property Value
EHCache (Easy Hibernate Cache)	`net.sf.ehcache.hibernate.Provider` (default)
OSCache (Open Symphony)	`net.sf.hibernate.cache.OSCacheProvider`
SwarmCache	`net.sf.hibernate.cache.Swarm` `CacheProvider`
JBoss TreeCache	`net.sf.hibernate.cache.TreeCache` `Provider`
Custom (User-Defined)	Fully qualified class name pointing to a `net.sf` `.hibernate.cache.CacheProvider` implementation

Table 10.7. Cache Options

Option	Comment
read-only	Only useful if your application reads (but does not update) data in the database. Especially useful if your cache provider supports automatic, regular cache expiration. You should also set `mutable=false` for the parent class/collection tag (see Chapter 5).
read-write	If JTA is not used, ensure that `Session.close()` or `Session.disconnect()` is used to complete all transactions.
nonstrict-read-write	Does not verify that two transactions will not affect the same data; this is left to the application.
	If JTA is not used, ensure that `Session.close()` or `Session.disconnect()` is used to complete all transactions.
transactional	Distributed transaction cache.

Using a Custom Cache

Understanding the interaction between a cache and your application can be very difficult. To help make it clearer, we have included below an example cache implementation that generates logging and statistics about your application's use of the cache (as generated by Hibernate).

Needless to say, don't use this custom cache in a production system.

Configuring the Custom Cache

For this test application, set the property `hibernate.cache` `.provider_class=com.cascadetg.ch10.DebugHashtableCache` `Provider` in your `hibernate.properties` file.

Table 10.8. Cache Options Supported by Provider

Cache	read-only	nonstrict-read-write	read-write	transactional
EHCache	Yes	Yes	Yes	
OSCache	Yes	Yes	Yes	
SwarmCache	Yes	Yes		
JBoss TreeCache	Yes			Yes

Custom Cache Provider

Listing 10.3 shows the options for our simple cache provider. Note that the statistical details are tracked for the allocated caches.

Listing 10.3 Custom Cache Provider

```
package com.cascadetg.ch10;

import java.util.Hashtable;

public class DebugHashtableCacheProvider implements
        net.sf.hibernate.cache.CacheProvider
{

    private static Hashtable caches = new Hashtable();

    public static Hashtable getCaches()
    {
        return caches;
    }

    public static String getCacheDetails()
    {
        StringBuffer newResult = new StringBuffer();
        java.util.Enumeration myCaches = caches.keys();
        while (myCaches.hasMoreElements())
        {
            String myCacheName = myCaches.nextElement()
                    .toString();
            newResult.append(myCacheName);
            newResult.append("\n");

            DebugHashtableCache myCache = (DebugHashtableCache)
                caches.get(myCacheName);

            newResult.append(myCache.getStats());
            newResult.append("\n\n");
        }

        return newResult.toString();
    }

    /** Creates a new instance of DebugHashtable */
    public DebugHashtableCacheProvider()
    {
    }
```

Listing 10.3   Custom cache provider (*continued*)

```
public net.sf.hibernate.cache.Cache buildCache(String str,
        java.util.Properties properties)
{
    System.out.println("New Cache Created");
    DebugHashtableCache newCache = new
        DebugHashtableCache();
    caches.put(str, newCache);
    return newCache;
}

public long nextTimestamp()
{
    return net.sf.hibernate.cache.Timestamper.next();
}
}
```

Custom Cache Implementation

Listing 10.4 shows the implementation of our simple cache. It's a pretty dumb cache—it just uses a `java.util.Hashtable` as the backing store. Of more interest is the use of `long` values to keep track of the number of accesses to the various cache methods. This can be useful for understanding the kind of access a section of code is generating. For example, you may wish to consider a different approach if your code generates a tremendous number of reads relative to writes.

Listing 10.4   Custom Cache Implementation

```
package com.cascadetg.ch10;

import net.sf.hibernate.cache.CacheException;
import net.sf.hibernate.cache.Timestamper;
import java.util.Hashtable;
import java.util.Map;
import org.apache.commons.logging.Log;
import org.apache.commons.logging.LogFactory;

public class DebugHashtableCache implements
        net.sf.hibernate.cache.Cache
{

    private static Log log = LogFactory
            .getLog(DebugHashtableCache.class);
```

(continues)

Listing 10.4   Custom Cache Implementation (*continued*)

```
private Map hashtable = new Hashtable(5000);

public void addStat(StringBuffer in, String label, long
value)
{
    in.append("\t");
    in.append(label);
    in.append(" : ");
    in.append(value);
    in.append("\n");
}

public String getStats()
{
    StringBuffer result = new StringBuffer();

    addStat(result, "get hits", get_hits);
    addStat(result, "get misses", get_misses);
    addStat(result, "put replacements", put_hits);
    addStat(result, "put new objects", put_misses);
    addStat(result, "locks", locks);
    addStat(result, "unlocks", unlocks);
    addStat(result, "remove existing", remove_hits);
    addStat(result, "remove unknown", remove_misses);
    addStat(result, "clears", clears);
    addStat(result, "destroys", destroys);

    return result.toString();
}

long get_hits = 0;

long get_misses = 0;

long put_hits = 0;

long put_misses = 0;

long locks = 0;

long unlocks = 0;

long remove_hits = 0;

long remove_misses = 0;
```

Listing 10.4   Custom Cache Implementation (*continued*)

```java
    long clears = 0;

    long destroys = 0;

    public Object get(Object key) throws CacheException
    {
        if (hashtable.get(key) == null)
        {
            log.info("get " + key.toString() + " missed");
            get_misses++;
        } else
        {
            log.info("get " + key.toString() + " hit");
            get_hits++;
        }

        return hashtable.get(key);
    }

    public void put(Object key, Object value)
            throws CacheException
    {
        log.info("put " + key.toString());
        if (hashtable.containsKey(key))
        {
            put_hits++;
        } else
        {
            put_misses++;
        }
        hashtable.put(key, value);
    }

    public void remove(Object key) throws CacheException
    {
        log.info("remove " + key.toString());
        if (hashtable.containsKey(key))
        {
            remove_hits++;
        } else
        {
            remove_misses++;
        }
        hashtable.remove(key);
    }
```

(*continues*)

Listing 10.4   Custom Cache Implementation (*continued*)

```
public void clear() throws CacheException
{
    log.info("clear ");
    clears++;
    hashtable.clear();
}

public void destroy() throws CacheException
{
    log.info("destroy ");
    destroys++;
}

public void lock(Object key) throws CacheException
{
    log.info("lock " + key.toString());
    locks++;
}

public void unlock(Object key) throws CacheException
{
    log.info("unlock " + key.toString());
    unlocks++;
}

public long nextTimestamp()
{
    return Timestamper.next();
}

public int getTimeout()
{
    return Timestamper.ONE_MS * 60000; //ie. 60 seconds
}

}
```

Cache Test Object

Listing 10.5 shows a simple mapping file used to test our object. In particular, note the use of the `cache` tag to indicate the type of cache management that should be performed.

Listing 10.5   Simple Performance Test Object Mapping File

```xml
<?xml version="1.0"?>

<!DOCTYPE hibernate-mapping PUBLIC
    "-//Hibernate/Hibernate Mapping DTD 2.0//EN"
    "http://hibernate.sourceforge.net/hibernate-mapping-
2.0.dtd">

<hibernate-mapping>
    <class name="com.cascadetg.ch10.PerfObject"
        dynamic-update="false" dynamic-insert="false">
        <cache usage="read-write" />

        <id name="id" column="id" type="long" >
            <generator class="native" />
        </id>

        <property name="value" type="java.lang.String"
            update="true" insert="true" column="comments" />
    </class>
</hibernate-mapping>
```

Listing 10.6 shows the source generated from the mapping file shown in Listing 10.5.

Listing 10.6   Simple Performance Test Object Java Source

```java
package com.cascadetg.ch10;

import java.io.Serializable;
import org.apache.commons.lang.builder.EqualsBuilder;
import org.apache.commons.lang.builder.HashCodeBuilder;
import org.apache.commons.lang.builder.ToStringBuilder;

/** @author Hibernate CodeGenerator */
public class PerfObject implements Serializable {

    /** identifier field */
    private Long id;

    /** nullable persistent field */
    private String value;

    /** full constructor */
```

(continues)

Listing 10.6   Simple Performance Test Object Java Source (*continued*)

```java
    public PerfObject(String value) {
        this.value = value;
    }

    /** default constructor */
    public PerfObject() {
    }

    public Long getId() {
        return this.id;
    }

    public void setId(Long id) {
        this.id = id;
    }

    public String getValue() {
        return this.value;
    }

    public void setValue(String value) {
        this.value = value;
    }

    public String toString() {
        return new ToStringBuilder(this)
            .append("id", getId())
            .toString();
    }

    public boolean equals(Object other) {
        if ( !(other instanceof PerfObject) ) return false;
        PerfObject castOther = (PerfObject) other;
        return new EqualsBuilder()
            .append(this.getId(), castOther.getId())
            .isEquals();
    }

    public int hashCode() {
        return new HashCodeBuilder()
            .append(getId())
            .toHashCode();
    }

}
```

Testing the Cache

Listing 10.7 shows a simple program that tests the cache. If you wish to test this using a larger number of objects, simply change `objects = 5` to a higher value.

Listing 10.7   Testing Cache Hits

```
package com.cascadetg.ch10;

/** Various Hibernate-related imports */
import java.io.FileInputStream;
import java.util.logging.LogManager;

import net.sf.hibernate.*;
import net.sf.hibernate.cfg.*;
import net.sf.hibernate.tool.hbm2ddl.SchemaUpdate;
import net.sf.hibernate.tool.hbm2ddl.SchemaExport;

public class CacheTest
{

    static long objects = 5;

    /** We use this session factory to create our sessions */
    public static SessionFactory sessionFactory;

    /**
     * Loads the Hibernate configuration information, sets up
     * the database and the Hibernate session factory.
     */
    public static void initialization()
    {
        System.out.println("initialization");
        try
        {
            Configuration myConfiguration = new
                Configuration();

            myConfiguration.addClass(PerfObject.class);

            new SchemaExport(myConfiguration).drop(true, true);

            // This is the code that updates the database to
            // the current schema.
```

(continues)

Listing 10.7   Testing Cache Hits (*continued*)

```
            new SchemaUpdate(myConfiguration)
                    .execute(true, true);
            // Sets up the session factory (used in the rest
            // of the application).
            sessionFactory = myConfiguration
                    .buildSessionFactory();

        } catch (Exception e)
        {
            e.printStackTrace();
        }
    }

    public static void createObjects()
    {
        System.out.println();
        System.out.println("createObjects");

        Session hibernateSession = null;
        Transaction myTransaction = null;
        try
        {
            hibernateSession = sessionFactory.openSession();

            for (int i = 0; i < objects; i++)
            {
                myTransaction = hibernateSession
                        .beginTransaction();

                PerfObject myPerfObject = new PerfObject();
                myPerfObject.setValue("");

                hibernateSession.save(myPerfObject);
                hibernateSession.flush();

                myTransaction.commit();
            }
        } catch (Exception e)
        {
            e.printStackTrace();
            try
            {
                myTransaction.rollback();
            } catch (Exception e2)
            {
                // Silent failure of transaction rollback
```

Listing 10.7   Testing Cache Hits (*continued*)

```
            }
        } finally
        {
            try
            {
                hibernateSession.close();
            } catch (Exception e2)
            {
                // Silent failure of session close
            }
        }

        // Explicitly evict the local session cache
        hibernateSession.clear();
    }

    public static void loadAllObjects()
    {
        System.out.println();
        System.out.println("loadAllObjects");

        Session hibernateSession = null;
        Transaction myTransaction = null;

        try
        {
            hibernateSession = sessionFactory.openSession();
            myTransaction =
                hibernateSession.beginTransaction();

            // In this example, we use the Criteria API. We
            // could also have used the HQL, but the
            // Criteria API allows us to express this
            // query more easily.

            // First indicate that we want to grab all of
            // the artifacts.
            Criteria query = hibernateSession
                    .createCriteria(PerfObject.class);

            // This actually performs the database request,
            // based on the query we've built.
```

(*continues*)

Listing 10.7   Testing Cache Hits (*continued*)

```
            java.util.Iterator results = query.list().iterator();

            PerfObject myPerfObject;

            // Because we are grabbing all of the artifacts and
            // artifact owners, we need to store the returned
            // artifacts.

            java.util.LinkedList retrievedArtifacts = new
                java.util.LinkedList();
            while (results.hasNext())
            {
                // Note that the result set is cast to the
                // Animal object directly - no manual
                // binding required.
                myPerfObject = (PerfObject) results.next();
                if (!retrievedArtifacts.contains(myPerfObject))
                        retrievedArtifacts.add(myPerfObject);

            }

            myTransaction.commit();
            hibernateSession.clear();
        } catch (Exception e)
        {
            e.printStackTrace();
            try
            {
                myTransaction.rollback();
            } catch (Exception e2)
            {
                // Silent failure of transaction rollback
            }
        } finally
        {
            try
            {
                if (hibernateSession != null)
                        hibernateSession.close();
            } catch (Exception e)
            {
                // Silent failure of session close
            }
        }
```

Listing 10.7   Testing Cache Hits (*continued*)

```
    }
    public static void main(String[] args)
    {
        initialization();
        createObjects();

        long timing = System.currentTimeMillis();
        loadAllObjects();
        System.out.println("Timing #1 : "
                + (System.currentTimeMillis() - timing));

        timing = System.currentTimeMillis();
        loadAllObjects();
        System.out.println("Timing #2 : "
                + (System.currentTimeMillis() - timing));

        timing = System.currentTimeMillis();
        loadAllObjects();
        System.out.println("Timing #3 : "
                + (System.currentTimeMillis() - timing));

        timing = System.currentTimeMillis();
        loadAllObjects();
        System.out.println("Timing #4 : "
                + (System.currentTimeMillis() - timing));

        timing = System.currentTimeMillis();
        loadAllObjects();
        System.out.println("Timing #5 : "
                + (System.currentTimeMillis() - timing));

        System.out.println(DebugHashtableCacheProvider
                .getCacheDetails());

    }
}
```

As can be seen from the output of the program shown in Listing 10.7, our simple application was able to cache the results from the first `loadAllObjects()` method, leading to lower timing values for the remaining access. This is reflected in the statistics for the cache, shown in terms of gets, puts, and so on.

Listing 10.8   Testing Cache Hits

```
initialization
New Cache Created

createObjects

loadAllObjects
Timing #1 : 40

loadAllObjects
Timing #2 : 10

loadAllObjects
Timing #3 : 0

loadAllObjects
Timing #4 : 10

loadAllObjects
Timing #5 : 0
com.cascadetg.ch10.PerfObject
        get hits : 20
        get misses : 5
        put replacements : 0
        put new objects : 5
        locks : 25
        unlocks : 25
        remove existing : 0
        remove unknown : 0
        clears : 0
        destroys : 0
```

CHAPTER **11**

Schema Management

One of Hibernate's most useful features is the automatic generation of schema manipulation commands. This feature, sometimes referred to as the ability to generate Data Definition Language (DDL) scripts, makes it possible (given a valid `*.hbm.xml` file) to create, update, and even drop tables in a target database. You can do this at runtime, during development, or via scripts generated for later use by a system administrator—an invaluable capability if you expect to support multiple target databases (during either development or deployment) or have a high degree of database schema change.

Hibernate supports two basic forms of DDL generation, **update** and **export**. Update is generally used within an application, targeting a specific database that may already contain a portion of the schema (and hence application data) but is missing schema components required by a new application. Export is used to generate the schema from scratch; it is especially useful if the application is not allowed to directly execute DDL (because, say, a database administrator is expected to perform these tasks).

Updating an Existing Schema

The tool `net.sf.hibernate.tool.hbm2ddl.SchemaUpdate` allows an application to bring a schema up to date with the expected schema based on a set of `*.hbm.xml` files. Typically, this is used to address a situation in which an incremental update to an application requires a relatively minor change, such as a new property.

Consider, for example, an application with a user object (and corresponding user table). You've decided to add a property to the user object to track the user's country code (previously the application only supported U.S. addresses). You make the change to your `*.hbm.xml` file and the corresponding Java code, and now would like to reflect the change in the deployed database. This can be done either from the command line, from an Ant task, or embedded within your application.

SchemaUpdate relies heavily on metadata returned by a database driver to understand the existing schema. For this reason, the ability of SchemaUpdate to operate properly can vary from driver to driver (and database to database). If you are unable to use SchemaUpdate with your preferred database, you may wish to use the SchemaExport tool (described later in this chapter) instead.

Schema Updates from within an Application

Listing 11.1 shows an example of SchemaUpdate embedded within an application. Note that a Configuration object is required, but a Session is not (obviously, you should perform any schema manipulation before working with the database).

Listing 11.1   SchemaUpdate Example

```
package com.cascadetg.ch11;

/** Various Hibernate-related imports */
import net.sf.hibernate.*;
import net.sf.hibernate.cfg.*;
import net.sf.hibernate.tool.hbm2ddl.SchemaUpdate;

public class SchemaUpdaterExample
{

    /** We use this session factory to create our sessions */
    public static SessionFactory sessionFactory;

    public static void main(String[] args)
    {
        initialization();
    }

    /**
     * Loads the Hibernate configuration information, sets up
     * the database and the Hibernate session factory.
     */
    public static void initialization()
    {
        System.out.println("initialization");
        try
```

Listing 11.1 SchemaUpdate Example (*continued*)

```
        {
            Configuration myConfiguration = new
                Configuration();

            myConfiguration
                    .addClass(com.cascadetg.ch03.Owner.class);
            myConfiguration
                    .addClass(com.cascadetg.ch03.Artifact
                        .class);

            // Load the *.hbm.xml files as set in the
            // config, and set the dialect.
            new SchemaUpdate(myConfiguration)
                    .execute(true, true);

        } catch (Exception e)
        {
            e.printStackTrace();
        }
    }
}
```

Command Line Schema Updates

To use SchemaUpdate from the command line, you have to use the command java net.sf.hibernate.tool.hbm2ddl.SchemaUpdate, passing in one or more of the command-line options shown in Table 11.1, followed by the path to the *.hbm.xml files.

Table 11.1. SchemaUpdate Command-Line Options

--quiet	Echo the script to the console
--properties= filename.properties	Specify the hibernate.properties file
--config= filename.cfg.xml	Specify the hibernate.cfg.xml file
--text	Do not execute the update
--naming= fully.qualified.class.name	Specify the naming policy to use (Hibernate ships with net.sf.hibernate.cfg.Default NamingStrategy (prefers mixed case) and net.sf.hibernate.cfg.ImprovedNamin gStrategy (prefers underscores).

Ant Task Schema Updates

In addition to the runtime and command-line options, you can also use a build-time Ant task, as shown in Listing 11.2.

Listing 11.2   SchemaUpdate Ant Task

```
<target name="schemaupdate">
    <taskdef name="schemaupdate"
        classname="net.sf.hibernate.tool.hbm2ddl
            .SchemaUpdateTask"
        classpathref="class.path"/>

    <schemaupdate
        properties="hibernate.properties"
        quiet="no">
        <fileset dir="src">
            <include name="**/*.hbm.xml"/>
        </fileset>
    </schemaupdate>
</target>
```

Generating Update and Drop Scripts

Hibernate also includes the `net.sf.hibernate.tool.hbm2ddl` `.SchemaExport` tool, which allows you to generate scripts for generating a schema (optionally generating DROP statements as well). The `SchemaExport` tool has several advantages over the `SchemaUpdate`:

- It can be run at development time, even if you don't have access to the target database.
- It doesn't rely on driver metadata.
- It may be necessary if your application's database connection is not allowed to perform DDL.
- It allows you to send the application's database requirements to a database administrator.

Like `SchemaUpdate`, `SchemaExport` can be run from the command line or from Ant. An example is also shown of how to use `SchemaExport` to simultaneously generate scripts for several databases.

Table 11.2. SchemaExport Command-Line Options

Option	Description
`--quiet`	Don't output the script to the console.
`--drop`	Only generate drop-table statements.
`--text`	Generate script but don't perform against the database.
`--output=my_schema.sql`	Specify the file name to output the script.
`--config=hibernate.cfg.xml`	Specify the Hibernate configuration XML file.
`--properties=hibernate.properties`	Specify the Hibernate configuration properties from a file.
`--format`	Format the generated SQL nicely in the script.
`--delimiter=;`	Set an end-of-line delimiter for the script.

Command-Line Script Generation

You can run `SchemaExport` from the command line using the command `java net.sf.hibernate.tool.hbm2ddl.SchemaExport options mapping_files`. The possible options are as shown in Table 11.2.

Ant Task Script Generation

Listing 11.3 shows an Ant task that can be used to generate a script. The meaning of the options is as shown in Table 11.2.

Listing 11.3 SchemaExport Ant Task

```
<target name="schemaexport">
    <taskdef name="schemaexport"
        classname="net.sf.hibernate.tool.hbm2ddl
            .SchemaExportTask"
        classpathref="class.path"/>

    <schemaexport
        properties="hibernate.properties"
        quiet="no"
        text="no"
        drop="no"
        delimiter=";"
        output="schema-export.sql">
        <fileset dir="src">
            <include name="**/*.hbm.xml"/>
```

(continues)

Listing 11.3 SchemaExport Ant Task (*continued*)

```
        </fileset>
    </schemaexport>
</target>
```

Generating Multiple Scripts

Hibernate has the advantageous ability of making it easier to support a wide range of databases. By taking advantage of SchemaExport, you can generate schema generation scripts for a wide variety of databases at development time and include them in the application distribution. This is obviously no substitute for testing, as Hibernate relies on the underlying database for a wide variety of features, but it can be helpful if you are interested in using an application with a new database.

Table 6.5 shows the list of dialects included with Hibernate 2.1.2. The sample code shown in Listing 11.4 takes advantage of this list to generate a set of schema generation scripts for a wide suite of databases. The suite of dialects is looped through, with an attempt made to generate scripts for the sample application shown in Chapter 3.

Listing 11.4 Generating Multiple Scripts

```
package com.cascadetg.ch11;

/** Various Hibernate-related imports */
import net.sf.hibernate.*;
import net.sf.hibernate.cfg.*;
import net.sf.hibernate.tool.hbm2ddl.SchemaExport;
import java.util.Properties;

public class SchemaGeneratorExample
{
    // System constants for the current platform directory
        token
    static String fileSep =
        System.getProperty("file.separator");

    /** We use this session factory to create our sessions */
    public static SessionFactory sessionFactory;

    static String[] db_dialects =
    { "DB2", //
            "net.sf.hibernate.dialect.DB2Dialect", //
            "DB2400", //
```

Listing 11.4   Generating Multiple Scripts

```
          "net.sf.hibernate.dialect.DB2400Dialect", //
          "Firebird", //
          "net.sf.hibernate.dialect.FirebirdDialect", //
          "FrontBase", //
          "net.sf.hibernate.dialect.FrontBaseDialect", //
          "Generic", //
          "net.sf.hibernate.dialect.GenericDialect", //
          "HypersonicSQL", //
          "net.sf.hibernate.dialect.HSQLDialect", //
          "Informix", //
          "net.sf.hibernate.dialect.InformixDialect", //
          "Informix9", //
          "net.sf.hibernate.dialect.Informix9Dialect", //
          "Ingres", //
          "net.sf.hibernate.dialect.IngresDialect", //
          "Interbase", //
          "net.sf.hibernate.dialect.InterbaseDialect", //
          "Mckoi SQL", //
          "net.sf.hibernate.dialect.MckoiDialect", //
          "Microsoft SQL Server", //
          "net.sf.hibernate.dialect.SQLServerDialect", //
          "MySQL", //
          "net.sf.hibernate.dialect.MySQLDialect", //
          "Oracle 9", //
          "net.sf.hibernate.dialect.Oracle9Dialect", //
          "Oracle", //
          "net.sf.hibernate.dialect.OracleDialect", //
          "Pointbase", //
          "net.sf.hibernate.dialect.PointbaseDialect", //
          "PostgreSQL", //
          "net.sf.hibernate.dialect.PostgreSQLDialect", //
          "Progress", //
          "net.sf.hibernate.dialect.ProgressDialect", //
          "SAP DB", //
          "net.sf.hibernate.dialect.SAPDBDialect", //
          "Sybase Anywhere", //
          "net.sf.hibernate.dialect.SybaseAnywhereDialect",
          "Sybase 11.9.2", //
          "net.sf.hibernate.dialect.Sybase11_9_2Dialect", //
          "Sybase", //
          "net.sf.hibernate.dialect.SybaseDialect",};

      public static void main(String[] args)
      {
```

(continues)

Listing 11.4   Generating Multiple Scripts (*continued*)

```java
        initialization();
}

/**
 * Loads the Hibernate configuration information, sets up the
 * database and the Hibernate session factory.
 */
public static void initialization()
{
    System.out.println("initialization");
    try
    {
        Configuration myConfiguration = new
            Configuration();

        myConfiguration
                .addClass(com.cascadetg.ch03.Owner.class);
        myConfiguration
                .addClass(com.cascadetg.ch03.Artifact
                    .class);

        Properties myProperties = new Properties();

        for (int i = 0; i < db_dialects.length; i = i + 2)
        {
            String dialect_name = db_dialects[i];
            String dialect_class = db_dialects[i + 1];

            String dialect_file =
                dialect_name.toLowerCase();
            dialect_file = dialect_file.replace(' ', '_');
            dialect_file += (".sql");

            String path = "com" + fileSep + "cascadetg"
                    + fileSep + "ch11" + fileSep;

            System.out.println("Generating " +
                dialect_name);

            // Note that this is the only Hibernate property
            // set.  In particular, there is no JDBC
            // connectivity data, nor are we specifying a
            // driver!
            myProperties.put("hibernate.dialect",
                    dialect_class);
```

Listing 11.4   Generating Multiple Scripts (*continued*)

```
            try
            {
                // Load the *.hbm.xml files as set in the
                // config, and set the dialect.
                SchemaExport mySchemaExport = new
                    SchemaExport(
                        myConfiguration, myProperties);

                mySchemaExport.setDelimiter(";");

                // Despite the name, the generated create
                // scripts WILL include drop statements at
                // the top of the script!
                mySchemaExport.setOutputFile(path + "create_"
                    + dialect_file);
                mySchemaExport.create(false, false) ;

                // Generates DROP statements only
                mySchemaExport.setOutputFile(path + "drop_"
                    + dialect_file);
                mySchemaExport.drop(false, false);

                System.out.println(dialect_name + " OK.");

            } catch (Exception e)
            {
                System.out.println(e.getMessage());
            }
        }

    } catch (Exception e)
    {
        e.printStackTrace();
    }
  }
}
```

Running the application in Listing 11.4 produces the results shown in Listing 11.5. As can be seen, the `native` identity generator is not supported by many databases. For broader support, a Hibernate-driven identity generator would be a better choice to support a wider range of databases (for more information on identity generation, see Chapter 6). Figure 11.1 shows the resulting schema script files.

Listing 11.5   Generating Multiple Scripts

```
initialization
Generating DB2
DB2 OK.
Generating DB2400
DB2400 OK.
Generating Firebird
Dialect does not support identity-key generation
Generating FrontBase
Dialect does not support identity-key generation
Generating Generic
Dialect does not support identity-key generation
Generating HypersonicSQL
HypersonicSQL OK.
Generating Informix
Informix OK.
Generating Informix9
Informix9 OK.
Generating Ingres
Dialect does not support identity-key generation
Generating Interbase
Dialect does not support identity-key generation
Generating Mckoi SQL
Dialect does not support identity-key generation
Generating Microsoft SQL Server
Microsoft SQL Server OK.
Generating MySQL
MySQL OK.
Generating Oracle 9
Dialect does not support identity-key generation
Generating Oracle
Dialect does not support identity-key generation
Generating Pointbase
Dialect does not support identity-key generation
Generating PostgreSQL
Dialect does not support identity-key generation
Generating Progress
Dialect does not support identity-key generation
Generating SAP DB
Dialect does not support identity-key generation
Generating Sybase Anywhere
Sybase Anywhere OK.
Generating Sybase 11.9.2
Sybase 11.9.2 OK.
Generating Sybase
Sybase OK.
```

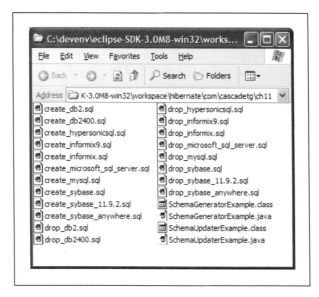

Figure 11.1. Generated Schema Scripts

CHAPTER **12**

Best Practices, Style Guide, Tips and Tricks

Hibernate supports several different systems for building applications. For example, you can start with Java objects (as shown in Chapter 3) or with an existing database (as shown in Chapter 4). If, as sometimes happens, you "inherit" a system, this may force your hand by making it necessary to start from an existing database.

In this chapter, we'll look at a few available technologies and solutions for reducing or improving your code. They aren't required but may make your life with Hibernate easier. They include:

- Reducing code with inversion of control.

- Reducing session-creation impact with `ThreadLocal`.

- Using Hibernate as an EJB BMP Solution.

- Integrating additional tools and technologies.

- Reviewing applications that use Hibernate.

- Strategies for getting started.

Hibernate is a popular technology, so watch the Hibernate Web site and forum (http://www.hibernate.org/) closely; there's always something interesting going on.

Reducing Code with Inversion of Control

Perhaps you wish to use Hibernate in a JSP application (as described in Chapter 2) but are unhappy with the copy-and-paste booking shown for managing transactions. If so, you can use anonymous inner classes to reduce bookkeeping while preserving control. This is popularly referred to as inversion of control, or IoC.

The term inversion of control refers to the notion that your code is handed to another class to actually be executed. Whenever you write code intended to run inside another application, you are, in a sense, inverting (or transferring) control of the execution environment to another system. In particular, the use in Java of anonymous inner classes in conjunction with a framework is dubbed "inversion of control."

Listing 12.1 shows the use of an anonymous inner class to actually perform the database access. Two independent operations are shown. Each operation is performed by an anonymous `HibernateSessionWrapper()` implementation of the `task()` method. The first operation demonstrates access to the database, the second is an example of error handling. Note that the code shows no exception-handling strategy; it is subsumed into the underlying `HibernateSession Wrapper` class.

Listing 12.1   Inversion of Control Example

```java
package com.cascadetg.ch12;

import java.util.Iterator;

public class IoCExample
{

    public static void main(String[] args)
    {
        // Need one global configuration
        HibernateSessionWrapper.initialization();

        // Create our task as an anonymous inner class.
        // Note, no exception handling needed, implicit
        // availability of a session.
        HibernateSessionWrapper myTask = new
        HibernateSessionWrapper()
        {

            Object task(Object in) throws Exception
            {
                net.sf.hibernate.Query myQuery = session
                        .createQuery((String) in);

                Iterator result = myQuery.list().iterator();

                session.flush();
```

Listing 12.1 Inversion of Control Example (*continued*)

```
                    return result;
            }
    };

    // Execute a bit of HQL and get the results
    Iterator result = (Iterator) myTask
            .perform("from Author");
    while (result.hasNext())
    {
        System.out.println(result.next().toString());
        System.out.flush();
    }

    // Create our task as an anonymous inner class.
    // Note, no exception handling needed, implicit
    // availability of a session.
    HibernateSessionWrapper myTask2 = new
    HibernateSessionWrapper()
    {

        Object task(Object in) throws Exception
        {
            throw new Exception();
        }
    };

    // Do the task.
    if (myTask2.perform() == null)
            System.out.println(myTask2.getException());
    }
}
```

The anonymous inner class in Listing 12.1 is a subclass of the abstract class shown in Listing 12.2. Only the `task()` method must be overridden. If the `task()` method fails because of an exception, the method automatically returns null, and additional methods are provided to determine the precise nature of the exception.

Listing 12.2 Inversion of Control Example

```
package com.cascadetg.ch12;

import net.sf.hibernate.*;
```

(*continues*)

Listing 12.2 Inversion of Control Example (*continued*)

```
import net.sf.hibernate.cfg.*;

public abstract class HibernateSessionWrapper
{

    /** This method must be overridden to actually do anything
     */
    abstract Object task(Object in) throws Exception;

    Session session = null;

    Transaction transaction = null;

    boolean stale = false;

    Exception problem = null;
    /**
     * Used to identify that a stale object was encountered as
     * part of the transaction.
     */
    public boolean isStaleOperation()
    {
        return stale;
    }

    public Exception getException()
    {
        return problem;
    }

    /** We use this session factory to create our sessions */
    public static SessionFactory sessionFactory;

    /**
     * Loads the Hibernate configuration information, sets up the
     * database and the Hibernate session factory.
     *
     * Should be customized for your application.
     */
    public static void initialization()
    {
        try
        {
            Configuration myConfiguration = new
                Configuration();
```

Listing 12.2   Inversion of Control Example (*continued*)

```
            myConfiguration
                    .addClass(com.cascadetg.ch02.Post.class);
            myConfiguration
                    .addClass(com.cascadetg.ch02.Author.class);

            // Sets up the session factory (used in the rest
            // of the application).
            sessionFactory = myConfiguration
                    .buildSessionFactory();
        } catch (Exception e)
        {
            e.printStackTrace();
        }
    }

    public Object perform()
    {
        return perform(null);
    }

    /**
     * Actually does the set-up for the session, as well as
     * execute the task. Handles all of the exceptions (you may
     * wish to customize this per your login preference)
     */
    public Object perform(Object in)
    {
        Object result = null;
        try
        {
            session = sessionFactory.openSession();
            transaction = session.beginTransaction();

            result = task(in);

            transaction.commit();

        } catch (StaleObjectStateException staleException)
        {
            stale = true;
            try
            {
                transaction.rollback();
            } catch (Exception e2)
            {
```

(*continues*)

Listing 12.2 Inversion of Control Example (*continued*)

```
            e2.printStackTrace();
        }
    } catch (Exception e)
    {
        result = null;
        problem = e;
        e.printStackTrace();
        try
        {
            transaction.rollback();
        } catch (Exception e2)
        {
            // Notify of a failure to roll the transaction
            // back
            e.printStackTrace();
        }
    } finally
    {
        try
        {
            if (session != null) session.close();
        } catch (Exception e)
        {
            // Silent failure of session close
        }
    }
    return result;
}
}
```

If you find the inversion of control style of development interesting, you may wish to investigate the Spring framework (http://www.springframework.org/). Spring is a more sophisticated IoC framework than the one shown in Listing 12.2; it provides a number of additional services (both specific to Hibernate and helpful for application development in general).

Reducing Session Creation Impact with `ThreadLocal`

You can reduce the impact of retrieving a new `Session` object for each thread by reusing the Session for a given object. As described in Chapter 6 and Chapter 9, a `Session` is not sharable across threads. The code in Listing 12.3 shows a Hibernate-recommended mechanism for maintaining a per-thread `Session` variable. The real work of this code is done in the `java.lang.ThreadLocal` class, which simplifies the use of a per-thread variable.

Listing 12.3 `ThreadLocal` Example

```java
import net.sf.hibernate.*;
import net.sf.hibernate.cfg.*;

public class HibernateUtil {

    private static final SessionFactory sessionFactory;

    static {
        try {
            sessionFactory =
                    new Configuration().configure()
                            .buildSessionFactory();
        } catch (HibernateException ex) {
            throw new RuntimeException(
                    "Exception building SessionFactory: "
                            + ex.getMessage(), ex);
        }
    }

    public static final java.lang.ThreadLocal
      session = new java.lang. ThreadLocal();

    public static Session currentSession() throws
    HibernateException {
        Session s = (Session) session.get();
        // Open a new Session, if this Thread has none yet
        if (s == null) {
            s = sessionFactory.openSession();
            session.set(s);
        }
        return s;
    }

    public static void discardSession() throws
    HibernateException {
        Session s = (Session) session.get();
        session.set(null);
        if (s != null)
            s.close();
    }
}
```

With luck, you should already have your `Session` management contained in a specific class with a static method, as shown in Chapter 2. The biggest difficulty with the pattern shown in Listing 12.3 is that a `Session` object can be rendered into an untenable state if a transaction-related exception is shown (Hibernate explicitly does **not** allow reuse of a `Session` object in this situation). This is why an additional `discardSession()` method is shown above; you need to ensure that the `Session` object is discarded if your application throws a transaction-related exception, as shown in the `discardSession()` method.

Using Hibernate as an EJB BMP Solution

Hibernate is intended to work in a wide variety of environments, and works well as a bean-managed persistence (BMP) solution when used in a variety of J2EE application servers. In fact, JBoss has indicated that a future version of its software will likely use Hibernate as the basis for container-managed persistence (CMP).

The development process for BMP and EJB varies tremendously from development environment to environment and therefore is beyond the scope of this text. Conceptually, however, you are relying on your J2EE application server to provide a variety of services, such as identity management, clustering, and JDBC connection pooling, when you use Hibernate to handle the actual generated persistence (specifically, the generated SQL). This affords several advantages, such as the ability to unit test your database access logic outside the context of a full application server and also the ability to understand the persistence performance characteristics of an application independent of the application server. Let's say, for example, that you develop an application intended to target three different application servers. By using Hibernate as your persistence mechanism, you can test your application against your target databases with a greater sense of independence for the tests with the different application servers.

In any event, Hibernate should at most be considered an alternative to EJB container-managed persistence, not the full EJB specification.

If you are interested in using Hibernate in conjunction with EJB, you will find descriptions of the general integration at http://hibernate.org/82.html and http://hibernate.org/166.html. A description of how to add Hibernate as a service to your JBoss installation can be found at http://hibernate.org/66.html.

Integrating with Other Technologies

Hibernate is a very popular package, and several developers have posted tips and tricks for integrating Hibernate with other packages. Table 12.1 shows a list, up to date as of this writing, of some of the products and technologies that in one form

Table 12.1. Technologies Integrated with Hibernate

Technology	Use	Page
Eclipse	Java IDE	http://www.midrangeserver.com/fhg/ fhg030304-story01.html
HiberClipse	Eclipse Plugin	http://sourceforge.net/projects/hiberclipse/
Hibernate JSP Tags	JSP Tags	http://sourceforge.net/projects/hibtags/
HibernateSynchronizer	Eclipse Plugin	http://sourceforge.net/projects/hibernatesynch/
Hibernator	Eclipse Plugin	http://sourceforge.net/projects/hibernator
IntelliJ IDEA	Java IDE	http://hibernate.org/108.html
JUnit	Unit Test Framework	http://hibernate.org/83.html
Log4j	Logging Toolkit	http://hibernate.org/97.html
Lucerne	Free Text Search Engine	http://hibernate.org/138.html
Maven	Project Management	http://hibernate.org/134.html
Pico	Lightweight Container	http://hibernate.org/174.html
Spring	Java IoC Framework	http://hibernate.org/110.html
Struts	Web MVC Framework	http://hibernate.org/105.html
Tangosol Coherence	Distributed Cache	http://hibernate.org/132.html
Tapestry	Web Application Framework	http://hibernate.org/96.html
Tomcat	Application Server	http://hibernate.org/114.html
WebSphere Application Developer (WASD) 5.x	IBM Java IDE	http://hibernate.org/173.html

or another have been integrated with Hibernate. For the latest information, consult the http://hibernate.org/ Web site.

Applications That Use Hibernate

Table 12.2 shows some applications that make use of Hibernate. If you wish to examine applications larger than those that can conveniently be included in a book like this one, you may wish to download and peruse the code for the open-source projects (and you may get ideas or useful tips from both the open-source and commercial products).

Table 12.2.   Products That Use Hibernate

Application	Use	Page
DeepBlack	Weblog	http://deepblack.blackcore.com/
Flock	News aggregator	http://flock.sourceforge.net/
Jagzilla	Bugzilla Interface	http://sourceforge.net/projects/jagzilla/
JasperReports	Reporting Tool	http://hibernate.org/79.html
JavaLobby Community Platform	Portal	http://sourceforge.net/projects/gotjava/
jboard	Bulletin Board	http://sourceforge.net/projects/jboard/
jBpm	Business Process Management	http://jbpm.org/
Liferay	Enterprise Portal	http://www.liferay.com/
openEF/J	Enterprise Application Framework	http://sourceforge.net/projects/openef/
OpenReports	Reporting Tool	http://sourceforge.net/projects/oreports
PersonalBlog	Weblog	http://sourceforge.net/projects/personalblog/
Phoo	Java Bot Suite	http://sourceforge.net/projects/phoo/
Roller Weblogger	Weblog	http://www.rollerweblogger.org/
TM4J	Topic Map Engine	http://tm4j.org/

Strategies for Getting Started

Throughout this text, I've tried to provide as balanced a set of recommendations as possible. In this section, I offer some general guidelines for those who are still unsure about the proper approach. Consider this section to reflect opinion only—and keep in mind that since I don't know your application's requirements, these recommendations should be taken with a grain of salt.

Where to Start?

My approach for working with Hibernate depends on whether or not there is an existing database. If you are starting with an existing database, use Middlegen (as described in Chapter 4). If the database schema is extremely stable, you may wish to use Middlegen to generate a first pass at the `*.hbm.xml` files, and then hand-tune them as needed. If you believe the schema is potentially subject to change, follow the guidelines for Middlegen as described in Chapter 4.

If you are starting from scratch, use the `*.hbm.xml` mapping as your canonical format, and generate both your Java and database schema based on that (as described in Chapter 2 and Chapter 11). I find that starting from Java (as described in Chapter 3) is most comfortable for developers who are accustomed to using XDoclet as a refuge from the complexity of EJB. I find it much easier to generate persistent objects from my mapping file than to rely on generating get/set methods in bulk and then inspecting the generated `*.hbm.xml` files.

Start with Many-to-One and One-to-Many

Make sure that you understand the many-to-one and one-to-many relationships before working on the more esoteric types shown in Chapter 7. The vast majority of databases can be modeled relatively conveniently using only these two basic relationships. Class and the more sophisticated relationships are useful tools, but you should feel comfortable with the basic relationships before tackling them.

Profile Database Fetching

When you are first starting out with Hibernate, the relationship between queries and lazy loading of objects can be confusing. You will probably find it especially difficult to understand the implications of the different data-loading strategies. Use the tools shown in Chapter 10 to inspect and time the SQL generated by Hibernate.

Put another way, make sure that you understand how your object graph is going to be traversed. How do you expect to access your data? Make sure that you understand as many as possible of the creation, retrieval, update, and delete (CRUD) operations on your objects.

CHAPTER **13**

Future Directions

Hibernate is a powerful technology intended to solve the problem of object/relational persistence. Hibernate 2.1.2 does this quite well, with a large suite of features (as demonstrated in this text). The developers of Hibernate expect future releases of the Hibernate 2.1.x line to provide bug fixes but no major changes. This chapter attempts to give a sense of the direction that will be taken both by Hibernate 3.0 and by the early draft specification of EJB 3.0.

Hibernate 3.0

Gavin King, the creator of Hibernate, quite wisely avoids speaking of new features and functionality, but he does offer a preliminary preview of possible future directions for Hibernate 3 in his weblog at http://blog.hibernate.org/cgi-bin/blosxom.cgi/2004/04/02#three. In addition, a Hibernate roadmap has been posted at http://hibernate.bluemars.net/200.html.

To summarize the points made, the following are on the horizon as possible directions for Hibernate 3:

Virtualization: Session-level filtering of data. For example, you may wish to allow only data that belongs to a particular user to be viewed across an entire Web application. The virtualization feature will allow you to specify this at the session, instead of in your application code. This feature will probably be of special interest to Web application developers.

More Complex Relationships: As described in Chapter 7, Hibernate already offers support for a variety of complex relationships. Hibernate 3 will allow the use of a single class for multiple tables, table-per-concrete-class mappings, and the ability to use SQL to specify more complex discriminators.

Representation Independence: Allows a persistence model to be represented using entirely dynamic objects, instead of persistent objects. At some point, you may have realized that most JavaBeans could just as easily be represented by a single object with a single get/set property method (as described by the Apache BeanUtils, http://jakarta.apache.org/commons/beanutils/). This feature allows for a much broader suite of dynamic (i.e., runtime) discovery and manipulation of data.

JDK 1.5 Support: For more information on JDK 1.5, see http://java .sun.com/j2se/. Annotations allow XDoclet-style metadata to be embedded in a Java class file and easily accessed at runtime. Generics allow for more type-safe collections (i.e., less casting, more reliable compile-type checking).

Stored Procedures: This would be quite relevant if you are working on an application with legacy stored procedures.

Event-Driven Design: While the life-cycle methods described in Chapter 6 are reasonable, Hibernate lacks a full event model. Currently, the only way to instrument Hibernate to perform certain tasks is to download the source for Hibernate and add your own hooks—and that is not the ideal situation.

New Parser Implementation: The grammar for HQL (as described in Chapter 8) is not fully documented and can be frustratingly vague in certain areas. Hibernate 3 should include a full grammar for HQL, as well as the ability to map new grammars on top of the existing implementation.

Declarative Session Management: Instead of session management constituting an explicit part of the application, Hibernate 3 will offer the ability to push this sort of detail into Hibernate and the session configuration.

Despite these changes, Hibernate 3 will not require JDK 1.5. As of this writing, Hibernate 3 is not even available as an alpha technology release.

EJB 3.0

At the present time, only the EJB 3.0 (Summer 2004 Early Draft Specification, http://jcp.org/aboutJava/communityprocess/edr/jsr220/index.html) has been made available. It is intended to obtain feedback from the community, but some probable aspects of the final release (including the clear influence of Hibernate 2.x for relational persistence) are already apparent.

Let's start by highlighting some of the similarities between EJB 3.0 and Hibernate 2.x. First and foremost, EJB 3.0 now bases container-managed persistence on plain old Java objects (POJO) with annotations, much like Hibernate's POJO + mapping file approach. From there, Hibernate's SessionManager and Session have been combined into a single EJB EntityManager class. EJB 3.0 now includes a Query class which allows for page control, similar to that of

Hibernate. You are expected to mark one end of an association as inverse. And so on.

Some of the differences between Hibernate and EJB 3.0 are a natural outgrowth of the reliance of EJB 3.0 on Java 2 Standard Edition 5.0 (J2SE 5.0). For example, there is no notion of a Hibernate `Configuration` class, because EJB 3.0 relies on J2SE 5.0 annotations in lieu of external XML files. Extensions to EJBQL make it look more like HQL, including support for named parameters, fetch, bulk update, and bulk delete. Collection semantics go beyond the support provided in Hibernate, leveraging J2SE 5.0 generics (see JSR 14, http://jcp.org/en/jsr/detail?id=14, for more information on generics).

Some features of EJB 3.0 go significantly beyond what is offered by Hibernate 2.x. These include:

- A defined distributed object environment.

- `Session`, `Message`, and `Entity` object distinctions.

- Additional object semantics and life cycles beyond object/relational persistence.

- Security permissions (including method-level security).

- Integrated resource-dependency references.

- Integrated support for exposing objects as Web services (JSR 181).

- A fully defined formal BNF description of the query language (important for robust parser implementations).

From the author's perspective, one of the most interesting advantages of EJB 3.0 as compared to Hibernate 2.1 HQL is the presence of a formal BNF for EJBQL. Backus Naur Form (BNF), as described at http://cui.unige.ch/db-research/Enseignement/analyseinfo/AboutBNF.html, is a formal description of a programming language. By providing a BNF, users can expect to see multiple parsers for a single language, allowing for richer and more innovative tools and solutions. For example, providing a BNF makes it much easier to produce a correct grammar for JavaCC, https://javacc.dev.java.net/. This in turn makes it much easier to produce alternative implementations for EJB 3.0 and to obtain rich support from tools—for example, automatic type-ahead in a text editor.

For a Hibernate developer, the most shocking change when moving to EJB 3.0 is likely to be the reliance on annotations to provide persistence metadata. Simply put, EJB 3.0 development with annotations (per JSR 175, http://jcp.org/en/jsr/detail?id=175) is most similar to Hibernate development with XDoclet (as described in Chapter 3). This eliminates the need for separate XML configuration files because the information is encoded directly in the class files. The formal annotation specification (combined with solid tool support) should alleviate some problems with the current, error-prone nature of XDoclet development, but concerns about embedding database configuration information in Java source remain. The tremendous simplification of the development process may prove able to manage these concerns.

Here and Now

Despite its potential benefits, it will probably be a good while before EJB 3.0 is suitable for production deployment. It requires J2SE 1.5, which as of this writing is still in beta.

Ironically, the best way to get a get a sense of the future is to start working with Hibernate 2.x today. Whatever your future choices may be, including Hibernate 3 or EJB 3.0, Hibernate 2.x will reduce your overall development time, make development more fun, and help you build your skill set for the next generation.

Index